FM 23-90

WAR DEPARTMENT FIELD MANUAL

81-MM
MORTAR M1

WAR DEPARTMENT • 22 APRIL 1943

DISCLAIMER:

THIS MANUAL IS SOLD FOR HISTORIC RESEARCH PURPOSES ONLY, AS AN ENTERTAINMENT. IT CONTAINS OBSOLETE INFORMATION AND IS NOT INTENDED TO BE USED AS PART OF AN ACTUAL OPERATION OF MAINTENANCE TRAINING PROGRAM. NO BOOK CAN SUBSTITUTE FOR PROPER TRAINING BY AN AUTHORIZED INSTRUCTOR.

WAR DEPARTMENT FIELD MANUAL

FM 23-90

81-MM

MORTAR M1

WAR DEPARTMENT • 22 APRIL 1943

United States Government Printing Office

Washington : 1947

WAR DEPARTMENT,

WASHINGTON, April 22, 1943.

FM 23–90, 81-mm Mortar M1, is published for the information and guidance of all concerned.

[A. G. 062.11 (2–24–43).]

BY ORDER OF THE SECRETARY OF WAR:

G. C. MARSHALL,
Chief of Staff.

OFFICIAL:

J. A. ULIO,
Major General,
The Adjutant General.

DISTRIBUTION:

B and H 2, 7, 17 (3) ; R 2, 7, 17 (5) ; Bn 2, 7, 19 (3) ; IC 2, 7, 17, 19 (10) ; C and H 9 (2).

For explanation of symbols see FM 21–6.

TABLE OF CONTENTS

	Paragraphs	Page
CHAPTER 1. Mechanical training.		
SECTION I. Description	1–3	1
II. Disassembling, assembling, mounting, and dismounting	4–5	6
III. Care, cleaning, and inspections	6–17	10
IV. Sighting equipment	18–19	21
V. Ammunition	20–32	25
VI. Destruction of ordnance matériel in event of imminent capture in combat zone	32.1–32.5	34
CHAPTER 2. Training of gunner.		
SECTION I. General	33	39
II. Compass	34	39
III. Spare parts and accessories	35–36	42
IV. Training exercises	37–44	45
V. Additional training	45–49	50
CHAPTER 3. Training for placing mortar in action	50–56	58
CHAPTER 4. Training of observer.		
SECTION I. Preparatory instruction	57–64	71
II. Squad conduct of fire	65–74	95
III. Combat expedients—rapid adjustment of fire	75	125
IV. Prearranged fires	76–82	131
CHAPTER 5. Marksmanship.		
SECTION I. Preparatory instruction	83–86	139
II. Examination	87–90	141
III. Qualification course, gunner's test	91–98	142
IV. Qualification course, expert's test	99–104	151
V. Targets, ranges, and range precautions	105–107	158
CHAPTER 6. Advanced training.		
SECTION I. Section conduct of fire	108–111	159
II. Employment of smoke	112–119	163
III. Fire control instruments	120–121	179
IV. Use of fire control instruments	122–123	203
CHAPTER 7. Field training.		
SECTION I. General	124–126	208
II. Preparatory exercises	127–130	208
III. Elementary firing exercises	131–137	211
IV. Advanced training exercises	138–143	218
CHAPTER 8. Advice to instructors.		
SECTION I. General	144–146	259
II. Mechanical training	147–152	259
III. Training of gunner and observer	153	265
IV. Training for placing mortar in action	154	265
V. Markmanship	155–156	266
VI. Field training	157–159	267
VII. Instruction on sand table	160	268
APPENDIX I. Firing tables and deflection-conversion table		270
APPENDIX II. Instruction card		278
APPENDIX III. Fire control instruments: Nomenclature and operative procedure, mortar platoon		279
INDEX		283

BASIC FIELD MANUAL

81-MM MORTAR M1

(This manual supersedes FM 23–90, May 7, 1942, including C 1, Jan. 12, 1943.)

Attention is directed to FM 21–7 for details as to how appropriate Training Films and Film Strips are intended to be used and how they are made available for use during training with the 81-mm mortar M1.

CHAPTER 1

MECHANICAL TRAINING

Paragraphs

SECTION I. Description _____ 1–3

II. Disassembling, assembling, mounting, and dismounting_____ 4–5

III. Care, cleaning, and inspections_____ 6–17

IV. Sighting equipment_____ 18–19

V. Ammunition_____ 20–32

VI. Destruction of ordnance matériel in event of imminent capture in combat zone_____ 32.1–32.5

SECTION I

DESCRIPTION

■ 1. CHARACTERISTICS.—The 81-mm mortar (fig. 1) is a smooth bore, muzzle loading, high angle fire weapon. The mortar is assembled into a single unit, while the mount consists of two units—the bipod and base plate. These three units—mortar, bipod, and base plate—form separate loads, each of which is light enough to be carried by one man. The mortar is attached to the bipod by means of a clamp and can be readily dismounted. It is fastened to the base plate by inserting the spherical projection of the base cap into one of the three seats of the socket and rotating the mortar 90°. A detailed list of the parts and equipment for the 81-mm mortar and mount may be found in Standard Nomenclature List A–33.

■ 2. GENERAL DATA.—General data of the 81-mm mortar and mount are as follows:

Weight:

Mortar and mount_____pounds__		136.0
Mortar_____do____		44.5
Bipod _____do____		46.5
Base plate _____do____		45.0
Over-all length of mortar_____inches__		49.5
Elevations (approximate) _____degrees__		40 to 85
Traverse, right or left (approximate)_____mils__		90
One turn of handwheel (approximate) mils__		15

Rate of fire, rounds per minute:

Maximum_____	30 to 35
Normal _____	18

Range (approximate):

HE shell:

6.92 pounds_____yards__	100 to 3,290
10.62 pounds_____do____	200 to 2,560
15.05 pounds_____do____	100 to 1,275

Chemical shell:

10.41 pounds_____do____	200 to 2,560
11.36 pounds_____do____	200 to 2,465
11.86 pounds_____do____	200 to 2,430

■ 3. DESCRIPTION.—*a. Mortar.*—(1) The mortar (fig. 2) consists of the barrel, the base cap, and the firing pin.

(2) The barrel is smooth bored and carefully finished in interior dimensions and surfaces.

(3) The base cap is hollowed and threaded to screw onto the barrel, thereby closing the breech end of the mortar. It terminates in a spherical projection, flattened on two sides, which fits into and locks in the socket of the base plate.

(4) The base cap is bored and threaded axially to receive the firing pin which, to prevent gas leakage, is screwed tightly into the base cap against a shoulder. When in place, the firing pin is held stationary with its point protruding through the base cap into the barrel.

b. Bipod.—(1) The bipod (fig. 3) consists of the legs, elevating mechanism assembly, and traversing mechanism assembly.

(2) The leg assembly consists of two tubular steel legs mounted on the trunnions of the gear case by a clevis joint. The legs terminate in feet with spikes. The spread of the legs is limited by an adjustable chain. A spring is interposed between the right end of the chain and the right leg to relieve the legs of shock during firing.

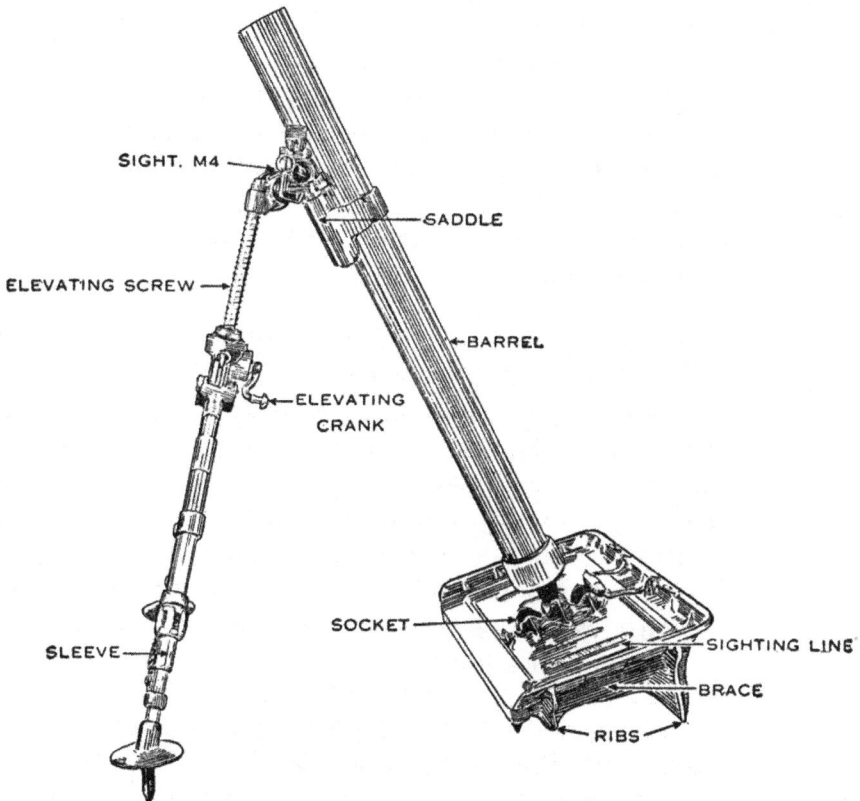

FIGURE 1.—81-mm mortar, mount, and sight M4.

(3) The left leg includes a cross-leveling mechanism. Cross-leveling is that operation by which the traversing screw is placed in a horizontal position. This operation, in turn, places the axis of the bore in a plane running vertically through the line on which the mortar is laid. This action removes any cant which may have been placed on the mortar. The cross-leveling mechanism consists of a sliding bracket, mounted on a sleeve, and an adjusting nut. The sliding bracket is connected with the guide tube by

a connecting rod. A movement of the sliding bracket up or down is transmitted to the mortar through the connecting rod, the elevating mechanism assembly, and the traversing mechanism assembly, causing a corresponding movement of the mortar. Thus the mortar may be cross-leveled by moving the sliding bracket. A locking nut attached to the sliding bracket locks it in any desired position on the sleeve. Final, accurate leveling is accomplished by rotating the adjusting nut on the upper part of the leg.

(4) The right leg contains no moving parts.

(5) The elevating mechanism assembly consists of a vertical screw moving in a guide tube. It is actuated by a bevel gear and pinion contained in the gear case. The gear and pinion are moved by the elevating crank. The top cover of the gear case contains an oil fitting for oiling the elevating screw, gear, and pinion.

(6) The traversing mechanism assembly consists of the traversing mechanism, shock absorbers, and clamp.

(7) The traversing mechanism consists of a horizontal screw operating in a yoke and actuated by a traversing handwheel. The yoke, which provides the bearings for the traversing screw, also serves as a connection between the mortar clamp, and the elevating mechanism. A level vial and a sight slot to receive the bracket of the sight are mounted on the yoke. The level vial is provided for cross-leveling purposes in the absence of a sight.

(8) The shock absorbers are designed to stabilize the mortar and mount during firing. They permit movement between the yoke and the clamp assembly and are countered by the resistance of two coil compression springs which are mounted in the shock absorber retainers of the saddle.

(9) The clamp, by means of which the barrel is clamped to the bipod, is in two sections. The lower half is called the saddle and includes the two shock absorber retainers with locking screws. The upper half is called the clamping collar. The two halves are hinged and can be locked tightly together by the clamp bolt. When so secured about the barrel of the mortar, they lock it firmly to the bipod.

c. *Base plate.*—The base plate (fig. 4) consists of a pressed steel body to which are welded a series of ribs and braces, a

BARREL ──→

BASE CAP ──→

SPHERICAL PROJECTION ──→

FIRING PIN ──→

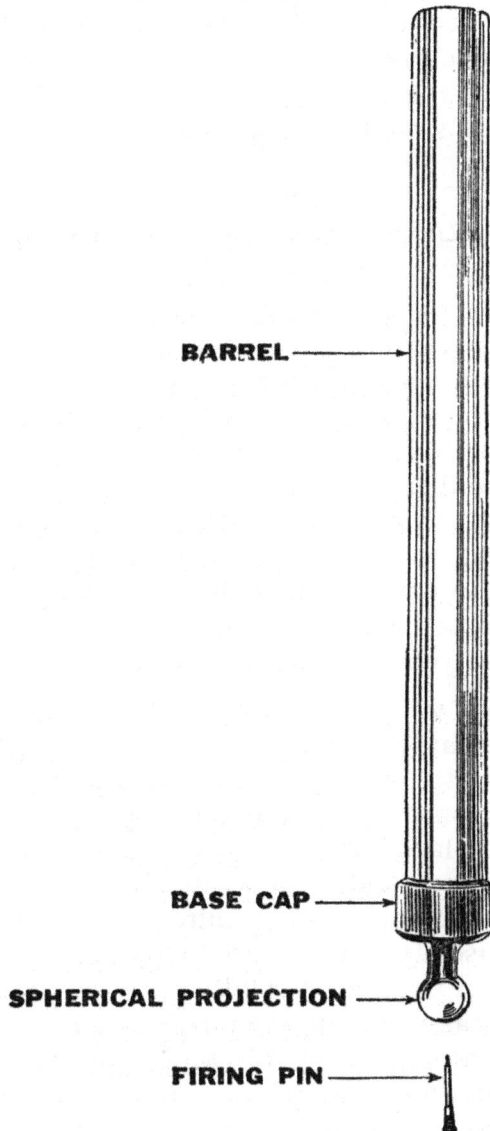

FIGURE 2.—Mortar.

front flange, three loops, two handle plates, and the socket. The socket carries three seats for the spherical projection of the base cap of the mortar. Normally, the spherical projection is placed in the center seat. However, as a result of firing, it may become necessary to move the spherical projection either to the forward or to the rear seat of the socket, in order to permit the base plate to be seated in the ground in an approximately horizontal position.

SECTION II

DISASSEMBLING, ASSEMBLING, MOUNTING, AND DISMOUNTING

■ 4. DISASSEMBLING AND ASSEMBLING.—The only part of the mortar, exclusive of the bipod and base plate, which may be removed by company personnel is the firing pin. This pin has a slotted head and is threaded into the base cap. The screw driver provided in the accessories chest should be used to unscrew the firing pin from the base cap. The firing pin is replaced by screwing it tightly into position after oiling the threads lightly. It should not be necessary to remove any parts of the bipod in the field for cleaning. If the working parts become inoperative because of wear and dirt, they should be repaired by ordnance personnel.

■ 5. MOUNTING AND DISMOUNTING.—a. *Base plate position.*— Prior to mounting the mortar, the direction of fire must be established by the placing of an aiming stake and a base plate stake to mark the location of the base plate. These two stakes are placed about 25 yards apart. The mortar may be fired, usually without impairing its accuracy, by placing the base plate on top of the ground so that its front edge is against the base plate stake and its long axis perpendicular to the direction of fire. The relative position of the base plate and the two stakes is indicated in figure 5.

The base plate will be firmly seated in average soil by the recoil of the first two or three rounds. However, when the mortar is to be mounted on a steep slope or on uneven ground, it may be necessary to prepare a horizontal surface upon which the base plate can be placed. The base plate is placed and alined by No. 3 man of the mortar squad.

b. *To mount the mortar.*—(1) After the direction of fire

is established and the base plate alined, the gunner (No. 1), lifts the bipod by placing his left hand on the traversing hand-wheel and his right hand on the sight slot. He moves to the front, faces the base plate, and positions the legs approximately 2 feet in front of the front flange of the base plate.

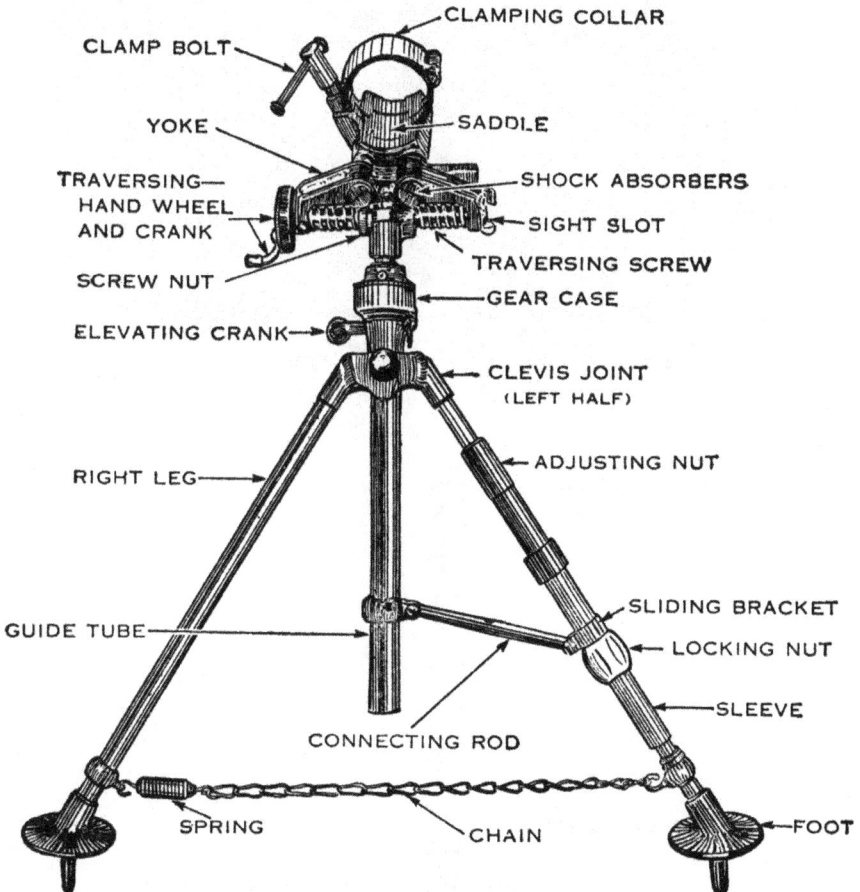

FIGURE 3.—Bipod.

He does this in such a manner that an extension of the right edge of the base plate would bisect the interval between the closed legs. Then, kneeling on his right knee in front of the bipod and supporting it with his left hand on the gear case, he unhooks the chain from its hook on the left leg and unwinds it from the legs. With his right hand, the gunner selects the end link of the extended chain and rehooks it on

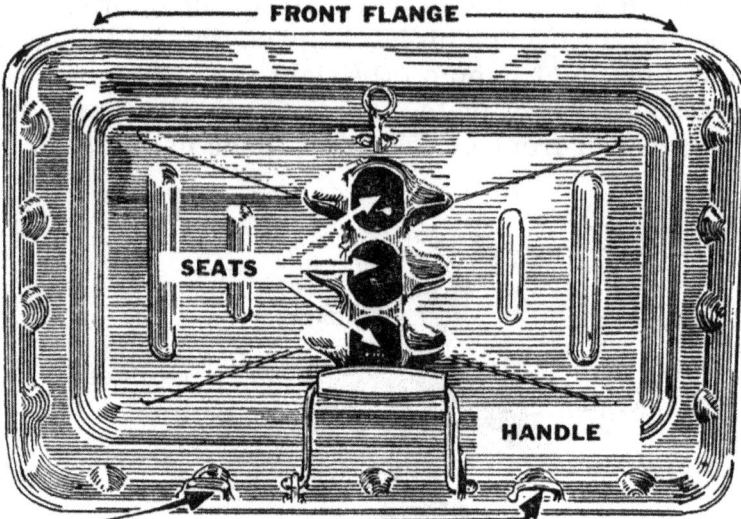

FRONT FLANGE

SEATS

HANDLE

LOOPS FOR CARRYING EQUIPMENT

FIGURE 4.—Base plate.

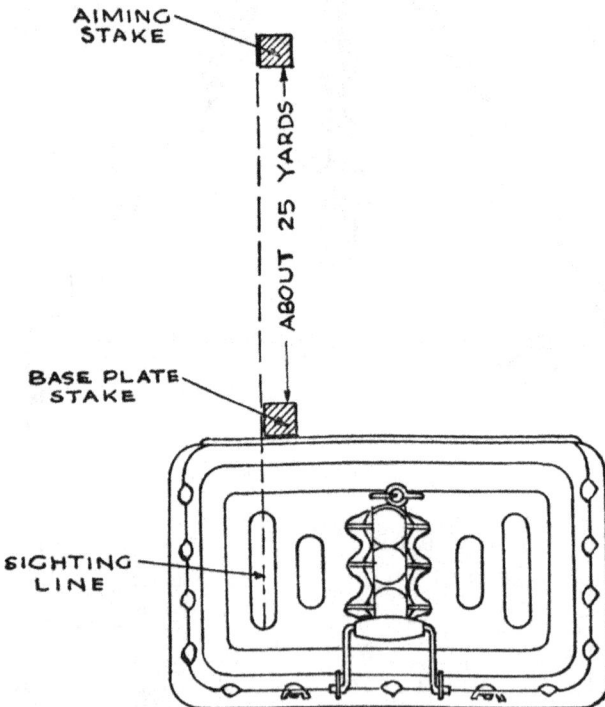

AIMING STAKE

ABOUT 25 YARDS

BASE PLATE STAKE

SIGHTING LINE

FIGURE 5.—Alinement of base plate.

the chain hook. Lifting the left leg, he opens the legs to the full extent of the spread chain (about 2½ feet). The gunner next places the traversing screw in a horizontal position by moving the guide tube to the left and centering the sleeve. This adjustment is made by rotating the adjusting nut until two fingers can be placed on the unpainted surface of the leg below the sleeve. He then tightens the locking nut.

(2) The gunner rises, rests the bipod against his legs, grasps the clamping collar with both hands, and with a quick upward and outward motion, unseats the saddle from its position behind the knob of the elevating crank. Supporting the bipod with his right hand by grasping the clamping collar, he moves to the left rear of the bipod and kneels on his right knee. He then places his left knee in front of the left leg of the bipod and supports the saddle with his left hand. His right hand remains on the clamping collar until No. 2 loosens the clamp bolt. The assistant gunner (No. 2) inserts the spherical projection of the mortar in the center seat of the socket and rotates the mortar 90° in order to lock the spherical projection in the seat of the base plate. He then grasps the rim of the muzzle with his left hand, loosens the clamp bolt with his right hand, opens the clamping collar, and places the mortar in position on the saddle. The gunner should support the saddle in such a manner that the under portion of the barrel rests squarely on the saddle. The gunner next closes the clamping collar and before the clamp bolt is tightened by the assistant gunner, raises or lowers the clamp so that the upper edge of the collar will be about 15 inches from the muzzle of the mortar. The assistant gunner tightens the bolt with either hand.

(3) The gunner turns the elevating crank 26 times to center the elevating screw, places the traversing crank in its operative position, removes the sight from the case, and mounts it on the mortar. He sets an elevation of 62° and a deflection of zero on the scales. He then directs the assistant gunner to move directly in front of the bipod and shift the legs until the vertical line in the collimator is alined approximately on the left edge of the aiming stake. During this movement, the gunner endeavors to keep the traversing screw level by movement of the adjusting nut and by signals to the

9

assistant gunner. He then centers the longitudinal level bubble, cross-levels with the adjusting nut only, and then lays accurately for direction by simultaneous operation of the traversing handwheel and the adjusting nut. He finally checks the lay for elevation.

c. *To dismount the mortar.*—(1) The gunner removes the sight and replaces it in the case. He next turns the elevating crank until the elevating screw is returned completely into the guide tube and the elevating crank is turned downward. He then centers the traversing screw nut on the traversing screw and returns the traversing crank to its inoperative position. He places his left knee in front of the left leg of the bipod and supports the saddle with his left hand. The assistant gunner places his left hand in the rim of the muzzle and loosens the clamp bolt with his right hand. After the assistant gunner raises the clamping collar and removes the mortar from the saddle, the gunner closes the clamping collar and assists No. 2 in tightening the bolt by holding it upright with the third finger of his left hand.

(2) From this point, the gunner and assistant gunner continue to dismount the mortar by reversing the operation of mounting. The locking nut is not retightened when dismounting the mortar.

NOTE.—In the preliminary stages of mechanical training, mounting of the mortar should proceed only to that point where the sight would be placed on the mortar. When the exercises described in paragraphs 37 to 42, inclusive, have been performed by squad members, training in mounting the mortar with sight attached should be undertaken.

SECTION III

CARE, CLEANING, AND INSPECTIONS

■ 6. CARE AND CLEANING.—The care and cleaning of the mortar and accessories are an essential duty which must be the personal responsibility of all personnel using this weapon. Experience has shown that these weapons become unserviceable through lack of proper care rather than from use.

■ 7. LUBRICANTS, CLEANING AGENTS, AND RUST PREVENTIVES.— The following are the only materials authorized and issued for cleaning and lubricating the mortar. The use of un-authorized materials such as abrasives is forbidden.

Cleaner, rifle bore.

Soda ash.

Issue soap.

Oil, lubricating, preservative, light.

Oil, lubricating, for aircraft instruments and machine guns.

Compound, rust preventive, light.

Solvent, dry cleaning.

Decontaminating agents.

a. Rifle bore cleaner.—(1) Rifle bore cleaner is issued for cleaning the bore of the mortar after firing. This material possesses rust preventive properties and will provide temporary protection against rust. It is preferable, however, to dry the bore immediately after using rifle bore cleaner and to apply a thin coat of light preservative lubricating oil to the metal.

(2) Rifle bore cleaner will freeze at temperatures below 32° F. If frozen, it must be thawed and shaken well before using. During freezing weather, closed containers should not be filled more than three-fourths full, as full containers will burst if the contents freeze.

b. Soda ash.—This is a white, odorless powder which is soluble in water. For use, this material is dissolved in water in the proportion of 1½ tablespoons of soda ash to 1 pint of boiling water, preferably, or else hot or cold water. This solution can be used to clean the bore when rifle bore cleaner is not available.

c. Soap.—A solution of soap should be used for cleaning the bore if rifle bore cleaner or soda ash are not available. Prepare the solution by dissolving issue soap which has been broken up in hot water in the proportion of ¼ pound soap chips to 1 gallon of water. This solution should be used hot but can also be used cold.

d. Light preservative lubricating oil.—This oil has rust-preventive as well as lubricating properties but cannot be depending upon to provide protection from rust for relatively long periods. It is used for the lubrication of all moving parts and for short term protection of the bore against rust. Preservative action results partly from the oily film on the metal parts and partly from chemical combination of inhibitors in the oil with the metal. It will protect the metal surfaces from rust though no appreciable film of oil is present on the metal parts. When used on moving parts it is necessary to maintain a thin film of oil to provide the necessary lubrication.

e. Lubricating oil for aircraft instruments and machine guns.—This oil may be used for lubricating the mortar matériel when light preservative lubricating oil is not available. It is an extremely light oil which relies entirely upon maintenance of the oil film to protect metal surfaces from rusting. When it is used as a preservative, the metal parts must be inspected daily for rust. They should then be cleaned and again coated lightly with the oil.

f. Light rust-preventive compound.—This compound is issued for the protection of metal parts for long periods of time while the parts are boxed and in storage. It can be applied with a brush at temperatures above 60° F., but the preferred method is to apply it hot, either by brushing or by dipping.

g. Dry-cleaning solvent.—This noncorrosive, petroleum solvent will remove grease, oil, or rust-preventive compound. Dry-cleaning solvent is highly inflammable and should not be used near open flames. Smoking is prohibited where dry-cleaning solvent is used. It is generally applied with rag swabs to large parts and used as a bath for small parts. The surfaces must be thoroughly dried with clean rags immediately after use of the solvent. Gloves should be worn by persons handling such parts after cleaning to avoid leaving finger marks, which are ordinarily acid and induce corrosion. Dry-cleaning solvent will attack and discolor rubber.

■ 8. CLEANING INSTRUMENTS.—*a.* The following are the only instruments authorized and issued for cleaning and lubricating the mortar. For complete list of accessories, see page 14, SNL A–33.

Brush, chamber, cleaning, M6.
Staff, cleaning, 50 inches, M2.
Tool, firing pin vent cleaning.
Oiler, oval, 3 ounces.

Gun, lubricating, pressure, pistol grip, flush type, 5 ounces.

Staff, cleaning, 6 feet 6 inches, M4 (aluminum). (Staff, cleaning, 6 feet 6 inches, M8 (wooden) may be issued in lieu of this item.)

b. See paragraph 36 for description of these instruments.

■ **9. CARE AND CLEANING WHEN NO FIRING IS DONE.**—*a. General.*—(1) This includes the care necessary to preserve the condition of the mortar and mount during the time when no firing is being done.

(2) Mortar matériel in the hands of troops should be inspected daily to insure proper condition and cleanliness. Training schedules should allow time for supervised cleaning on each day this matériel is used.

b. Bore.—(1) To clean the bore, attach cotton waste to the cleaning staff and insert the waste into the bore at the muzzle end. Move the staff forward and backward several times and replace with clean waste. This cleaning removes accumulations of dust, dirt, and thickened oil in the bore.

(2) Repeat until the waste comes out clean.

(3) After the bore has been thoroughly cleaned, saturate clean waste with light preservative lubricating oil and push it through the bore.

(4) Wash the outside of the barrel with soap solution, rinse with clean water, and dry.

Caution: When cleaning the bore, be careful not to foul the waste on the firing pin.

c. Firing pin.—(1) Remove the firing pin.

(2) Wrap cotton waste around the chamber cleaning brush and insert into the firing pin vent. Clean the vent by moving the waste back and forth through the vent. Make sure that the waste goes all the way through the vent. Repeat with clean waste until the waste comes out clean.

(3) After the vent has been thoroughly cleaned, saturate clean waste with light preservative lubricating oil and push it in the out of the vent.

(4) Clean the firing pin with waste.

(5) Oil the firing pin with clean waste which is wet with light preservative lubricating oil.

(6) Check the threads in the base cap and on the firing pin to make sure that no lint is present.

(7) Assemble the firing pin to the base cap.

d. Mount.—(1) All parts of the bipod and base plate must be kept clean and free from foreign matter. All moving parts and polished surfaces must be kept coated with oil.

(2) To clean the screw threads and crevices, use a small cleaning brush or small stick.

(3) To clean the metal surfaces, rub with a dry cloth to remove moisture, perspiration, and dirt. Then wipe with a cloth wet with a small quantity of light preservative lubricating oil. This protective film must be maintained at all times.

(4) For oiling parts of the bipod, seven flush-type lubricating fittings have been provided. They are found as follows:

One on connecting rod bracket.
One on gear case.
One on rear half of the left leg clevis.
One on leg clevis, retainer, rear.
Three in yoke.

When oiling is required, apply light preservative lubricating oil to these points by means of the lubricating gun.

■ 10. Preparatory to Firing.—Before firing, take the following steps to insure efficient functioning of the mortar:

a. Inspect the three units.

b. Clean the bore and firing pin with clean, dry waste. Do not apply any oil to these parts before firing.

c. Thoroughly clean and lightly oil all metal moving parts with light preservative lubricating oil. Do not use grease.

d. Mount the mortar for firing.

■ 11. After Firing.—*a. General.*—(1) The bores of all mortars must be thoroughly cleaned by the evening of the day in which they are fired. They should be cleaned in the same manner for the next 3 days.

(2) Firing the mortar causes powder and primer fouling to collect in the bore and on the firing pin. This fouling absorbs and retains moisture from the air, thereby causing rust. These deposits can be removed by cleaning with rifle bore cleaner, soda ash solution, soap solution, or water.

b. Cleaning procedure after firing.—(1) Clean bore (*c* or *d* below) and all working parts. If this cannot be done at once, apply oil carefully to prevent rust.

(2) At the first opportunity, clean, oil, and inspect all parts and make needed repairs and replacements.

(3) On assembly, check operation of the bipod to insure that functioning is correct.

c. Cleaning bore with rifle bore cleaner.—(1) Remove the firing pin.

(2) Assemble clean cotton waste to the cleaning staff and saturate the waste with rifle bore cleaner. Insert the waste into the muzzle and push it back and forth through the bore of the barrel by means of the cleaning staff.

(3) Repeat the operation with clean waste two or three times. Care should be used to insure that the swab goes all the way through the bore before the direction is changed.

(4) Follow this with dry waste until it comes out clean and dry.

(5) Examine the bore carefully for cleanliness. If it is not free of all residue, repeat the cleaning process.

(6) Clean the firing pin with a rag saturated with rifle bore cleaner. Dry the firing pin.

(7) Wrap cotton waste around the chamber cleaning brush and saturate it with rifle bore cleaner. Clean the vent by pushing the waste back and forth through the vent. Repeat with clean waste several times. Follow this with dry waste until it comes out clean and dry.

(8) When the vent and bore are both thoroughly clean and dry, apply light preservative lubricating oil to them by means of waste.

(9) Make sure no lint is on the firing pin threads, oil the pin, and replace it in the base cap.

d. Cleaning the bore with soda ash or soap solution.—(1) Use soda ash solution if rifle bore cleaner is not available, and soap solution or plain water if neither of these is available.

(2) Clean the vent and firing pin as described in *c* (9) above, using a liberal quantity of the soda ash or soap solution in place of the rifle bore cleaner.

(3) Rinse the parts with clean water to remove the washing material.

(4) Dry the parts by using clean waste. Thoroughly swab barrel until it is perfectly dry and clean.

(5) When the bore, vent, and firing pin are clean and dry, saturate waste in light preservative lubricating oil and push it through the bore. Oil the vent and firing pin and assemble the pin to the base cap.

e. *Mount.*—(1) Wipe the bipod clean, taking care to remove dirt from all crevices. Thoroughly clean all moving parts with dry-cleaning solvent, using a small stick covered with waste to remove dirt from all recesses.

(2) Dry all parts thoroughly.

(3) Wipe all moving parts and polished surfaces with a rag wet with light preservative lubricating oil.

(4) Apply light preservative lubricating oil to the seven flush-type lubricating fittings.

(5) Operate the handwheel and cranks so as to distribute the oil over the working surfaces.

f. *Exterior surfaces.*—Wipe off exterior of the mortar with a dry cloth to remove dampness, dirt, and perspiration.

g. *Accessories.*—Inspect, clean, and oil the accessories.

h. *Complete cleaning.*—Complete cleaning should be accomplished as soon as possible after firing. If the mortar is not to be fired in the next few days, repeat the procedure outlined above for 3 days.

■ 12. ON THE RANGE OR IN THE FIELD.—The mortar must be kept clean and properly lubricated. To obtain its maximum efficiency, the following points must be observed:

a. Never fire a mortar with any dust, dirt, mud, or snow in the bore.

b. Keep the bore free from oil and dirt when firing.

c. Never leave waste or other obstruction in the bore or on the firing pin.

d. If the bipod gives indication of lack of lubrication and excessive friction, apply additional oil to the parts subjected to this friction.

e. All sliding surfaces should be oiled frequently and freely to insure perfect functioning of the mount.

f. In general, it should not be necessary to remove any of the parts of the bipod in the field for cleaning. However, if the mechanism of the bipod becomes very dirty, it should be disassembled for the necessary cleaning and lubrication by ordnance personnel.

g. In emergencies when the prescribed lubricant is not available, use lubricating oil for aircraft instruments and machine guns or any clean, light mineral oil such as engine oil.

■ 13. PREPARATION FOR STORAGE.—*a.* Light preservative lubricating oil is the most suitable oil for short-time protection of the mechanism of the mortar. It is effective for storage for periods of 2 to 6 weeks, depending on climatic conditions. However, mortars in short-time storage must be inspected every 5 days, and the preservative film should be renewed if necessary. For longer periods of time, they will be protected with light rust-preventive compound.

b. Light rust-preventive compound is a semisolid material. It is efficient for preserving the polished surfaces and the bore for a period of 1 year or less, depending upon climatic and storage conditions.

c. The mortar should be cleaned and prepared for storage with particular care. The bore, all parts of the bipod, and the exterior of the mortar should be thoroughly cleaned with dry-cleaning solvent and then dried completely with clean rags. In damp climates particular care must be taken to see that the rags are dry. After drying a metal part the bare hands should not touch that part. All metal parts should then be coated with either light preservative lubricating oil or light rust-preventive compound, depending on the length of storage required. Application of the rust-preventive compound to the bore is best done by dipping waste in the compound and running it through the bore two or three times by means of the staff. The firing pin and base cap should be removed, thoroughly coated with rust-preventive compound, and then reassembled. The wooden supports of the packing box must be painted with rust-preventive compound before storing the mortar. Place it in the wooden packing box, handling it with oiled rags. Under no circumstances will a mortar be placed in storage while contained in a cloth or other cover, or with a plug in the bore. Such covers collect moisture, which causes the weapon to rust.

■ 14. CLEANING WEAPONS RECEIVED FROM STORAGE.—Weapons which have been stored in accordance with the preceding paragraphs will be coated either with light preservative lubricating oil or with light rust-preventive compounds. Weapons received from ordnance storage will in general be coated with rust-preventive compound. Use dry-cleaning solvent to dissolve and remove all traces of the compound or oil. Take particular care that all small parts and springs are cleaned thoroughly. Failure to do this may cause stiff or slow action at normal temperatures and will certainly do so when the rust-preventive compound congeals at low temperatures. After using this cleaning solvent, be sure to dry all parts by wiping with dry cloths. Then follow the instructions in paragraph 9.

■ 15. CARE AND CLEANING UNDER UNUSUAL CONDITIONS.—a. In cold climates.—(1) It is necessary that the moving parts of the weapon be kept absolutely free from moisture. It also has been found that excess oil or rust-preventive compound on the working parts will solidify to such an extent as to cause sluggish operation or complete failure.

(2) Clean all parts thoroughly with dry-cleaning solvent before use in temperatures below 0° F. The working surfaces or parts which show signs of wear may be lubricated by rubbing with a cloth which has been saturated with light preservative lubricating oil and wrung out.

(3) When brought indoors, the matériel should first be allowed to come to room temperature. It should then be wiped completely dry of the moisture which will have condensed on the cold metal surfaces and oiled thoroughly with light preservative lubricating oil.

(4) If possible, such condensation should be avoided by providing a cold place in which to keep the mortar when not in use, for example, a separate cold room, or when in the field, proper cover set up outdoors.

(5) If the mortar has been fired, it should be thoroughly cleaned and oiled. The bore may be swabbed out with oily waste, and when the weapon reaches room temperature, thoroughly cleaned and oiled as described in paragraph 11.

(6) Before firing, the weapon should be cleaned and oiled as described in paragraph 10.

(7) The bore and firing pin should be entirely free of oil before firing.

b. *In tropical climates.*—(1) In tropical climates where temperature and humidity are high, or where salt air is present, and during rainy seasons, the weapon should be inspected thoroughly every day and kept lightly oiled when not in use.

(2) Care should be exercised to see that unexposed parts and surfaces are kept clean and oiled.

(3) Light preservative lubricating oil should be used for lubrication.

c. *In hot, dry climates.*—(1) In hot, dry climates where sand and dust are apt to get into the mechanism and bore, the weapons should be wiped clean daily, or oftener if necessary.

(2) When the weapon is being used under sandy conditions, all lubricant should be wiped from the matériel. This will prevent sand carried by the wind from sticking to the lubricant and forming an abrasive compound which will ruin the mechanism.

(3) Immediately upon leaving sandy terrain, the weapon must be relubricated with light preservative lubricating oil.

(4) Perspiration from the hands is a contributing factor to rust because it contains acid. Consequently metal parts should be wiped dry frequently.

(5) During sand or dust storms, the muzzle should be kept covered whenever possible.

■ 16. CARE DURING GAS ATTACK.—*a.* (1) It is important to prevent the chemicals used in a gas attack from getting in or on the mortar and ammunition. When a gas attack is anticipated, steps will be taken to cover and protect the mortar, ammunition, bipod, spare parts, and accessories.

(2) Apply oil to the surfaces of all the parts of the weapon, ammunition, and spare parts.

(3) If the mortar is not to be used during the gas attack, the oiled weapon should be covered or placed in a container so that it cannot come into contact with any contaminating chemicals.

(4) After the attack, if the matériel has not been contaminated, it should be cleaned with dry-cleaning solvent.

(5) Prepare for use as described in paragraph 9 or 10 according to requirements.

b. Decontamination.—(1) A complete suit of impermeable clothing and a service gas mask must be worn for decontamination.

(2) Matériel contaminated with chemicals other than mustard or lewisite must be cleaned as soon as possible with dry-cleaning solvent or denatured alcohol.

(3) Do not allow the chemical agents to come into contact with the skin. Always burn or bury all rags or wiping materials used for decontamination. Extreme caution should be taken to protect men against fumes created by burning.

(4) If the surface of the matériel is coated with grease or oil and has been in a mustard or lewisite attack, first remove the grease or oil by wiping with rags saturated with dry-cleaning solvent.

(5) Decontaminate unpainted metal surfaces with a solution of agent, decontaminating, noncorrosive. Prepare this by mixing 1 part of agent, decontaminating, noncorrosive, to 15 parts solvent (acetylene tetrachloride) by weight.

(6) Decontaminate painted surfaces with a bleaching solution. Prepare this by mixing equal parts by weight of agent, decontaminating (chloride of lime) and water.

(7) After decontamination, clean the matériel thoroughly and prepare for use as described in paragraph 9 or 10 according to requirements.

c. References.—Detailed information on decontamination is contained in FM 21–40, TM 9–850 and 3–220.

■ 17. INSPECTION.—The following instructions with reference to inspection will be carefully observed by all concerned:

Points to be inspected in order of inspection	*Points to observe*
a. Mortar.	*a.* Note general appearance and cleanliness of the bore.
b. Firing pin.	*b.* Examine for fouling, rust, or foreign substance on the point.

Points to be inspected in order of inspection	Points to observe
c. Bipod.	c. Note general appearance. Oil fittings should be encircled by a red ring. All moving parts should be properly lubricated.
(1) Elevating mechanism.	(1) Elevate and depress the mortar. The mechanism should operate without binding, excess play, or undue backlash.
(2) Traversing mechanism.	(2) Traverse the mortar. The mechanism should operate smoothly without binding or undue backlash.
(3) Cross-leveling mechanism.	(3) Operate the mechanism. It should function properly without excess play. The level vial should be clear, and index marks for centering the bubble should be distinct.
d. Base plate.	d. Note general appearance. The edges of the free recesses in the socket should be smooth and without bur.
e. Sight and its mounting.	e. Note whether the operating condition of the sight or rigidity of its mounting has been impaired. (See TM 9–60.)

Section IV

SIGHTING EQUIPMENT

■ 18. AIMING POSTS.—a. Aiming posts are supplied with the 81-mm mortar M1 as follows:

1 aiming post M7, 3 feet 10 inches long, for pack transport only.

1 aiming post M9, 2 feet long, for all uses.

1 aiming post M8, 6 feet long, for other than pack transport.

b. In addition to the issued aiming posts, it is advisable to have available with the squad equipment at least three improvised wooden aiming stakes. These may be prepared locally with approximately the following dimensions: 2 inches x 1 inch x 3 feet.

■ 19. SIGHT M4 (fig 6).—a. General description.—The sight M4, provided with the 81-mm mortar for laying in elevation and direction, is likewise the standard sight for the 60-mm mortar. The sight includes a collimator, elevating and lateral deflection mechanisms, and longitudinal and cross levels, all supported by a bracket with a dovetailed base which fits in a slot in the mortar yoke and latches in place. The levels when centered indicate the elevation and deflection angles, respectively, to be measured in true vertical and horizontal planes. The longitudinal level also provides a datum line for elevation settings. The collimator, the direction sighting device of the sight, consists of a vertical translucent line in the opaque field of the eyepiece, inclosed within a rectangular tube. When the sight is level, the collimator establishes a vertical line in the field of view, the line of sight with a normal lateral deflection setting being parallel to the plane of fire. The bracket upon which the collimator and open sight are mounted can be pivoted so that the assembly may be moved in elevation as required to bring the aiming point into the field of view; this motion has no effect on elevation indications. The sight is removed for traveling, and a carrying case for it is provided.

   b. Detailed description, sight M4.—This sight (fig. 6) is now furnished with the 81-mm mortar M1. Elevation in degrees is indicated on the elevation scale, graduated in 10° steps, supplemented by a micrometer graduated in ¼° steps. Deflection in mils is indicated on the deflection scale, which is graduated in 5-mil steps. Directions of motion for left and right deflections are indicated by the letters L and R and arrows near the index. Deflection is limited to ±150 mils, and a zero indication corresponds to the normal setting (line of sight parallel to the plane of fire). The collimator and the open sight directly below it have vertical reference lines and may be placed as desired in elevation. With the collimator moved to the extreme rear and an elevation setting of 40°, the elevation of the overhead portion of the open sight is 2° below the axis of the mortar tube, a feature of service in determining the approximate minimum elevation for clearing nearby objects.

   c. Operation.—(1) Remove the sight from the carrying case and insert the dovetailed base of the bracket in the slot of the mortar yoke. When the sight is fully inserted, the

latch will snap into place, securing the sight in position.
Check to see that the sight is firmly seated, latched, and free
from motion.

(2) Set the elevation and lateral deflection to the desired
values.   Range elevation data are obtainable from the pertinent firing table.   The angle of elevation is measured in
degrees.   Deflection angles are indicated in mils.

(3) Operate the elevating crank, centering the bubble in
the longitudinal level.   Then traverse until the vertical line

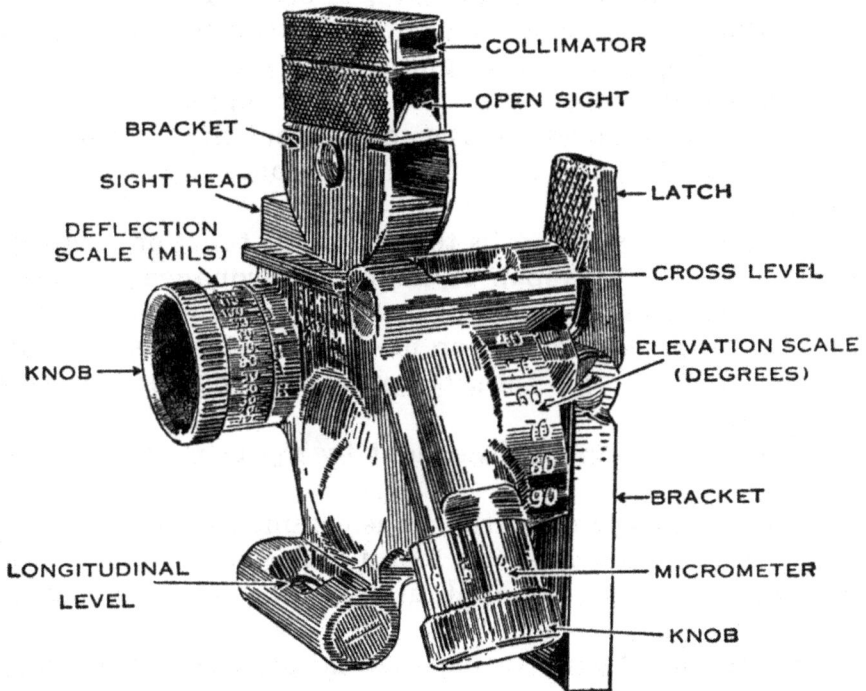

FIGURE 6.—Sight M4

of the collimator is laid on the aiming point (stake) and, *at
the same time,* move the adjusting nut in the same direction
as the traversing handwheel is moved in order to cross-level.
The mortar is then properly laid for elevation and direction.

(4) The sight should be removed prior to the firing of the
first three rounds or until such time as the base plate is
firmly seated.

(5) To remove the sight for traveling, depress the latch
to release the bracket (see fig. 11②), withdraw the sight and

place it in the carrying case provided, with the elevation scale set at 40°.

d. Tests and adjustments.—Proper alinement of the levels, pivots, and collimator is accomplished at the factory. No facilities are ordinarily available for verification in the field, and no adjustment by the using arm is permitted.

e. Care and preservation.—(1) The sight is a rugged instrument but will not stand abuse or rough handling. Inaccuracy or malfunctioning will result from such mistreatment. Care must be taken to avoid striking or otherwise injuring any part of the sight—particularly burring or denting the locating surface of the sight bracket and mortar yoke.

(2) When it is not in use, the sight should be kept in the carrying case provided. It is essential that the sight be kept as dry as possible and that it is never placed in the carrying case while wet.

(3) Any sight which fails to indicate or function correctly is to be turned in for repair by competent ordnance personnel.

(4) No painting of the sight by the using arm is permitted.

(5) Elevation and deflection mechanisms have stops limiting their motion. Do not attempt to turn the knobs beyond these limits.

(6) No disassembly of the sight by the using arm is permitted.

(7) Keep the optical parts of the collimator clean and dry. For wiping these parts, use lens tissue paper. The use of polishing liquids, pastes, or abrasives is prohibited for polishing optical parts.

(8) Occasionally oil the exposed moving parts of the sight with a small quantity of light preservative lubricating oil or lubricating oil for aircraft instruments and machine guns. Keep the dovetailed surface of the bracket and the mating surface of the mortar yoke thinly coated with light preservative lubricating oil or light rust-preventive compound. To prevent accumulation of dust and grit, wipe off excess lubricant that seeps from moving parts.

SECTION V

AMMUNITION

■ 20. GENERAL.—The information in this section pertaining to several types of semifixed complete rounds authorized for use in the 81–mm mortar M1 includes a description of the round, means of identification, care, use, and ballistic data.

■ 21. CLASSIFICATION.—Based upon use, the principal classifications of ammunition for the mortar are—
    a. High explosive, light, for use against personnel (fig. 7①).
    b. High explosive, heavy, for demolitions against shelters and accessory defenses (fig. 7②).
    c. Smoke, for blinding enemy observation (similar in construction and appearance to the shell, M56).
    d. Practice, for training purposes.

■ 22. AMMUNITION LOT NUMBER.—When ammunition is manufactured, an ammunition lot number, which becomes an essential part of the marking, is assigned in accordance with pertinent specifications. This ammunition lot number is stamped or marked on every loaded complete round, on packing containers, and on the accompanying ammunition data card. It is required for all purposes of record, including reports on condition, functioning, and accidents in which the ammunition might be involved.

■ 23. IDENTIFICATION.—*a. Marking on fiber containers.*—The contents of fiber containers are readily identified by the markings. Additional data pertaining to the round contained therein are included on the ammunition data card packed with the round in the fiber container.
    b. Color of projectiles.—All projectiles are painted to prevent rust and, by means of the color, to provide a ready method of identification as to type. The color scheme is as follows:
    (1) High explosive projectiles, yellow.
    (2) Smoke projectiles, gray with narrow yellow band.
    (3) Practice, blue.
    (4) Training, black.

c. Markings on round.—The complete round when removed from its fiber container is identified by the following information stenciled thereon:

(1) Caliber of mortar in which fired.

(2) Kind of filler.

(3) Model of shell.

(4) Ammunition lot number.

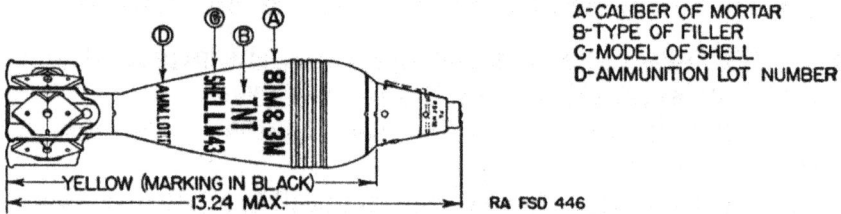

① M43, 81-mm mortar (with PDF M52).

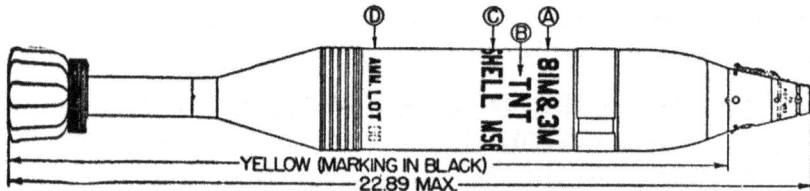

② M56, 81-mm mortar (with PDF M53).

FIGURE 7.—HE shell.

■ 24. CARE, HANDLING, AND PRESERVATION.—*a.* Ammunition is made and packed to withstand all conditions ordinarily encountered in the field. However, ammunition is adversely affected by moisture and high temperature, and should be protected accordingly.

b. Complete rounds, being fuzed, must be handled with due care at all times. The explosive elements in primers and fuzes are particularly sensitive to strong shock and high temperature.

c. The moisture-resistant seal of the fiber container should not be broken until the ammunition is to be used. Where a large number of rounds (15 or more per squad) must be prepared prior to a combat mission, the rounds may be removed from the containers, the propellent increments adjusted, and the safety wires removed. The fin assembly of each round should then be reinserted in the container to protect the powder.

d. Do not attempt to disassemble any fuze.

e. Protect the ammunition carefully from mud, sand, dirt, and water. Free the round of such foreign matter before firing. Should it get wet or dirty, wipe it off at once.

f. Do not allow the ammunition, particularly the propellent increments, to be exposed to the direct rays of the sun for any length of time. More uniform firing is obtained if the rounds are at the same temperature.

g. Just before firing, remove the safety wire from the fuze.

h. When firing, enter the round into the mortar, cartridge end first. When the projectile is released to slide down the bore, remove the hand promptly from the muzzle.

i. When rounds have been prepared for firing, but are not used, return them to their original packing and mark them appropriately. In subsequent firing use such rounds first.

j. Do not handle duds. After firing, fuzes are extremely dangerous.

■ 25. STORAGE.—Whenever practicable, ammunition should be stored under cover. Should it be necessary to leave the ammunition in the open, it should be raised at least 6 inches from the ground, and the pile should be covered with a double thickness of tarpaulin. Suitable trenches should be dug to prevent water from flowing under the pile.

■ 26. AUTHORIZED ROUNDS.—*a. General.*—(1) With the exception of the M45 shell, the 81-mm mortar ammunition is standard for use in this mortar. The M45 shell is limited standard. The 81-mm mortar ammunition is issued as fuzed complete rounds.

(2) Because of its stabilizing fins, this ammunition, even though fired from a smooth bore mortar, is stable in flight and strikes nose end first. A point detonating impact type of fuze is fitted to the nose of the shell. The propelling charge, consisting of an ignition cartridge and propellent increments, is attached to the base end of the projectile. The increments of the charge are removable to provide for zone firing. When fired, the projectile carries the fired ignition cartridge case with it. The mortar is then ready for the next round.

b. *Designation of rounds.*—The rounds authorized for use in the mortar, 81-mm, M1 are listed below. The designation completely identifies the ammunition as to type and model.

AMMUNITION FOR 81-MM MORTAR M1

Nomenclature	Prescribed fuzes		Approximate weight as fired
	Model	Action	
Service ammunition			*Pounds*
Shell, HE, M43 w/PDF [1]	M45	SQ-D	6.92
Shell, HE, M43 w/PDF [1]	M52	SQ	6.92
Shell, HE, M43A1 w/PDF [1]	M52	SQ	6.92
Shell, HE, M45 w/PDF [2]	M45	SQ-D	15.01
Shell, HE, M45B1 w/PDF [2]	M53	Del	15.05
Shell, HE, M56 w/PDF [2]	M53	Del	10.62
Shell, smoke, FS, M57 w/PDF [2]	M52	SQ	11.86
Shell, smoke, WP, M57 w/PDF [2]	M52	SQ	11.36
Shell, gas, persistent, HS, M57 w/PDF [2]	M52	SQ	10.41
Target practice ammunition			
Shell, practice, M43 w/PDF [1]	M52	SQ	6.92
Shell, practice, M43A1 w/PDF [1]	M52	SQ	6.92
Shell, practice, M43 w/PDF [1]	M45	SQ-D	6.92
Shell, practice, M44 w/PDF	M52	SQ	6.92
Projectile, training, M68 [3]			10.75

SQ—superquick; Del—delay; PDF—point detonating fuze.

[1] Full (outer zone) propelling charge, when fired in 81-mm mortar, consists of an ignition cartridge and six propellent increments. Full charge is assembled to the base of the shell, as issued.

[2] Full (outer zone) propelling charge consists of an ignition cartridge and 4 propellent increments when fired in 81-mm mortar. Full charge is assembled to the base of the shell, as issued.

[3] Uses ignition cartridge only.

■ 27. PREPARATION FOR FIRING.—This ammunition, which is issued as assembled complete rounds, is prepared for firing as follows:

a. Adjust propelling charge for the zone to be fired (par. 28).

b. Remove safety wire from fuze (par. 54).

■ **28. PROPELLING CHARGES.**—*a. G e n e r a l.*—The propelling charges for mortar ammunition are divided into parts to provide for zone firing.

b. M43 shell.—The full (outer zone) charge consists of an ignition cartridge and six equal increments (bundles of sheet powder or capsules of granular powder) assembled to the base of the round as issued. One increment is fitted into each of the spaces between the blades of the fin. To prepare the charge for firing inner zones, it is only necessary to remove those increments not required. This shell is limited standard.

c. M45 shell.—The full (outer zone) charge consists of an ignition cartridge and four equal propellent increments (bundles of sheet powder or capsules of granular powder) assembled to the base of the round as issued. One increment is fitted into each of the four spaces between the blades of the fin. To prepare the charge for firing inner zones it is only necessary to remove those increments not required.

d. M56 and M57 shell.—The full (outer zone) charge consists of an ignition cartridge and four propellent increments (bundles of sheet powder) assembled to the base of the round as issued. The increments are held against the forward edge of the fin by means of a propellent holder. To prepare the charge for firing inner zones it is only necessary to remove those increments not required.

NOTE.—Unused increments will be destroyed at the firing line by burning. Because of high combustibility, extreme care should be taken in igniting the increments.

e. M68 training projectile.—An ignition cartridge is the only propelling charge provided for this projectile.

■ **29. FUZES M52 AND M53.**—*a. General.*—Fuzes used on 81-mm shells are classified as bore-safe (detonator-safe), that is, they are fitted with safety devices by which the explosive train is so interrupted that prior to firing and subsequent to firing, while the projectile is still in the barrel of the mortar, premature action of the bursting charge is prevented should any of the more sensitive elements, the primer or detonator, malfunction.

b. Types.—(1) The *superquick* fuze (M52) is designed to function before any penetration occurs, permitting the maximum surface effect of fragmentation of the shell.

(2) The *delay* fuze (M53) is designed to allow penetration of targets before detonating, thereby producing a demolition effect.

c. Safety features and functioning of fuze M52 (fig. 8).— (1) *Safety features.*—(a) The *safety wire* inserted through the body of the fuze and the set-back pin, thereby locking all moveable parts in their original safe position. The safety wire is pulled just prior to firing.

(b) The *set-back pin*, held in place by the safety wire, in turn locks the safety pin in position. The set-back pin is supported by a spring and is positioned in a recess of the safety pin. Until the set-back pin moves out of this recess, the safety pin is locked in the body of the fuze.

(c) The *safety pin*, held in place by the set-back pin, is the main locking device of the fuze. It holds the slider (which contains the primer and detonator) in its retracted position and prevents premature alinement of the various elements of the powder train.

(2) *Functioning.*—(a) The fuze M52 is not armed until the primer and slider detonator are alined with the firing pin and booster lead. The first step in the arming of the fuze is the removal of the safety wire just before firing. The shell, when inserted in the barrel, slides down until the primer of the ignition cartridge strikes the firing pin of the mortar. The combined forces of the shell striking the breech of the mortar and the blow delivered to the shell by the propelling charge gases cause the inertia of the set-back pin to overcome the resistance of the set-back pin spring and permit the set-back pin to move toward the base of the fuze. This movement withdraws the shank of the set-back pin from the recess of the safety pin. The safety pin, now being released by the set-back pin, is thrown outward by the action of the safety pin spring, but is prevented from leaving the fuze by striking and bearing against the bore of the mortar.

At this time, the safety pin has not moved far enough to disengage the slider, and the slider remains locked in its unarmed position.

(b) When the shell leaves the muzzle and the restraint on the safety pin is released, the pin and spring fly out of the fuze, thereby releasing the slider. Under the action of the slider spring, the slider is forced to the opposite end of its

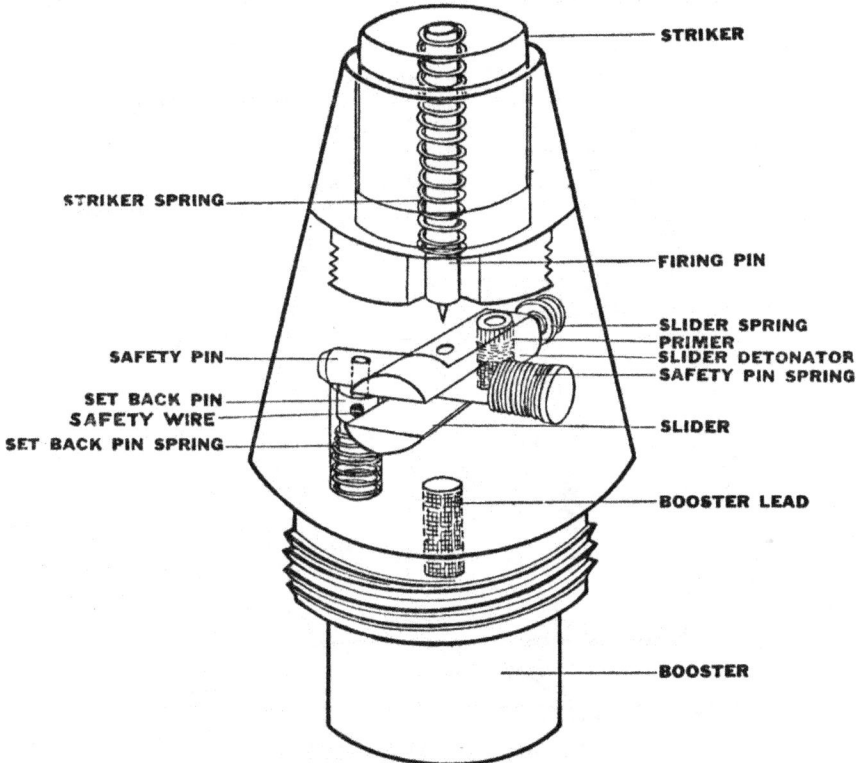

FIGURE 8.—Fuze M52.

chamber. The slider locking pin, pressed upward by its spring and guided by a groove in the lower surface of the slider, is lined up with a recess in the slider. The spring forces it into the recess, locking the slider in position and completing the powder train. At this time, the fuze is completely armed.

(c) When the shell hits the ground, the striker is compressed and drives the firing pin into the primer of the slider. The flash from the primer ignites the detonator, which in turn explodes the booster lead and the booster. The explosion of the booster detonates the TNT filler in the body of the shell.

d. Safety features and functioning of fuze M53 (fig. 9)—The fuze is constructed with the three safety features of the fuze M52 and an additional feature called the shear wire. The shear wire hold the striker and firing pin unit away from the primer. This wire will resist a severe blow, so

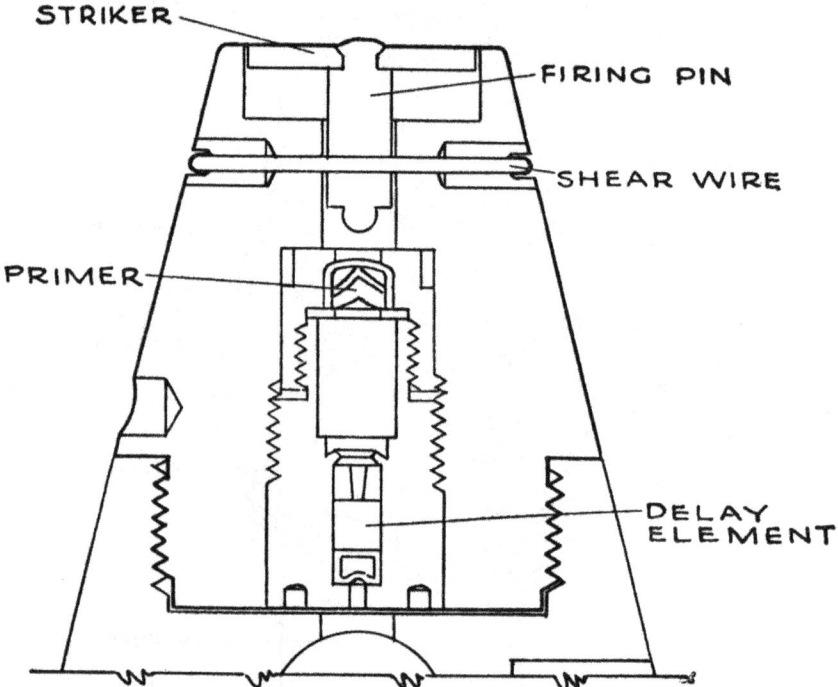

FIGURE 9.—Fuze M53.

that even when the fuze is armed it will be comparatively safe.

The fuze M53 has a different striker and a separate primer (not part of the slider) but is otherwise similar in construction and functioning to the fuze M52.

■ 30. FUZE, PDF, M45.—*a. Description.*—This limited standard fuze is a combination superquick and short delay type identified by "PDF, M45" stamped on the body. For use in the field, it is issued assembled to the shell as a component of the complete round. The fuze is set by rotating the head assembly to bring either the knurled button SQ or the engraved line D into alinement with the common reference point (knurled button and line) on the body. Two concealed spring-actuated pins aid in locating the exact position of alinement and hold the head in the position as set. The setting may be changed before firing, although the setting should be made before the cotter pin has been removed. Since the knurled buttons and the engraved line can be felt by the fingers, the setting can be made in the dark.

b. Preparation for firing.—(1) *Superquick action.*—Since the superquick fuze is set for superquick action before shipment, it is only necessary to remove the cotter pin to prepare the fuze for firing. The strip of adhesive tape which holds the ring against the fuze is removed first; then the ring is pulled to withdraw the cotter pin.

(2) *Delayed action.*—To prepare the delay fuze for action, the head assembly is rotated so that the engraved reference lines are in alinement; the cotter pin is removed before firing.

■ 31. TRAINING PROJECTILE M68.—This projectile has a solid cast body, a standard fin assembly, weighs approximately 10.75 pounds, and is propelled by an ignition cartridge only. The projectile contains no bursting charge and, due to the increased weight, has a maximum range of about 330 yards. Extra fin assemblies come in containers and serve as replacements in the event the assembly used with the projectile becomes unserviceable. There are furnished with each bundle a firing table for the training projectile, a hook with which to recover the projectile in the event that it becomes embedded in soft earth, and an extractor to remove fired cartridges. This projectile is of considerable value as a training aid (pars. 70 and 74).

■ 32. FIRING TABLES.—*a.* For the purpose of converting ranges in yards into elevations in degrees, firing tables are provided. These tables, printed on convenient cards, include a deflection-conversion table (see app. I) and instructions as to their use. In each bundle of ammunition a pertinent firing table will be found. Firing tables for instructional use may be obtained on requisition.

b. Tables applicable to the various types of 81-mm shell are as follows:

FT–81–B–3 (abridged) : For firing shell, HE, M43, M43A1, and practice shell, M43, M43A1, and M44.

FT–81–C–2 (abridged) : For firing shell, HE, M46, and shell, chemical M57 (FS), and M57 (WP).

FT–81–D–1 (abridged) : For firing shell, HE, M45.

FT–81–F–1 (abridged) : For projectile, training, M68.

c. Extracts of current firing tables are contained in appendix I.

d. Use.—(1) Since mortar fire is usually adjusted fire (par. 69), the gunner should select for his initial round a charge zone which permits a subsequent increase or decrease in range without changing the charge. The zone selected should be such that fire for adjustment and fire for effect can be completed without changing to another charge. Where the gunner has a choice betwen two charge zones, latitude in firing being provided in both, he will select the lower charge (see par. 66*b*(3)), since less dispersion results with the lower charge.

(2) It may be necessary (though undesirable), in subsequent adjustment of fire, to change to a higher elevation and charge. In such a case, the gunner will continue to use the higher charge until fire for effect has been delivered on that particular target. Fire adjustment is less accurate where there is a shift between charge zones during adjustment.

SECTION VI

DESTRUCTION OF ORDNANCE MATÉRIEL IN EVENT OF IMMINENT CAPTURE IN COMBAT ZONE

■ 32.1 GENERAL PRINCIPLES.—*a.* Tactical situations may arise when, owing to limitations of time or transportation, it will become impossible to evacuate all equipment. In such situations it is imperative that all matériel which cannot be evacuated be destroyed to prevent—

(1) Its capture intact by the enemy.

(2) Its use by the enemy, if captured, against our own troops.

b. (1) Methods for the destruction of mortars, their accessories, and ammunition, subject to capture or abandonment in the combat zone must be adequate, uniform, and easily followed in the field.

(2) Destruction must be as complete as the available time, equipment, and personnel will permit. If thorough destruction of all parts cannot be completed, those parts essential for the use of the mortar should be destroyed. Other parts which cannot easily be duplicated by the enemy should be ruined or removed. *The same essential parts must be destroyed on all like units to prevent the enemy's constructing one complete unit from several damaged ones by consolidation of serviceable parts.*

(3) The destruction of matériel is a command decision and will be ordered and carried out only on authority delegated by the division or higher commander. The standing operating procedure of the division may prescribe the conditions under which unit commanders will be authorized to destroy matériel.

c. To accomplish adequate and uniform destruction of matériel, it is essential that—

(1) All echelons prepare plans for the destruction of matériel in the event of imminent capture. Variations in the time available in which to effect the required destruction, and in the amount and nature of the matériel to be destroyed, as well as variations in the number of men available with whom to effect this destruction, dictate considerable flexibility in the preparation of plans.

(2) All echelons be trained to effect the desired destruction of matériel issued to them. *Training will not involve the actual destruction of matériel.*

■ **32.2. METHODS.**—*a.* The destruction procedures outlined are arranged *in order of effectiveness.* Destruction should be accomplished by method No. 1, if possible. If method No. 1 cannot be used, destruction or disposition should be accomplished by one of the other methods outlined, in the priority shown.

b. The sequence outlined should be adhered to, whichever method is used. Uniformity of destruction will then be obtained, whether or not the method is carried to completion.

c. Certain of the methods outlined require special tools and materials, such as TNT and incendiary grenades, which may not normally be items of issue. The issue of such special tools and materials, and the conditions under which destruction will be effected, *are command decisions in each case.*

d. Mortar.—(1) *Sight.*—Detach the sight. If evacuation is possible, carry away the sight; if evacuation is not possible, thoroughly smash the sight.

(2) *Barrel.*—(*a*) *Method No. 1.*—Place a complete round, with 24 propellent increments attached, and with the safety

FIGURE 9.1—Demolition of mortars, using excess increments.

wire in fuze not withdrawn, part way into the mortar barrel. Block the round in this position by jamming a stick, small-arms cartridge, or loop of ¼-inch or larger cord between the round and the side of the mortar barrel; a cord (or rope) 100 feet long is attached to the stick, cartridge, or loop. Take a covered position (see fig. 9.1) and pull the cord (or rope) to cause the round to slide down the barrel and be fired. The excess pressure caused by the large number of increments will burst the base end of the barrel. The danger zone is at least 100 yards. Elapsed time by this method: 1 minute.

(*b*) *Method No. 2.*—Drop two M14 incendiary grenades into the tube and ignite. One of the grenades should be equipped with a 15-second Bickford fuze, if available; otherwise the standard Buchon fuze may be used. Elapsed time by this method: 1 minute.

■ 32.3 AMMUNITION.—*a. General.*—Time will not usually permit the deliberate destruction of all the ammunition in forward combat areas. When time permits, ammunition on hand may be destroyed by firing the shells rapidly in the direction of the enemy. Large amounts, when sufficient time and materials are available, may be destroyed by the following methods, which will require from 30 to 60 minutes, within the regiment. (For methods and safety precautions, see ch. 4, TM 9–1900.)

b. Unpacked ammunition.—(1) Stack ammunition in small piles. Stack or pile most of the available gasoline in cans and drums around the ammunition. Throw onto the pile all available inflammable materials such as rags, scrap wood, and brush. Pour the remaining available gasoline over the pile. Sufficient inflammable material must be used to insure a very hot fire. Ignite the gasoline and take cover. (Small-arms ammunition may be heaped.)

(2) HE shells can be destroyed by sympathetic detonation, using TNT. Stack the ammunition in two stacks, about 3 inches apart, with the fuzes in each stack toward each other. Place TNT charges between the stacks, using a minimum of 1 pound of TNT for every 10 rounds of ammunition. Detonate all TNT charges simultaneously from cover.

c. Packed ammunition.—(1) Stack the bundled ammunition in small piles. Cover with all available inflammable materials, such as rags, scrap wood, brush, and gasoline in drums or cans. Pour gasoline over the pile. Ignite the gasoline and take cover. (Small-arms ammunition must be broken out of the boxes or cartons before burning.)

(2) (a) The destruction of packed ammunition by sympathetic detonation with TNT is not advocated for use in forward combat zones. To insure satisfactory destruction involves putting TNT in alternate bundles of ammunition, a time-consuming job.

(b) In rear areas or fixed installations, sympathetic detonation may be used to destroy large ammunition supplies if destruction by burning is not feasible. Stack the bundles. In each bundle of each row, place sufficient TNT blocks to insure the use of 1 pound of TNT for every 10 rounds of 81-mm ammunition. Place the TNT blocks at the fuze end of the rounds. Detonate all TNT charges simultaneously. See FM 5–25 for details of demolition planning and procedure.

■ 32.4. FIRE-CONTROL EQUIPMENT.—All fire-control equipment, including optical sights and binoculars, is difficult to replace. *Fire-control equipment should be the last equipment to be destroyed, if there is any chance that personnel will be able to evacuate it.* If evacuation of personnel is not possible, inflammable items such as firing tables, drawing boards, mil scales, and alidades (improvised) will be burned; all optical equipment such as compasses, binoculars (M3, and type EE), aiming circles, and range finders will be thoroughly smashed.

■ 32.5. DESTRUCTION OF CAPTURED ENEMY MATÉRIEL.—Captured enemy matériel which is not suitable for repair and issue to troops may be destroyed, in general, in the same manner as for equivalent United States equipment. In general, it should be destroyed before our own equipment.

CHAPTER 2

TRAINING OF GUNNER

Paragraphs
SECTION I. General _____ 33
II. Compass_____ 34
III. Spare parts and accessories_____ 35-36
IV. Training exercises_____ 37-44
V. Additional training _____ 45-49

SECTION I

GENERAL

■ 33. GENERAL.—The purpose of this chapter is to provide instruction and training for the gunner in the form of instructional material and exercises. The subject matter is restricted to that which pertains to the training of the gunner. The method of instruction will be as outlined in chapter 8. The sequences of instruction are progressive.

SECTION II

COMPASS

■ 34. LENSATIC COMPASS.—*a. Types.*—The lensatic compass is standard for fire control use with the 81-mm mortar; several similar models are issued. The prismatic compass may be used for fire control, but the watch compass is unsuitable for such use.

b. Description.—The latest type of lensatic compass is shown in figure 10. The carrying case, to which is attached a brass holding ring, is made of plastic. The hinged eyepiece contains a magnifying lens and is slotted on the end for sighting. The raising of the eyepiece releases the compass card. The compass card, pivoted in the center, is doubly graduated, the outer scale reading in mils, the inner scale reading in degrees. A compass stop plunger is provided on the side of the case. The hinged cover is slotted and contains a vertical wire for sighting. This wire is marked at each end by a luminous dot. The glass cover of the compass box is movable and is provided with a luminous line for use at night.

c. Use.—(1) In mortar units the lensatic compass is used primarily for measuring magnetic azimuths. It may also be used as a marching compass.

(2) If practicable, in order to obtain an accurate mil scale reading, the compass should be rested on a level surface, or on a flat-topped aiming stake. It may, however, be read when held in the hands, using the holding ring for support. The index line in some of the newer instruments is excessively broad. To obtain uniform readings, the *left edge* of the index should be consistently read whenever broad index lines are noted.

(3) The instrument must be held with the card as nearly level as possible to permit the needle to swing freely.

d. Operation.—(1) *To measure azimuth.*—Raise the eyepiece and cover; sight through the slot in the eyepiece and sighting wire on cover. Rotate the compass until the line of sight bisects the object to which azimuth is desired. Without altering the position of the compass, read the azimuth desired on the proper scale, looking through the eyepiece lens.

(2) *To lay off azimuth from observer's position.*—Rotate the compass until the given azimuth is opposite the index. Without disturbing the position of the compass, have an aiming stake placed on the line of sight of the compass.

(3) *To read back-azimuth from given object to observer.*—Proceed as in (1) above. If the azimuth thus determined is less than 3,200 mils, add 3,200 mils; if it is 3,200 mils or more, subtract 3,200 mils. The result is the back-azimuth desired.

(4) *To place observer on given azimuth from given point.*—The observer places himself approximately on the required line and reads the azimuth to the point as in (1) above. Holding the line of sight on the point, he moves to the right or left as required until the desired azimuth is opposite the index. A movement to the right decreases the reading; to the left increases it.

(5) *To determine horizontal angle between two points from position of observer.*—Read the azimuth to each point and

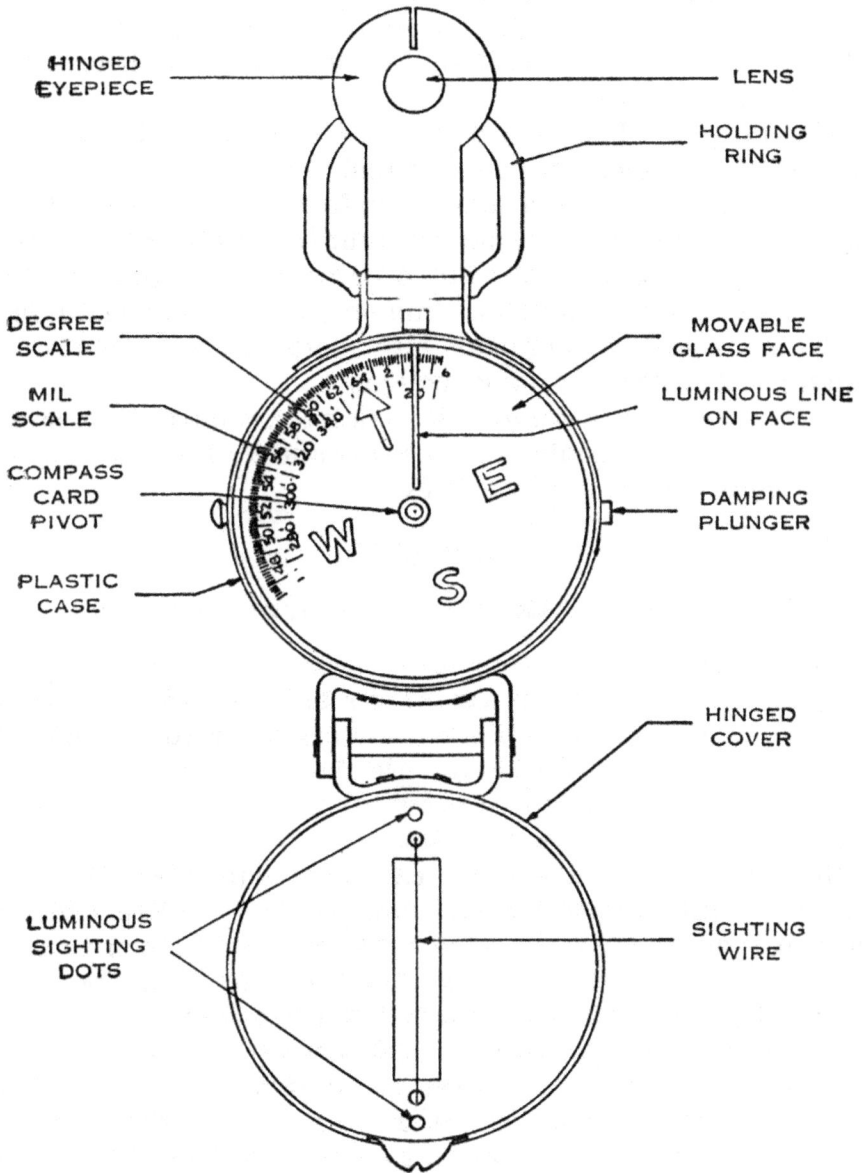

FIGURE 10.—Lensatic compass.

subtract the smaller reading from the larger. The difference is the required angle.

(6) *To lay off azimuth at night.*—(*a*) Using a flashlight or other source of illumination when in a covered position, turn the compass until the desired reading on the dial is opposite the fixed luminous index.

(*b*) Move the luminous line on the crystal to coincide with the north arrow on the compass dial.

(*c*) Without using a light, move to the position from which the azimuth is to be determined. Hold the compass level and rotate until the north arrow on the compass dial coincides with the luminous line on the crystal. The luminous index and the luminous sight dots on the hinged cover then point in the desired direction.

e. Care and preservation.—Although the compass is strongly constructed, the needle pivot bearing and its jewelled support must be protected against shocks.

SECTION III

SPARE PARTS AND ACCESSORIES

■ 35. SPARE PARTS.—*a. General.*—Parts become unserviceable through breakage or through wear resulting from continuous usage. For this reason, spare parts are provided for replacement purposes. These parts are divided into two groups, spare parts and basic spare parts. They should be kept clean and lightly oiled to prevent rust.

b. Spare parts.—These are extra parts provided with the mortars and mounts for replacing those most likely to fail and are employed by the using arms in making minor repairs. Sets of spare parts should be kept as complete as possible. The allowances of spare parts are prescribed in pertinent Standard Nomenclature Lists (SNL A–33).

c. Basic spare parts.—These are sets of spare parts provided for use by ordnance maintenance companies. These spare parts are of no interest to line troops except that, in an emergency, a part may be drawn from the maintenance company.

■ 36. ACCESSORIES.—Accessories include tools required for assembling and disassembling, supplies for the cleaning and preservation of the matériel, and covers, tool rolls, chests, etc., necessary for storage and protection when the mortars and mounts are not in use or when traveling. Accessories should not be used for purposes other than those prescribed and when not in use should be stored in the places or receptacles provided. There are a number of accessories listed in SNL A–33, the names or general characteristics of which indicate their uses or application. Therefore, no detailed description or method of use is outlined herein. However, accessories embodying special features or having special uses are described below:

a. *Bag, ammunition, M2.*—The ammunition bag is a reinforced strip of canvas with a central opening which admits the head of the ammunition carrier. Pockets are provided in front and rear to carry the ammunition.

b. *Brush, chamber cleaning, M6.*—The bristle brush having a twisted wire body is used to clean fouling from the firing pin vent of the mortar.

c. *Chest, accessory, M3.*—The steel accessory chest is a commercial-type chest provided for the storage and protection of equipment, cleaning material and small stores, and miscellaneous spare parts.

d. *Cover, muzzle, M307.*—The leather muzzle cover is used for protection of the mortar bore from foreign matter and moisture. This cover is not used when the mortar is pack transported.

e. *Cover, traversing screw, M505.*—The cylindrical leather cover is used to cover the traversing screw mechanism when the bipod is to be manhandled.

f. *Pad, shoulder, M2.*—The shoulder pad consists of two pads, one for the left and one for the right shoulder. They are strapped together and provide protection for the shoulders of the members of the squad.

g. *Staff, cleaning, M4 (aluminum).*—The cleaning staff has a four-prong fork fastened at one end to hold rags or waste with which the firing pin and bore of the mortar may be cleaned.

h. *Staff, cleaning, M8 (wooden).*—This item is similar to the M4 cleaning staff.

i. *Strap, carrying, M1.*—The carrying strap, M1, consists of a V-shaped strap and a pad. The strap is fastened to the link and loops of the base plate and slipped over the shoulders. The pad eases the load on the carrier's back.

j. Tool, firing pin vent cleaning.—The round steel tool has a flattened, pointed cleaning end by which the firing pin vent of the mortar may be cleaned.

k. Oval oiler.—The oval oiler is used to lubricate and apply oil to flat and exposed surfaces that require oil but have no fittings. A cap is provided to protect the tip of the oiler and prevent loss of oil when the oiler is not used.

l. Flush-type pressure lubricating gun.—This lubricating gun is used to apply oil to the flush-type, lubricating fittings located on the bipod.

m. Camouflage net.—The camouflage net is a woven netting, 12 feet by 12 feet, issued to the squad for the purpose of camouflaging a mortar position against air observation.

n. Accessories for pack transport.—(1) *Cinch, M7.*—The cinch has an olive-drab cotton duck body with a steel loop at one end and a two-bar loop for adjusting purposes at the other. Adjustable leather straps are attached at either end for securing the cinch to the pack saddle to prevent the bundled ammunition from slipping.

(2) *Cinch, M12.*—This cinch is similar to the cinch, M7, but it has a leather facing on its body which is slotted to permit the center brace of the base plate to enter when being secured.

(3) *Cover, muzzle, M310.*—This cover will be used only when the mortar is pack transported.

(4) *Frame, ammunition, M4.*—The frame, composed of rear, center, and front braces held together by longitudinal bars, is secured to the pack saddle by screws and nuts. The three extension bars assembled to the frame are adjustable to suit the bundled ammunition.

(5) *Hanger, mortar, M1.*—The braces and brackets of the mortar hanger M1 are shaped and located to form a convenient arrangement for transporting the base plate and accessory chest. Two straps secure the hanger to the near side of the pack saddle.

(6) *Hanger, mortar, M2.*—The components of the hanger, M2 are constructed so that there are three compartments, one each for the mortar, bipod, and cleaning staff, M2. The

hanger is secured to the offside of the pack saddle by two straps.

(7) *Staff, cleaning, M10.*—The wooden cleaning staff has a four-prong fork fastened at one end to hold the rags or waste with which the firing pin and bore of the mortar may be cleaned. It is shorter than the cleaning staff M9.

SECTION IV

TRAINING EXERCISES

■ 37. CHECKING SEAT OF SIGHT AND CORRECT REMOVAL PROCE-DURE.—*a.* The purpose of this exercise is to teach the gunner the procedure for checking the seating (latching) of the sight in the slot on the mortar yoke and the method of removing the sight without disturbing the lay of the mortar.

b. The instructor explains that the gunner automatically checks the seating of the sight in the slot every time he places it on the mortar. He emphasizes the fact that failure to check the seating of the sight may cause a serious waste of time and ammunition during fire for adjustment, since true angles of elevation, corresponding to the elevations set on the sight, can only be laid on the mortar when the sight is securely latched. He demonstrates the procedure as follows (fig. 11①): He mounts a sight on the mortar, apparently latched in place, then places his left index finger against the sight slot and underneath the body of the sight. With his left thumb extending over the cross-level and the remaining fingers of the left hand grasping the under portion of the sight body, he attempts to lift the sight out of the slot. If the sight has been properly inserted, the hook on the latch will continue to engage the notch in the sight slot.

c. The instructor explains that, to prevent damage to the sight while the first three rounds are being fired, the sight is removed before firing the rounds. To avoid disturbing the lay of the mortar, the gunner removes the sight with care. The instructor demonstrates the method as follows (fig. 11②): From a standing position, he places the fingers of his left hand as in *b* above. With his right thumb, he exerts pressure on the knurled portion of the latch and places the remaining fingers of his right hand on top of the yoke. The upward pressure of the left hand is counteracted by the pressure exerted on the yoke with the fingers of the right hand. By this method, the least disturbance in the lay of the mortar results.

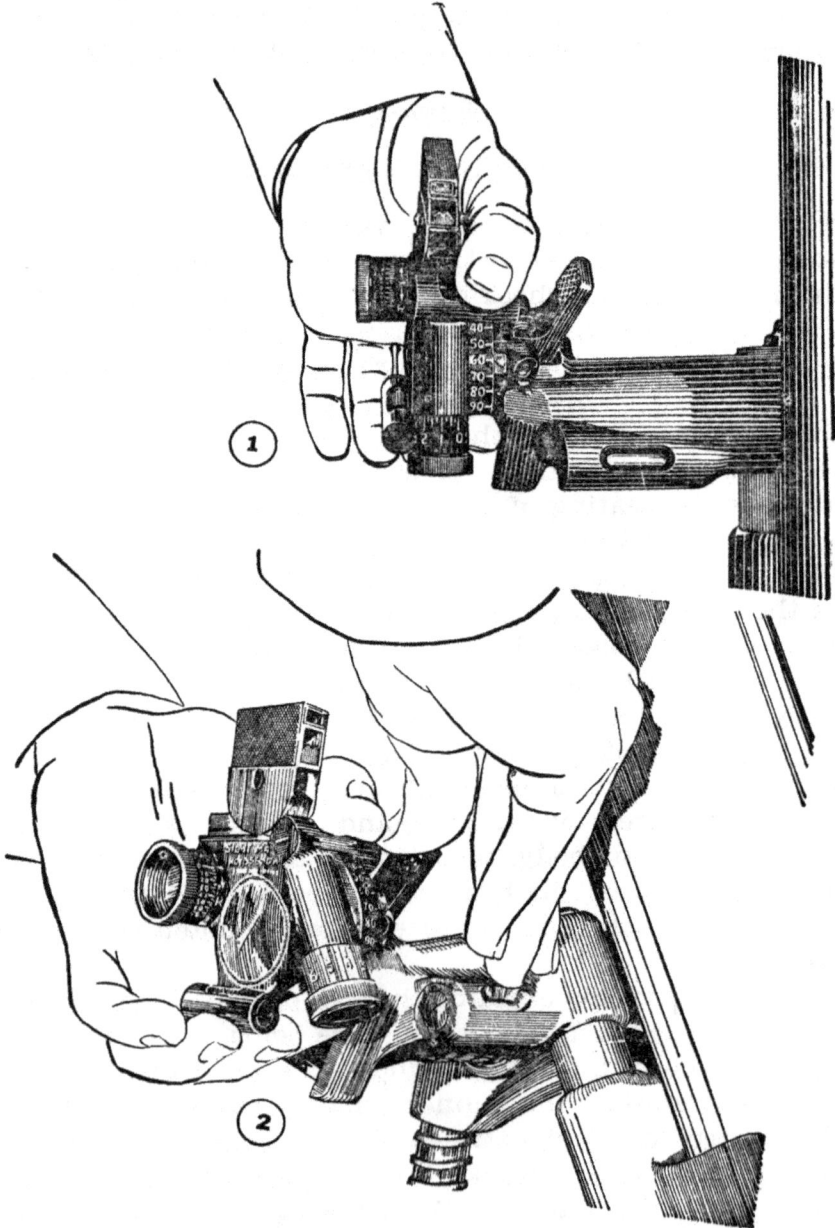

FIGURE 11.—Checking the seat, sight M4, and removal of sight M4.

d. For practice, the instructor has the class divided into small groups, each reporting to a previously trained assistant who supervises the practical work.

■ 38. SIGHT SETTING.—*a.* The purpose of this exercise is to teach the gunner to operate the sight.

b. Holding the sight in his hand, the instructor names the principal parts of the sight and describes their functions to the assembled groups. He explains how to determine and set off deflections as described in paragraph 19.

c. He then explains how to set off elevation and deflection as described in paragraph 19, illustrating this by several examples. He explains that to place a right deflection on the sight, the gunner pulls the knob toward him; to set a left deflection on the scale, the knob is pushed away from him.

d. To demonstrate the group method of conducting this exercise, the instructor uses two trained men, one to act as gunner and the other as group instructor. He requires the gunner to set off a given deflection and elevation and to explain the operation as he performs it. The group instructor checks each detail and points out any errors made.

■ 39. LAYING FOR ELEVATION.—*a.* The purpose of this exercise is to teach the gunner to determine the angle of elevation and the charge for any given range, to lay the mortar in elevation, and to check for mask clearance.

b. The instructor explains the use of the firing table and the way in which to find the correct angle of elevation and charge for any required range (par. 32). He then explains the method of laying for elevation as follows: The gunner, having determined the correct charge, informs No. 2 of the charge requirements in the fire order; for example, CHARGE 2, or CHARGE ZERO. No. 2 then prepares the round. After setting an angle of elevation on the sight, the gunner lays for elevation by manipulating the elevating crank until the bubble in the longitudinal level is centered.

c. The instructor explains that mask clearance is determined as follows: When an elevation of 40° is set on the sight and the bracket on which the collimator is mounted is tilted to its extreme upward position, the line of sight through the open sight will be 2° *below* the axis of the bore. Accordingly

47

if the line of sight clears the mask, the mortar shell will like-wise clear it.   A careful check must be made to see that the path of the projectile will not pass through overhead branches of trees.   Mask clearance and overhead interfer-ence can usually be determined more quickly by sighting along the top of the barrel with the eye placed near the base cap.   If it is not safe to fire, the gunner announces, "Not safe to fire."

d. To demonstrate the method of conducting this exercise, the instructor has two trained men act as gunner and group instructor, respectively.   The group instructor announces a range and requires the gunner to determine the correct angle of elevation, announce the charge, lay the mortar for eleva-tion, and determine mask clearance.   The group instructor checks each operation and explains any errors made.

■ 40. CROSS-LEVELING.—*a.* The purpose of this exercise is to give the gunner necessary training and practice in cross-leveling.   Continuous practice is essential for the gunner to obtain the required manual dexterity in this important operation.

b. The instructor stresses the fact that the two movements of traversing and cross-leveling are combined in a simul-taneous operation; this is necessary in order to avoid delay in laying the mortar and in manipulating the mortar for dis-tributed fire.   He points out that, in traversing and cross-leveling, the right hand operates the traversing handwheel and the left hand the adjusting nut at the same time; both hands are turned in the same relative direction in order to keep the cross-level bubble centered during traverse.   Ap-proximately four turns of the traversing handwheel should be taken to one-half turn of the adjusting nut.   (This ratio may vary with different mortars.)

c. To demonstrate this exercise, the instructor has a trained gunner position the traversing screw nut on one side of the yoke and cross-level by means of the adjusting nut.   The gunner then demonstrates traversing the full width of the traversing screw, keeping the mortar cross-leveled at all times by watching the cross-level bubble of the sight.

d. For practice, the instructor has the class divided into small groups, each reporting to a previously trained assistant who supervises the practical work. This exercise should be repeated at various times during the course of the training.

e. When the gunner becomes more proficient in this exercise, the instruction may be varied by having the gunner watch the white line of the collimator during traverse and attempt to keep it in a vertical plane at all times. Upon completing the entire amount of traverse, he can check his estimate of a vertical position against the cross-level bubble.

f. The gunner, while laying for direction (par. 41), keeps the white line of the collimator in a vertical position. In this way he keeps the mortar approximately cross-leveled while traversing. When the mortar is sighted on the left edge of the aiming stake, a slight movement of the adjusting nut will complete the cross-leveling.

■ 41. LAYING FOR DIRECTION.—*a.* The purpose of this exercise is to teach the gunner to lay accurately for direction.

b. The instructor makes the following explanation to the assembled groups: accurate firing is possible only if the vertical line of the collimator is laid exactly the same for each round fired at the same target, with the mortar accurately cross-leveled. If an aiming stake is used, the gunner must lay so that the vertical line of the collimator is made to coincide with the left edge of the stake. If an aiming point other than a stake is used, the gunner must select a clearly defined vertical edge on which to lay. To place the vertical line of the collimator on the aiming point, the mortar must be traversed and cross-leveled simultaneously. In aiming, the eye should be held at a distance of 3 to 10 inches from the lense of the collimator and in such a position that both the aiming point and the vertical line of the collimator are visible. No attempt is made to look through the collimator, since this is impossible.

c. To demonstrate the method of conducting this exercise, the instructor has two trained men act as gunner and group instructor, respectively. The group instructor lays the mortar, repeats the explanation described above, and requires the gunner to observe the aim. He then requires the gunner to relay on the same aiming point several times. After each laying the instructor checks the gunner's aim and the cross-leveling of the mortar. He then traverses the mortar to the right or left to disturb the aim (par. 150).

■ 42. LAYING FOR ELEVATION AND DIRECTION.—*a*. The purpose of this exercise is to teach the gunner to follow a chronological procedure from the issuance of the initial fire order to the moment when the gunner orders FIRE.

b. The instructor emphasizes the fact that a standardized procedure for setting the sight and laying the mortar for elevation and direction is necessary in order speedily and accurately to prepare the mortar for firing. He explains that the sight is an angle measuring instrument on which setting of deflections and elevations may be made without affecting the axis of the bore. Therefore, the mortar barrel must be laid (pointed) by manipulating the traversing handwheel (to bring the vertical line of the collimator back on the aiming stake) and by manipulating the elevating crank (to center the bubble in the longitudinal level). The mortar must also be cross-leveled during this process (par. 40).

c. To demonstrate the method of conducting this exercise, the instructor has two trained men (a squad leader and a gunner) demonstrate the procedure described in (1) and (2) below, while he explains each step of the operation.

(1) The mortar is mounted as prescribed in paragraph 5*b*. The squad leader issues an initial fire order, for example, HE, LIGHT, LEFT 40, STAKE, 800, ONE ROUND. The gunner, holding the firing table in his right hand, repeats the elements of the fire order. He immediately sets the deflection "left 40" on the deflection scale of the sight with his left hand, then looks at the firing table to find the angle of elevation and the charge required for the range of 800 yards. He announces the charge and sets the elevation scale of the sight at the required angle.

(2) Since the angles of elevation and deflection have been measured on the sight, the elevating crank and traversing handwheel must be turned in the proper direction to lay the mortar correctly. Therefore, the gunner turns the elevating crank until the longitudinal level bubble is centered and rotates the adjusting nut until the cross-level bubble is centered. He checks the vertical line of the collimator and simultaneously turns the adjusting nut and traversing hand-

wheel in the same direction until the vertical line is laid on the left edge of the aiming stake. Again he checks the cross-level bubble and the longitudinal level bubble. When the gunner has accurately laid the mortar, he orders: FIRE.

(3) The instructor may have the squad leader issue a subsequent fire order and require the gunner to follow the procedure described above. Upon completion of the explanation and demonstration, the groups return to their squad equipment where the squad instructors conduct the practical work.

NOTE.—When the deflection in an initial fire order exceeds 60 mils, the gunner does not attempt to lay off the deflection with the traversing handwheel. He sets the deflection on the scale of the sight, directs No. 2 to move the bipod until the vertical line of the collimator is approximately on the left edge of the stake, and re-lays accurately with the handwheel. For subsequent adjustments for deflection, a maximum traverse to the right or left may now be obtained on the screw.

■ 43. LAYING FOR DIRECTION BY AZIMUTH.—*a.* The purpose of this exercise is to teach the gunner to lay the mortar on a given azimuth.

b. The instructor explains how to read azimuths, using the lensatic compass. He points out that when the vertical wire in the cover is alined with the aiming point, the azimuth of the line compass-aiming point appears opposite the index. He then explains that because the mortar is normally located in defilade it may be necessary to lay it by compass azimuth when the direct alinement method cannot be used (par. 59).

c. To demonstrate the method of conducting this exercise, he has a group of three trained men (a gunner, No. 2, and No. 3) demonstrate the method described in (1) and (2) below, while he explains each step of the operation.

(1) After the squad leader has indicated the position for the mortar, No. 1 drives a stake in the ground to mark the position of the base plate. Making sure that the mortar and other metallic equipment are at a distance of not less than 10 yards from the position, the gunner rests his compass on the stake and rotates it until the azimuth announced by the squad leader is laid off on the mil scale. He then directs No. 2 to drive an aiming stake on this azimuth at a distance of about 25 yards. No. 3 alines the base plate for direction.

(2) As soon as the base plate is in position, the mortar is mounted as described in paragraph 5b. With the initial setting placed on the sight, the gunner directs No. 2 to shift the bipod until the vertical line of the collimator is approximately on the left edge of the aiming stake. He lays for elevation, cross-levels, and then lays accurately for direction.

■ 44. MANIPULATION OF MORTAR FOR TRAVERSING AND SEARCHING FIRE.—a. The purpose of this exercise is to teach the gunner the coordination required for simultaneous use of the traversing handwheel and the adjusting nut; determination of the necessary number of turns of the elevating crank; and the sequence necessary to engage targets that require a combination of distributed fire called traversing and searching fire.

b. The instructor first explains the technique of distributing fire laterally (traversing) and in depth ((searching) by manipulation of the mortar. He then explains that it may be necessary to combine these two types of fire and that a definite operating sequence must be followed.

c. To demonstrate the method of conducting this exercise, he has a group of three trained men, a squad leader (observer), a gunner (No. 1), and an assistant gunner (No. 2) demonstrate the method described below while he explains each step of the operation.

d. The mortar is mounted as prescribed in paragraph 5b, with an aiming stake set at a convenient distance. The mortar is laid on the left edge of the stake, with the deflection scale set at zero and the traversing screw approximately centered. The elevation scale is set at 62° and the longitudinal level centered.

(1) The squad leader gives a fire order, for example:

SEARCH 900–1,000.

TRAVERSE RIGHT FOUR TURNS.

NINE ROUNDS.

(2) The gunner repeats each element of the fire order and, upon hearing the words "Search 900–1,000," places his thumb opposite the range of 900 yards on the firing table* and selects the lowest charge zone which will include the extreme range (1,000 yards) as given in the fire order. He then notes that the elevation for the range 900 is 59°; he sets his eleva-

_____

*Abridged Firing Table, 81-mm Mortar, M1, Shell, HE, M43A1.

tion on the elevation scale of the sight and announces, "Charge 1." He next reads the difference in degrees between the limiting ranges (app. I) and translates the number of degrees (disregarding fractions) to the number of turns of the elevating crank between range bounds, and announces, "Down 10 turns." (If the limits are given with the greater range first, that is, 1,000–900, the command would be: UP 10 TURNS.)

(3) With the traversing handwheel, the gunner turns the traversing screw off center enough to allow him to traverse twice the number of turns announced in the fire order. He directs No. 2 to move the bipod legs until the white line of the collimator is approximately laid on the left edge of the aiming stake. He then centers the bubble in the longitudinal level, cross-levels, and lays accurately with the traversing handwheel while keeping the mortar cross-leveled. When he is satisfied with the laying of the mortar, he commands: FIRE. He then executes the remainder of the operation as ordered, in the following manner: After firing the first round (simulated), he traverses right 4 turns, keeping the mortar cross-leveled, and commands: FIRE for the second round; he traverses right 4 more turns and commands: FIRE for the third round; for the fourth round he turns the elevating crank down 10 turns, checks the cross-level, and commands: FIRE; then he traverses left 4 turns and commands: FIRE for the fifth round; he traverses left 4 more turns and commands: FIRE for the sixth round; again he turns the elevating crank down 10 turns, checks the cross-level, and commands: FIRE for the seventh round; traverses right 4 turns and commands: FIRE for the eighth round; he traverses right 4 more turns and commands: FIRE for the ninth round, and announces, "Rounds complete."

SECTION V

ADDITIONAL TRAINING

■ 45. MARKING BASE DEFLECTION.—In order to facilitate rapid adjustment on new targets and to mark accurately targets already engaged, it is necessary to establish an origin of shift as early as possible. This origin of shift for the squad is usually the first target engaged or any clearly defined point in the target area. It is called the "base point," and the deflection of this point is called "base deflection." Base deflection is marked on the ground as soon as adjustment is completed upon the base point, or in case the base point is the initial target, as soon as fire for effect on the target is completed, so as not to interfere with the fire. When the immediate engagement of another target is not anticipated, the observer establishes the direction to the base point by commanding: MARK BASE DEFLECTION. After firing the last round for effect (in drill, after the last practice shift in elevation and deflection), the mortar is checked for cross-level and resighted on the stake which marks the direction to the target now to be established as the base point. This alinement on the base point is marked by setting up a stake on the established line. This is done by turning the deflection scale to zero, taking care not to disturb the lay of the mortar. No. 3 resets the stake on which the mortar was first alined so that the stake will now be alined with the vertical line of the collimator. After being reset, this stake is known as the *base stake*. The deflection of the base point is now zero. When base deflection is marked, the gunner centers the traversing screw, directs No. 2 to move the bipod and re-lays on the stake. Space is now provided on the screw for deflection corrections to the right or left when new targets are engaged.

■ 46. PLACING ADDITIONAL AIMING STAKES.—*a. General.*— Since the maximum deflection which can be set on the sight is 150 mils to the right or left of zero, it becomes necessary to set out additional stakes. These are established at 150-mil intervals to the right and left of the base stake and make possible the laying of the mortar on targets located at more than 150 mils to the right and left of the base point. In the attack these stakes are placed, without further command, immediately after marking the base deflection. At least two additional stakes should be placed. In a defensive position, they should be placed immediately after the direction to the base point has been established. At least four additional stakes should be placed. Whenever the situation permits, the stakes should be driven at least 15 yards from the mortar.

b. Procedure.—(1) *For two stakes.*—With the deflection scale at zero and the mortar cross-leveled, the base deflection is marked. Without moving the mortar, the gunner sets the deflection scale at right 150 mils and directs No. 2 in the driving of the *left stake* so that the left edge of the stake is in alinement with the vertical line of the collimator. This stake is then 150 mils to the left of the *base stake*. The gunner then rotates the deflection knob until the scale registers left 150 mils and has No. 2 drive the *right stake*. These stakes now make possible the engagement of targets 300 mils to the right and left of the *base stake,* because, with the deflection scale set at zero, a movement of the bipod to place the vertical line of the collimator on the *right* (or *left*) *stake* will permit the setting of an additional 150 mils on the deflection scale of the sight. Therefore, with two additional stakes, a frontage of 600 mils can be covered. Example: To engage a new target which is 225 mils to the left of the base point, the observer's fire order, so far as it concerns direction, would be: LEFT 75, LEFT STAKE.

(2) *For four stakes.*—Having established the base stake, to place two additional stakes to the right, the gunner sets right 150 mils on the deflection scale (the vertical line of the collimator is then pointed to the left) and directs No. 2 to move the bipod legs until the line of the collimator is placed approximately on the left edge of the *base stake*. He lays accurately with the traversing handwheel, cross-leveling simultaneously. The gunner rotates the deflection knob until the scale registers zero. Without moving the mortar, he directs No. 3 to drive the *first right stake,* so that its left edge is on line with the collimator. He once more rotates the deflection knob in the same direction until he has laid off another 150 mils left. No. 3 is then directed to drive the *second right stake.* To place two additional stakes to the left of the *base stake,* the gunner repeats the process in the opposite direction. These stakes are designated as the *first left stake* and the *second left stake.* A frontage of 900 mils can be covered with four additional stakes. For employment of these stakes, see paragraphs 141 and 142.

■ 47. NIGHT FIRING.—*a. Laying.*—When it is necessary to fire the 81-mm mortar at night, an aiming stake with a night firing device attached (*b* below) is set up and used as an aiming point.   Sights are set by the light of a shaded flashlight.   In order to see the vertical line of the collimator (or the open sight), a shaded flashlight, produced by covering the lens with black paper pierced with a small pin, is held just above the front of the collimator and at a slight angle so that the light will be placed on the front of the collimator.   With a flashlight in this position, the white line of the collimator shows as clearly at night as in daylight.   Additional methods of laying the mortar at night are described in paragraph 143*f*.

b. *Devices.*—Night firing devices may be improvised.   For example, a cross-shaped slit is cut in the end of a tin can and covered with a thin white cloth to keep the glare out of the gunner's eyes; or the lid of the can is removed, a heavy black cross is marked on a sheet of paper, and the paper is fastened over the open end.   Several holes are punched in the other end of the can.   In one side of the can a rough cross-shaped slit is cut and the edges are bent inward to admit and hold a candle.   Several nail holes are punched above and on each side of the point where the flame of the candle will be.   A lighted candle is inserted in the can, which is then attached to the aiming stake.   A flashlight may be used instead of a candle for illumination of the aiming stake.

c. *Data.*—Firing data should be prepared during daylight and recorded on a range card, as described in paragraph 79. If the mortar position is to be occupied at night and there has been no opportunity to prepare data in advance, any night firing must be based on data prepared from an aerial photograph or map.   Such data are only as accurate as the aerial photograph or map and the skill and accuracy of the computer (par. 123).

■ 48. FIRING WITHOUT SIGHTS.—The mortar is not rendered useless because of loss or destruction of the sight or the dovetail slot.

a. *Direction.*—The gunner lays the mortar in direction, from a position in rear, by having No. 2 shift the bipod legs until the left edge of the barrel is alined on the aiming stake.

b. *Elevation.*—With the elevating screw centered, the gunner must estimate the angle of elevation announced in the initial fire order of the squad leader.   Placing himself to one side of the mortar, the gunner directs No. 2 to move the bipod legs or the position of the clamping collar so that the desired angle of elevation will be obtained. No. 2 may make small changes with the elevating crank, but it is important that the elevating screw be as nearly centered as possible. The laying of the mortar for direction should be checked.

c. The observer announces changes in deflection and elevation in terms of number of turns of the traversing handwheel and elevating crank; the gunner manipulates both mechanisms in the direction indicated by the observer in his fire orders (par. 71). The gunner cross-levels by means of the bubble located on the yoke.

■ 49. DIRECT LAYING.—Since the mortar is usually located in defiladed positions, it is rarely possible to lay directly on the target. There may be situations, however, where no defilade is available or where speed in destroying a target is more essential than cover. Usually such a position is a temporary one and will be evacuated as soon as the target is destroyed. In such a situation, the squad leader should point out the target or its direction to the gunner and direct that the mortar be mounted immediately and without stakes. If the target is indistinct and the squad leader (observer) has indicated only its direction, he should lay the mortar himself as soon as it is mounted. The mortar is laid and fired in the same manner as described for indirect laying except that one clearly defined edge or point of the target should be used as the aiming point. If it is apparent that the bursts may obscure the target from observation, any suitable aiming point in the target area may be used. Its deflection should be measured by the observer from a position near the mortar and announced as initial deflection.

CHAPTER 3

TRAINING FOR PLACING MORTAR IN ACTION

■ 50. TRAINING WITH MORTAR EQUIPMENT.—*a.* The primary purpose of mortar drill is to teach all members of the mortar squad the duties of each member in carrying the mortar and equipment, in executing simple movements with the mortar and equipment, and in serving the mortar during firing. In the initial phases of mortar drill, individual weapons need not be carried. However, upon entering advanced drill, they should be required as items of equipment.

b. The most important consideration is the development of accuracy. When accuracy has been obtained, emphasis is placed on the development of speed. The various commands for controlling the initial actions of the squad are listed below:

(1) *Secure equipment for mortar drill.*—At the appropriate command, the men fall out and secure equipment as listed in table I. In combat, where the squad may be in any one of several formations and the equipment may be on motors, carts, or packs, the command will be: OFF TRUCKS (OFF CARTS; OFF PACKS).

(2) *Ground equipment.*—At the original assembly with equipment, and at all halts except IN PLACE, HALT, loads are grounded without command as indicated in table I and figure 12.

(3) *Carry equipment.*—This command is given before starting any movement on foot, with loads taken as described in table I and figures 13 and 14.

■ 51. MOVEMENTS FOR THE SQUAD AND INDIVIDUALS.—*a. To move off.*—The squad having taken equipment, the squad leader commands or signals: SQUAD COLUMN. The men form an irregular column behind the squad leader. In this formation the squad follows the squad leader at his command: FOLLOW ME.

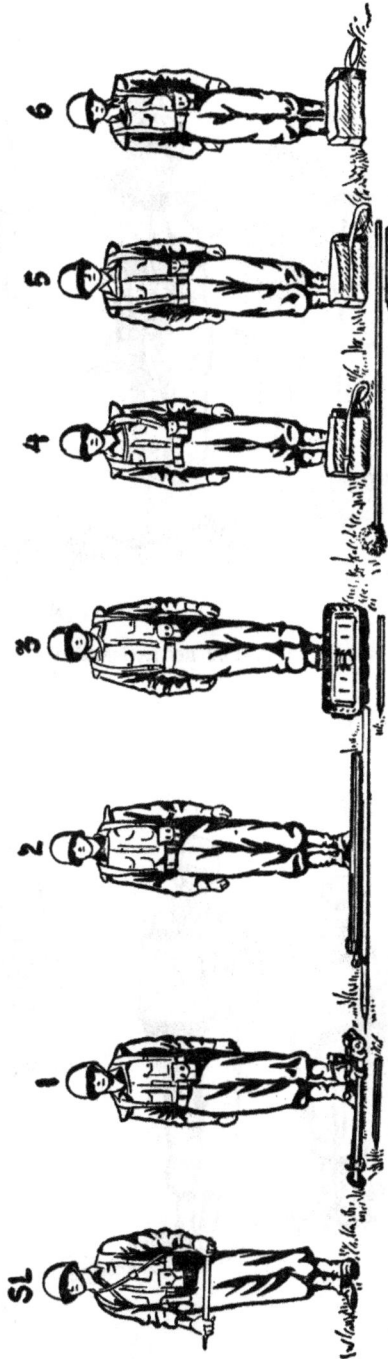

FIGURE 12.—81-mm mortar squad.

FIGURE 13.—81-mm mortar squad with single load.

FIGURE 14.—81-mm mortar squad with two-man load.

TABLE I.—*Securing, grounding, and carrying equipment*

| Personnel | SECURE EQUIPMENT | | GROUND EQUIPMENT | CARRY EQUIPMENT | |
	Drill	Combat		Single load (fig. 13)	Two-man load (fig. 14)
Squad leader.	Sight. Compass (lensatic). Firing pin and screw driver. Firing tables. 1 aiming post M9. 1 flashlight.	Sight. Compass (lensatic). Firing pin and screw driver. Firing tables. 1 aiming post M9. 1 flashlight.			
No. 1	Bipod. Shoulder pads. 1 aiming stake (improvised). (1 ammunition bag for two-man load.)	Bipod. Shoulder pads. 1 aiming stake (improvised). (1 ammunition bag for two-man load.)	Places bipod in front of him, legs to the right, and elevating crank up. Aiming stake in front of the bipod, point to the right.	Places bipod on right shoulder, feet to front and clamping collar down. Carries aiming stake in left hand.	Carries bipod suspended on cleaning staff, assisted by No. 4. Carries six rounds of dummy or 81-mm, M43A1, ammunition.
No. 2	Mortar. Shoulder pads. 1 aiming post M8. (1 ammunition bag for two-man load.)	Mortar. Shoulder pads. 1 aiming post M8. (1 ammunition bag for two-man load.)	Places mortar in front of him, spherical projection to the right; aiming post in front of the mortar, point to the right.	Places mortar on his right shoulder, spherical projection to the front. Aiming post held in left hand.	Carries mortar suspended on aiming post M8, assisted by No. 5. Three aiming stakes placed in barrel. Carries six rounds of dummy or 81-mm, M43A1, ammunition.

TABLE I.—Securing, grounding, and carrying equipment

Personnel	SECURE EQUIPMENT		GROUND EQUIPMENT	CARRY EQUIPMENT	
	Drill	Combat		Single load (fig. 13)	Two-man load (fig. 14)
No. 3	Base plate. 1 aiming stake (improvised).	Base plate. 1 aiming stake (improvised).	Places base plate in front of him, handle to the rear. Aiming stake in front of the base plate, point to the right.	Lifts the base plate with his right hand. Aiming stake held in left hand.	Carries base plate strapped to his back, by means of the carrying strap M1.
No. 4	Shoulder pads. Cleaning staff. 1 ammunition bag. (Six rounds dummy).	Shoulder pads. Cleaning staff. 1 ammunition bag. (Six rounds 81-mm, M43A1, or 4 rounds 81-mm, M56 or M57).	Places the ammunition bag on ground in front of him, shoulder loop to the left. Places cleaning staff in front of bag, waste end to the right.	Puts on the ammunition bag and carries cleaning staff in right hand.	Assists No. 1 in carrying the bipod. Carries six rounds of dummy or 81-mm, M43A1, ammunition.
No. 5	Shoulder pads. 1 ammunition bag. (Six rounds dummy). 1 aiming stake (improvised).	Shoulder pads. 1 ammunition bag. (Six rounds 81-mm, M43A1, or 4 rounds 81-mm, M56 or M57). 1 aiming stake (improvised).	Places ammunition bag on ground, shoulder loop to the left. Aiming stake in front of bag, point to the right.	Puts on ammunition bag. Aiming stake held in right hand.	Assists No. 2 in carrying mortar. Carries six rounds of dummy or 81-mm, M43A1, ammunition.

No. 6-----	Shoulder pads----- 1 ammunition bag----- (Six rounds dummy).	Same as No. 5 (except for aiming stake).	Same as No. 5 (except for aiming stake).	Same as No. 5 (except for aiming stake).	Carries six rounds of dummy or 81-mm, M43A1, ammunition.
No. 7-----	Usually remains with truck. May participate in drill.	Compass (watch)-----			May carry additional ammunition.

b. To change numbers.—At any time during the drill, **the** squad leader may command: FALL OUT ONE. At this command, No. 1 takes the position of No. 6, and all other numbered members of the squad move up one number. This rotation in drill is made in order to train all members **of** the squad in the duties of other members.

■ 52. ACTION.—*a.* The squad being in any formation, to prepare the mortar to fire upon a target, the command is: ACTION.

b. All members of the squad except the squad leader ground their loads.

c. The squad leader indicates the approximate position for the mortar by placing the sight case on the ground and gives the direction of fire by—

(1) Placing an aiming stake and directing the placing of **a** base plate stake (direction by the direct alinement method described in par. 59).

(2) Announcing the magnetic azimuth (direction by **the** azimuth method described in par. 59).

d. If the first method (*c*(1) above) is used, No. 1 drives a stake at the position indicated for the base plate and **as** alined by the squad leader. If the second method (*c*(2) above) is used, No. 1 receives the compass from the squad leader and drives a base plate stake at the indicated location. No. 1, using the compass, then directs No. 2 in placing an aiming stake to establish the direction of fire.

e. The squad leader moves to a position from which he **can** observe and control the fire.

f. As soon as the direction of fire is established, the mortar is mounted as prescribed in paragraph 5.

g. Members of the squad then take posts as follows:

(1) No. 1 kneels on his right knee on the left of the mortar in a position convenient to the sight M4 and the traversing and elevating mechanisms (fig. 15).

(2) No. 2 stands or kneels on the right side of the mortar near the muzzle and facing it.

(3) No. 3 posts himself where he can supply ammunition to No. 2.

(4) Nos. 4, 5, and 6 are echeloned to the right and left rear where they can supply ammunition to No. 3.

■ 53. PRECAUTIONS.—*a. Before firing.*—See that—
   (1) The mortar is properly mounted (par. 5).
   (2) The mortar is locked to the base plate.
   (3) The clamp bolt is secure.
   (4) The locking nut is secure.

FIGURE 15.—81-mm mortar squad at posts.

   (5) The chain is adjusted to limit the spread of the bipod legs.
   (6) The bore is clean.
   (7) Each shell is clean—particularly the bourrelet.
   (8) The fuze safety pin of each shell is in place.
   b. During firing.—(1) From time to time check to be sure that the clamp bolt and locking nut are tight.
   (2) Swab the bore after every ten rounds.

(3) Check frequently to see that the base plate and bipod positions are safe for firing.

(4) If it is not clearly apparent from observation that the shell will clear the mask, check the clearance as prescribed in paragraph 39.

■ 54. To FIRE MORTAR.—*a. Squad leader.*—The squad leader gives an initial fire order as described in paragraph 61.

b. Gunner.—(1) Consults the firing table after checking or resetting the deflection on the sight (par. 42).

(2) Announces the charge to be used, for example, "Charge 1."

(3) Sets the elevation on the sight for the range announced.

(4) Lays for elevation.

(5) Lays for deflection and cross-levels simultaneously.

(6) Removes the sight during the firing of the first three rounds or until the base plate is firmly seated.

(7) Orders: FIRE.

(8) Places his left foot on the base plate to assist seating during the firing of the first three rounds.

c. Ammunition handler No. 3.—(1) Removes the round (dummy) from the ammunition bag or container.

(2) Hands the round to No. 2.

(3) When the gunner announces the charge, No. 3 repeats the command and withdraws the necessary number of increments from the metal fins in order to leave in place the announced charge.

(4) No. 3 extracts the safety wire, when this has not been previously done, while No. 2 holds the round.

d. Assistant gunner No. 2.—(1) Takes the shell from No. 3 in both hands; right hand, palm up, around the fuze; left hand, palm down, grasping the lower part of the shell body near the fin assembly.

(2) Holds the shell firmly while No. 3 removes the necessary number of increments in order to leave the announced charge in place and pulls out the safety wire. *No. 2 will test the tension of the safety pin spring by pressing and releasing the pin with his thumb. If the safety pin becomes unseated, the round will not be fired but will be placed in a safe location for destruction by ordnance personnel.*

(3) Upon the gunner's command FIRE, he starts the shell into the muzzle, fuze end up, both hands retaining their grasp (fig. 15). He is careful not to disturb the lay of the mortar during the loading process.

(4) Releases the shell so that it slides down the bore. In releasing the shell, he instantly withdraws the hands, head, and upper part of the body from the muzzle in order to avoid the blast which occurs as the round is discharged. In withdrawing the hands, the right hand is moved under the muzzle and the left hand directly away from the muzzle so that they do not pass in front of it. The head and upper part of the body are turned to the left. He places his right foot on the base plate to assist in seating it during the firing of the first three rounds.

■ 55. MISFIRES.—*a. General.*—(1) Frequently during mortar drill when the squad has simulated firing the mortar, using a dummy round or training projectile with the ignition cartridge removed, the squad leader announces "Misfire" and requires the mortar crew to remove the misfire as prescribed in *b* below.

(2) A misfire occurs when a round is loaded into the barrel of the mortar but fails to fire. The round may hang in the barrel without striking the firing pin, or it may strike the firing pin and fail to function.

b. Removal of round after misfire.—(1) When any doubt exists as to whether or not the round has struck the firing pin, No. 1 will kick the barrel with his heel. Under training conditions, *or when battle conditions permit,* the mortar crew should wait at least 1 minute before removing the round in order to avoid an accident caused by a possible delayed action of the igniting cartridge. If the barrel is kicked at any time during the removal process, No. 1 will make sure that no person is in front of the muzzle of the barrel. During this period, No. 1 tests the barrel for heat. If the heat of the barrel is excessive, No. 1 should use an ammunition bag to protect his hands. No. 2 then places his right leg behind and bracing the right leg of the bipod and unscrews the clamp bolt far enough to allow the mortar to be rotated. No. 1 rotates the mortar until it is unlocked from the base plate. No. 2 then reclamps the mortar and places his right hand, palm up, under the barrel near the muzzle, and his left hand, palm down, on top of the barrel. The thumbs of both hands should be placed alongside the forefingers. Care is taken that no part of either hand is in front of the muzzle.

(2) No. 1 lifts the base of the mortar until the round slides slowly toward the muzzle. *Under no circumstance will the base of the mortar be lowered again below a horizontal position until the round has been removed from the barrel.* As soon as the round has started forward, *and not before,* No. 2 places the thumb of each hand over the muzzle and stops the round as the point of the fuze reaches the muzzle. He then passes the round to No. 3, who inspects it to determine the cause of the misfire. If the primer of the ignition cartridge is dented, the round, with the safety wire replaced, should be laid to one side and later destroyed. If the primer is undented, the gunner should invert the mortar and shake it to dislodge any remnants from the last round fired which may have remained in the barrel.

(3) No. 1 lowers the mortar to insert the spherical projection in the socket. No. 2 unscrews the clamp bolt, and No. 1 rotates the mortar to lock it into the base plate. No. 2 tightens the clamp bolt, and firing is then resumed. If another misfire occurs, No. 1 inspects the firing pin to see that it is clean and tightly screwed into the base cap.

NOTE.—If the extremely unlikely situation exists where the safety pin springs clear of the fuze body, the round should be carefully placed in a safe location for destruction by Ordnance personnel.

c. Causes.—The propelling charge may not function because of—

(1) Defective primer or ignition cartridge.
(2) Defective, damaged, or loose firing pin.
(3) Firing pin fouled or obstructed by remnants from previous rounds.
(4) Fouled bore.
(5) Excess oil in bore.
(6) Cartridge not fully inserted in container.
(7) Misalined stabilizing fin.
(8) Foreign matter or excess paint on bourrelet.

■ 56. OUT OF ACTION.—*a.* At the squad leader's command OUT OF ACTION, the mortar is dismounted as prescribed in paragraph 5*c*. All members of the squad secure equipment and form as directed by the squad leader.

b. When the mortar is to be carried a considerable distance, the squad leader may command: OUT OF ACTION, TWO-MAN LOAD. The mortar is prepared for transport as described in table I.

c. The squad should be trained in the rapid occupation of alternate and supplementary firing positions. At the

FIGURE 16.—Two-man carry, method for lifting.

command: OUT OF ACTION, TWO-MAN CARRY, the mortar is prepared for rapid movement in the following manner.

(1) No. 1 removes the sight, places it in the carrying case, and slings it over his right shoulder. He then checks to see that at least one-half of the elevating screw is exposed. Next, from a standing position (fig. 16), he places his left hand on the sight slot, palm to the rear, and his right hand over the adjusting nut.

(2) No. 2, from a standing position, turns the traversing

crank to its inoperative position, grasps the traversing hand-wheel with his right hand and the right leg with his left hand about three-quarters of the way down the leg.

(3) No. 3, from a kneeling position in rear of the base plate, lifts the front edge of the base plate to permit Nos. 1 and 2 to swing the bipod to the rear and hook the flanges of the bipod feet under the base plate. (Where the base plate has

FIGURE 17.—Two-man carry.

been seated by firing, No. 3 must jerk the base plate loose before lifting the front edge.)

(4) When the feet of the bipod have been secured in this fashion, Nos. 1 and 2 may move off at double time with their load (fig. 17). Upon arrival at the new firing position, the mortar can be rapidly placed in action.

CHAPTER 4

TRAINING OF OBSERVER

Paragraphs
Section I. Preparatory instruction_____ 57–64
       II. Squad conduct of fire_____ 65–74
      III. Combat expedients—rapid adjustment of fire____   75
       IV. Prearranged fires_____ 76–82

Section I

PREPARATORY INSTRUCTION

■ 57. General.—To perform his duties efficiently, the observer (squad leader) must first learn and master the mechanical requirements of his training in order that the technical phases, involving judgment and initiative, may receive his undivided attention. Experience in combat indicates that the ability of the observer is the most vital single factor in the effective delivery of fire.

■ 58. Preparation of Initial Data.—*a.* Usually the requirements in the preparation of fire data make it necessary that this information be computed in the shortest time. Consequently, the methods employed must be quick and simple. To provide the necessary data with a minimum delay, the observation post should, wherever possible, be close enough to the mortar position to permit the observer to see both the target and the mortar position.

b. The information needed in the preparation of initial fire data is—

(1) Initial direction of fire (par. 59).

(2) Initial range (par. 60).

■ 59. Determination of Initial Direction of Fire.—In order to protect the mortar crew, the mortar usually is located in defilade. From this location, the gunner will neither be able to see the target nor to lay the vertical line of the collimator directly on the target. Consequently, it becomes necessary to establish an auxiliary aiming point in order to lay on the line mortar–target and on the initial direction of fire. This auxiliary aiming point may be an aiming stake or some clearly defined object, such as the trunk of a tree or the corner of a building. The method selected to establish this aiming point depends on whether the observation post is on the line mortar–target, or to one side of this line.

a. *Observation post on line mortar–target.*—When the observation post is on the line mortar–target, the observer may determine the direction of fire by either of two ways: he may aline aiming stakes directly on the line mortar–target, or he may first determine the magnetic azimuth of that line and direct the gunner to aline the stakes. These two methods are described as follows:

(1) *Direct alinement method.*—This method is preferable when both the mortar and target can be seen from a point

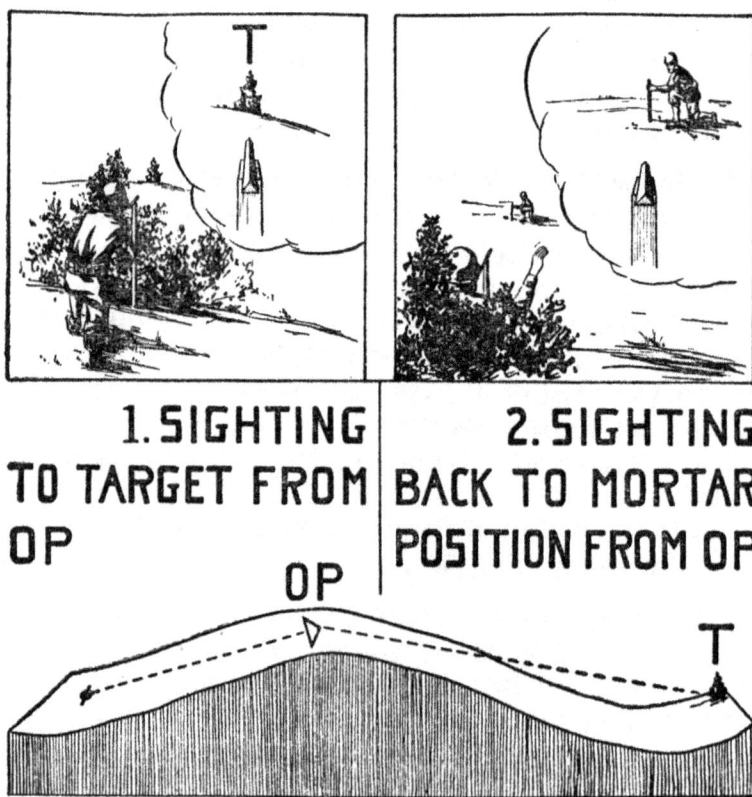

FIGURE 18.—Direct alinement method.

very **near** the mortar position (within about 50 yards).
Under such conditions it is usually the simpler and more
accurate method.

(a) *Mortar position not fixed* (fig. 18).

1. *Normal method.*—The observer moves forward to a
position from which he can see both the mortar
position and the target.   He places himself on the
line mortar–target and drives an aiming stake on
this line.   He then places an alidade on the stake
and alines the edge of it on the target.   (The
alidade may be any suitable straightedge, that is,
another stake, a ruler, or a pencil.)   Without
disturbing the position of this improvised alidade
and using the same edge, he sights back to the
mortar position and directs that the base plate
stake be driven on this line of sight to mark the
location of the base plate.   If the first stake is
at such a distance or is in such a position that it
cannot be clearly seen from the mortar position,
a second stake, to be used as an aiming stake, is
driven on the line mortar–target about 25 yards
from the base plate stake.   The mortar is then
mounted and laid on the aiming stake.

2. *Expedient.*—Where the tactical situation does not
permit the alinement of stakes and the mortar
must be placed in action rapidly, the observer
may establish initial direction of fire as follows:
Select some object situated in the general direction of fire and direct the gunner to mount and
lay the mortar on this object with the deflection
scale set at zero.   The observer may even direct
the gunner to lay the mortar on a distant object,
such as a gap in a stand of trees or on an odd-
shaped tree, provided the mortar crew is partially defiladed from hostile fire.   By using the
object upon which the mortar is laid as a reference point, the mortar may be laid on a target
to the right or left of this point by reading the
angle in mils between the object and the target

and laying the corresponding deflection on the mortar. After the mortar is laid on a reference point, additional aiming stakes may be placed for engaging targets located more than 150 mils to the right or left of the reference point.

(b) *Mortar position fixed.*—Where the base plate has been seated by previous firing and a new direction of fire must be established, the observer may order the placement of additional aiming stakes (par. 46), or he may aline the mortar as follows:

1. Repeat the procedure in (a)1 above, to include the point where the observer sights back to the mortar position. Note the position of the stake with respect to the line mortar–target. If the stake is off the line, move it in the required direction and repeat the procedure outlined above until alinement has been secured.

2. If necessary, a second stake may be placed about 25 yards from the mortar position to facilitate laying.

(2) *Azimuth method* (fig. 19).—(a) This method is used when the observer cannot see the mortar position at his observation post. This may be due to terrain features such as intervening woods, intervening masks, tall underbrush, or scrub growth which prevent the establishment of stakes as described in (1) above.

(b) The observer indicates the mortar position, moves to his observation post (in front or in rear of the mortar), being accompanied by a member of the squad as messenger. The observer places himself approximately on the line mortar–target (to aid in establishing this line, the observer should select a landmark at or near the mortar position before moving to his observation post), reads the magnetic azimuth in mils to the target. He then sends a messenger back to the mortar with the compass and a written notation of the azimuth. When the compass is returned to the mortar position, the gunner drives a stake to support the compass, lays off the recorded azimuth, and directs No. 2 to place an aiming stake on the line of sight of the instrument. During this operation, the mortar and mount must be removed at least 10 yards from the compass to reduce magnetic disturbance. The compass support stake can then be used as a base plate stake to aline the base plate for direction.

(3) *Exercise in determining direction.*—(*a*) The purpose of this exercise is to teach the observer the method of establishing the direction of fire of the mortar when the observation post is on the line mortar-target.

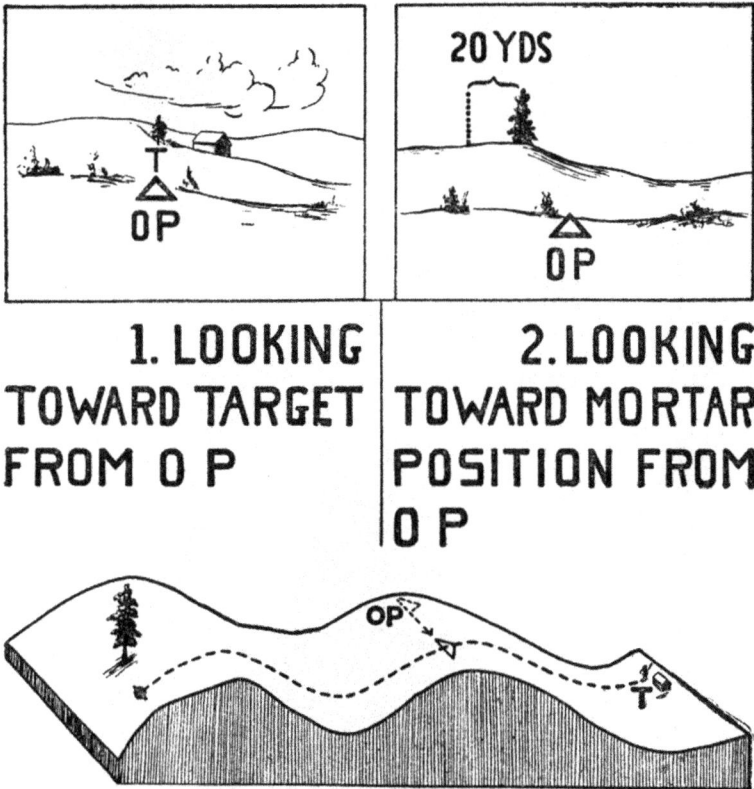

1. LOOKING TOWARD TARGET FROM O P

2. LOOKING TOWARD MORTAR POSITION FROM O P

FIGURE 19.—Azimuth method.

(*b*) The instructor explains and demonstrates the exercise as follows: Using a qualified man as observer, he explains to the assembled groups the direct alinement method of establishing direction, as described in *a*(1) above, and requires the observer to demonstrate each step as it is explained. The groups are then returned to their equipment and required to go through the exercise as demonstrated, each man in turn acting as observer.

(c) The groups are then assembled, and the instructor explains the azimuth method of determining direction, as described in a(2) above. Each step is demonstrated, and upon completion, each group instructor will require every man to go through the prescribed exercise.

FIGURE 20.—Parallel line method.

b. *Observation post to flank of line mortar–target.*—To determine the direction of fire when the observation post is to the flank of the line mortar–target, the observer must first determine the azimuth of this line. Two methods are described below:

(1) *Parallel line method.*—This method is simple, rapid, and accurate enough for field use. The observer estimates the shortest distance from his position (observation post) to the line mortar–target. He selects an object on the ground which is on the same side of the line mortar–target and at the same distance from this line as himself. With a compass, he reads the magnetic azimuth from his position to the selected object. This is the azimuth of the line mortar–target. For example, in figure 20, the observer at point O estimates the shortest distance to the line mortar-target as 125 yards. He then selects some object to his front which is 125 yards from the line mortar–target. Such a point in this case would be on the line O–X. The azimuth of the line O–X, therefore, is the same as the azimuth of the line mortar–target.

(2) *Compass-and-mil method.*—(a) The observer at his observation post computes, for example, the following data (fig. 21):

The azimuth O–T=2,300 mils.

The range O–T=1,700 yards.

The distance O–MT=125 yards.

(b) He then obtains the correction angle in mils by reference to the deflection-conversion table, or by using the mil formula.

(c) He next adds or subtracts the mil correction from the azimuth read. The word MOLARS (mortar on left, add; right, subtract) may aid the observer in remembering the correct procedure in making the mil correction.

> 1. *By use of deflection-conversion table.*—Using the data in (2)(a) above, the observer refers to his deflection-conversion table (app. I), reads down the left column headed *range in yards* to 1,700 and then reads across the top line headed *deflection in yards* to column 125. Reading right from 1,700 and down from 125, he finds the figure 75 at the junction of the two columns. This 75 is the correction angle in mils to be added to or

subtracted from the azimuth read. He adds 75 mils to 2,300 mils to obtain the azimuth of the line mortar–target (2,375 mils), since the mortar is on the left of his observation post. This table

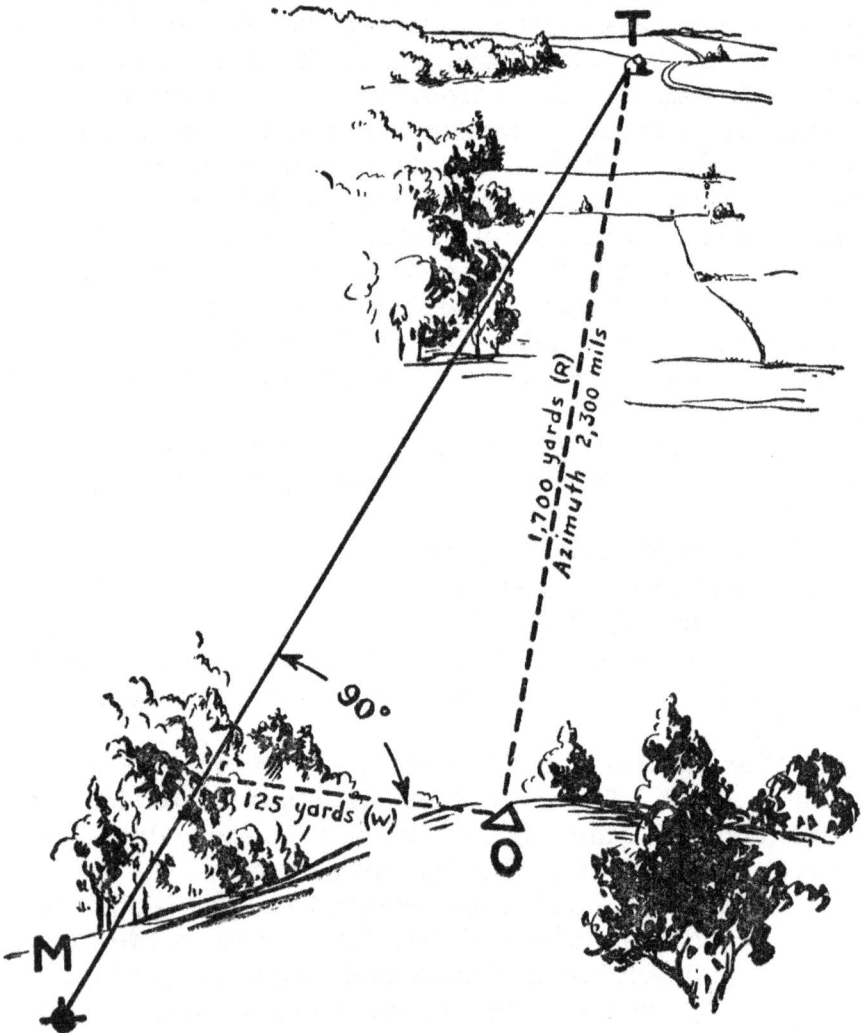

FIGURE 21.—Compass-and-mil method.

should be used, wherever possible, for rapid solution of compass-and-mil problems. The table is printed on the reverse side of the firing table for shell, HE, M43A1, and is based on the mil formula.

NOTE.—*a. The mil.*—The unit of angular measure is the mil. Ordinarily, angles are measured in degrees, but in computing firing data for mortars and certain other weapons, a unit of measure called a mil is used. A mil may be defined as the angle measured by an arc the length of which is $\frac{1}{1000}$ of its radius. Thus, if the distance from O to A is 1,000 units of any designated measure (shown as yards in sketch below), and the dis-

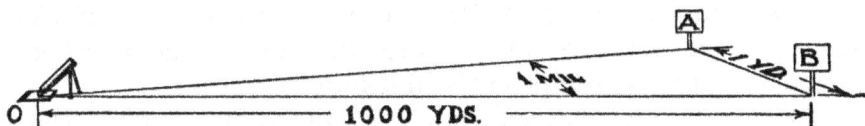

A
1 MIL
B
1 YD
O |————— 1000 YDS. —————|

tance from A to B measured along the arc AB, drawn with O as the center, is 1 unit (shown as 1 yard in sketch below), then the angle AOB is 1 mil. Similarly, at 500 yards 1 mil subtends an arc the width of which is ½ yard; and at 2,000 yards, 1 mil subtends an arc the width of which is 2 yards. An angle of 1 mil is very small, for the difference in direction between lines forming such an angle is slight. For example, imagine two strings 1,000 yards long drawn taut so that they lie straight along the ground. Suppose these strings are tied together at one end and at the other end are separated by an arc of just one yard. The angle thus formed is a *true* mil. Suppose another mil is measured off in the same way next to the first mil, and that this operation is continued until the entire circle is completed. It would be found that it would take 6,283 (1,000 times 2Π) angles of 1 mil each to complete the circle.

b. As 6,283 is an inconvenient number to use in making calculations for firing data, 6,400 is used instead. Thus the circle is divided into 6,400 equal angles; and, in military parlance, each of these angles is called a mil. The difference between this mil and the true mil is so very small that the error is negligible in computing firing data.

2. By use of mil formula.—Where the deflection-conversion table is not available, or where ranges are less than 500 yards, the mil formula, $M=\frac{1,000W}{R}$, must be used. The observer, using the data in (2)(a) above, substitutes in the formula as follows:

$$M=\frac{1,000 \times 125}{1,700}$$

M represents mils (the correction angle to be found);

W represents the unit of width; and *R* the unit of length. The result is 73.6 (or 75 mils, to the nearest 5), which is added to the original azimuth.

(3) *Exercise in determining direction.*—(*a*) The purpose of this exercise is to teach the observer the method of determining the azimuth of the line mortar–target from an observation post which is to the flank of this line.

(*b*) For this exercise, a number of simulated mortar positions and targets are selected in advance. It is desirable to have as many set-ups as there are groups to be instructed. Each should include a mortar position designated by a flag or marker, a well-defined target, and an observation post. Paragraph 59*b* (1) and (2) may be used as a guide in arranging set-ups. Each should have a carefully checked solution previously prepared and should be numbered so that the groups under instruction may be rotated.

(*c*) To the assembled groups, the instructor explains the methods of determining the azimuth of the line mortar–target as described in 59*b*(1) and (2). To do this, he uses a blackboard or chart illustrating figures 20 and 21 and works out several examples similar to the one contained in (1) and (2) above.

(*d*) Each group is then assigned to a set-up in which the group instructor requires each man to solve the problem and to turn in his individual solution. The group instructor corrects any mistakes in the solution, allowing a 15 percent error in range estimation. The groups are rotated through the different set-ups.

■ 60. DETERMINATION OF RANGE.—*a. General.*—As soon as the direction of fire is established, the observer determines the initial range to the target. To do this, he uses the most efficient method available. However, since a range finder, map, or other means is rarely available, he must usually estimate the range by eye.

b. Exercises in range estimation.—The purpose of exercises in range estimation is to teach the observer to estimate ranges by eye with the minimum of error. As estimation by eye must be depended upon in combat, all men should be trained in this method. Stress should be laid on estimating ranges between 200 and 1,500 yards. The estimation by eye of untrained men is little better than a guess, and the average error of such men is at least 15 percent of the range. A definite system of range estimation, frequently practiced, is the only way to make estimation by eye sufficiently reliable.

c. Method of estimation by eye.—(1) Estimation by eye consists in measuring the range by applying to it a unit of measure 100 yards long. The method is the same as that employed in measuring the length of a board with a ruler. The only difference is that the soldier's unit of measure is applied mentally. Thorough familiarity with the 100-yard unit and its appearance on different kinds of ground and at different distances will enable the estimator to apply it with a fair degree of accuracy.

(2) Knowledge of terrain, life in the open, and training in scouting and patrolling are helpful in range estimation.

(3) Application of the unit of measure beyond 500 yards is difficult. For this reason, in ranges over 500 yards, it is better to select a point halfway to the target, apply the 100-yard unit up to this halfway point, and multiply the estimated distance by two (fig. 22).

(4) The average of a number of estimates by different men is generally more accurate than a single estimate. However, in combat the unit leader must usually rely on his own estimation.

d. Conditions affecting the appearance of objects.—(1) Conditions of light and terrain have considerable effect upon the appearance of objects, making them appear sometimes much nearer and at other times much more distant than they really are. The effect of these conditions on the appearance of the first 100 yards is negligible.

(2) In some situations, much of the ground between the observer and the target is hidden from view, and the application of the unit of measure to the hidden portion of the ground is impossible; the appearance of objects is the only guide.

(3) If there is a considerable stretch of visible ground ex-

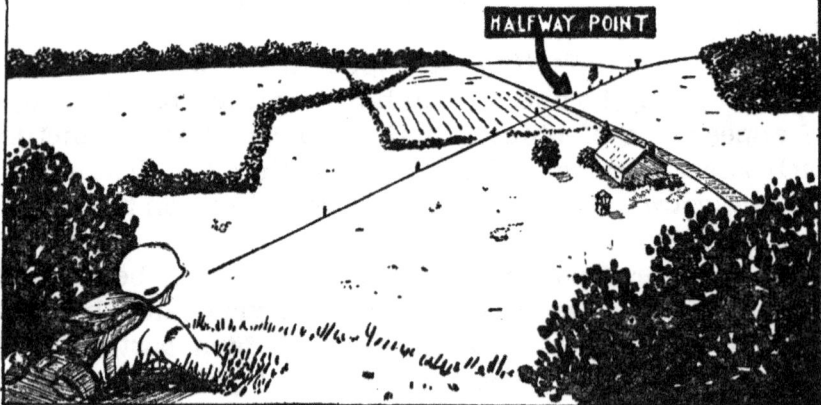

FIGURE 22.—Range estimation, application unit of measure.

tending from the far edge of a depression to the target, it is best to estimate the distance to the far edge of the depression, judging by the appearance of objects, and then to apply the unit of measure over the remaining distance to the target.

(4) Whenever the appearance of objects is used as a basis for range estimation, the observer must make allowances for the effects noted below (fig. 23).

(*a*) Objects seem nearer when—

1. Looking over water, snow, or uniform surface like a wheat field.
2. The color of the object contrasts sharply with the color of the background.
3. Looking over a depression, most of which is hidden.
4. Looking from a height downward.
5. The object is in a bright light.
6. In the clear atmosphere of high altitudes.

(*b*) Objects seem more distant when—

1. There is a poor light or fog.
2. One object is partially hidden.
3. Looking over a depression, all of which is visible.
4. Looking from low ground toward higher ground.

e. Exercises.—(1) The unit of measure, 100 yards, is previously staked out over varied ground, using markers that are visible up to 500 yards. The men are required to become thoroughly familiar with the appearance of the unit of measure at various ranges. They do this by moving away from and in prolongation of the lines staked out and studying the appearance of the unit from distances of 100, 200, 300, and 400 yards (fig. 24).

(2) Ranges up to 900 yards are measured accurately and marked at every 100 yards by large markers or target frames, each bearing a number to indicate its range. Men undergoing instruction are then placed about 25 yards to one side of the prolonged line of markers and directed to place a card, hat, or some other object before their eyes so as to cover from view all of the markers. They are then directed to apply the unit of measure five times along a straight line in the general direction but slightly to one side of the markers. When they have selected the final point reached by mentally applying

FIGURE 23.—Range estimation, appearance of objects.

the unit to the ground five times, the eye cover is removed and the estimations of the successive 100-yard points and the final point are checked against the markers. Accuracy is gained by repeating the exercise.

(3) Ranges greater than 500 yards are then considered. With the markers concealed from view in the same manner as explained in (2) above, men estimate the ranges to points which are obviously over 500 yards distant and a little to one

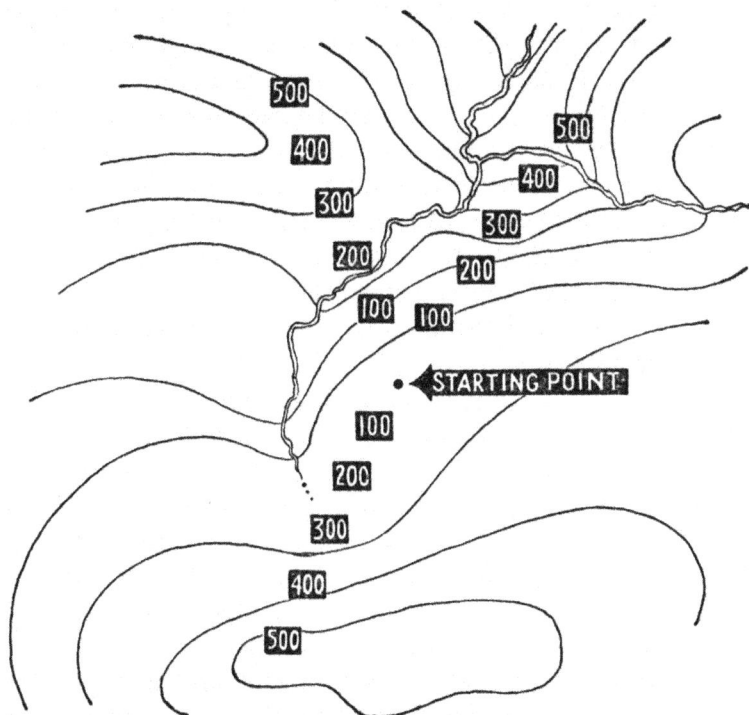

FIGURE 24.—Range estimation, lay-out.

side of the line of markers. As soon as they have announced each range, they remove their eye covers and check the range to the target and to the halfway point by means of the markers.

(4) From a suitable point, ranges are previously measured to objects within 2,000 yards. The instructor conducts the class to the point, where the men are required to estimate the ranges to the various objects that are pointed out by the instructor, writing their estimates upon paper previously issued.

Thirty seconds are allowed for each estimate. When all ranges have been estimated, the papers are collected and the true ranges are announced to the class. Individual estimates and squad averages are posted on bulletin boards accessible to all members of the class.

■ 61. FIRE ORDERS.—a. *General.*—(1) The observer causes his squad to open fire on a target and controls the fire after it has been opened by his fire orders. These orders contain necessary data to enable the squad to lay the mortar correctly and to fire at the proper range and with the proper ammunition. The elements of a fire order are given in a definite sequence in order to accustom the squad to execute them in a definite routine. Whenever practicable, fire orders are given orally. When oral orders are not practicable, arm-and-hand signals, messengers, or sound-powered telephone may be used. The elements of oral fire orders and the arm-and-hand signals are repeated by the gunner.

(2) Deflections and ranges are announced as illustrated in the following example:

10	one zero
25	two five
300	three hundred
875	eight seven five
1,400	one four hundred
2,000	two thousand
1,925	one nine two five
2,050	two zero five zero

(3) Fire is begun at the gunner's command FIRE, after he has received the last element of the observer's fire order. If the observer desires the mortar to be fired at his command, he includes the words UPON COMMAND as the next to the last element of his fire order. Fire is stopped at the observer's command CEASE FIRING, but in an emergency anyone present may give the command CEASE FIRING.

(4) Fire orders are classed as initial fire orders and subsequent fire orders.

b. *Initial fire orders.*—(1) The initial fire order, which contains the data necessary to lay the mortar and fire the first round, includes the elements listed below in their correct sequence:

(*a*) Type of shell.

(*b*) Deflection.

(*c*) Aiming point.

(*d*) Range.

(*e*) Number of rounds.

(2) The type of shell is announced as "HE, light (heavy); practice (smoke)."

(3) If the initial direction of fire has been marked by an aiming stake, the deflection setting is announced as "Zero." If the initial direction of fire has been determined with reference to a base point (par. 45) or another target, the setting is announced as "Right (left) so much." The word "deflection" is not used in the order. The gunner sets the deflection scale of the sight immediately.

(4) The aiming point is announced as STAKE when only one aiming stake is used. When more than one stake is used, this element is announced as "Right stake," "Left stake," or "Base stake."

(5) The initial range to the target is announced as a number of yards ending with a multiple of 25 and without the words "range" and "yards," as, for example, 1,600. The gunner sets the sight at the corresponding elevation shown in the firing table (app. I).

(6) The number of rounds is the last element of the initial fire order, and it is the squad leader's command to the gunner to fire the mortar when laid.

(7) The following are examples of initial fire orders:

HE, LIGHT	HE, LIGHT
ZERO	RIGHT 20
STAKE	RIGHT STAKE
1,000	850
ONE ROUND	ONE ROUND

c. Subsequent fire orders.—(1) Subsequent fire orders contain only the data which are to be changed and the number of rounds to be fired. The elements, listed in their correct sequence, are as follows:

(*a*) Deflection correction (if any).

(b) Range (if changed).

(c) Number of rounds.

(2) In subsequent fire orders, the number of rounds is always announced, since this element is the observer's command of execution. Only such other elements as differ from the initial fire order are announced.

(3) The elements of a subsequent fire order for fire on a point target may be expressed as follows:

(a) *Fire for adjustment.*

LEFT 50	LEFT 30	950
1,200	ONE ROUND	ONE ROUND
ONE ROUND		

(b) *Fire for effect.*

1,225

THREE ROUNDS

d. Arm-and-hand signals.—(1) When the distance between the squad observation post is so great or battle noises are such that the observer cannot make his fire orders heard, and when more accurate means of communication are not available, arm-and-hand signals are used. Arm-and-hand signals are given by the observer while facing the mortar position for which the signals are intended. Deflection signals are executed in the direction toward which the correction is to be made, regardless of which arm is used. The signal indicating the number of rounds automatically becomes the command of execution. Since the elements of the fire order for effect on area targets are not transmitted easily by arm-and-hand signals, they are transmitted usually by voice or messenger.

(2) As there are no prescribed signals for indicating the elements of an initial fire order, the following are suggested as a guide:

(a) For type of ammunition, HE, light, is understood unless otherwise indicated; for HE, heavy, a closed fist may be placed under the chin; for smoke, the palms of both hands may be placed over the eyes.

(b) Zero deflection is understood unless otherwise indicated.

(c) The aiming point will be known by the gunner, or will have been previously indicated by the observer. Hence, no signal need be given.

(3) The arm-and-hand signals essential for use in mortar firing are given below.

(a) *Are you ready?*—The first signal in any series is, "Are you ready?" Extend the arm toward the gunner, hand raised, fingers extended and joined, palm toward the gunner.

(b) *Deflection right (left).*—Facing the mortar, extend one arm toward the gunner; swing the hand and arm horizontally in the direction in which the fire is to be shifted, palm turned in that direction. The first sweeping horizontal movement of the hand represents a 5-mil change in deflection. Each subsequent movement of the hand, after return to the starting position, represents an additional 5-mil change in deflection.

(c) *Range or change in elevation.*—Facing the mortar, raise one arm laterally until horizontal, arm extended and fist closed. For each range increment of 100 yards, swing the arm, fully extended, to an overhead position and return to the horizontal. For each 25-yard increase, the fist is thrust upward, vertically, from the shoulder to the full extent of the arm and returned. For each subsequent fire order, a complete signal sequence, including the range requirements, is given.

(d) *One round.*—Extend one arm above the head, palm toward the gunner; cut the hand sharply downward.

(e) *Three rounds.*—Extend one arm above the head, hand open; flex the wrist, making a quick, choppy, lateral movement with the hand.

■ 62. EXERCISE IN FIRE ORDERS.—*a.* The purpose of this exercise is to teach the observer to give rapid, accurate, and complete oral fire orders.

b. The instructor assembles the men who are to receive this instruction. He explains that the observer controls the fire of his mortar by fire orders which contain the firing data to be used. He also explains that such orders must be brief and accurate and must include all the essential data shown in paragraph 61. He further explains that there are two classes of fire orders as follows:

(1) Initial fire orders, which contain the data for firing the first round on each target; and

(2) Subsequent fire orders, which continue the fire on the target and which contain only the data to be changed in correcting errors in range and deflection of the preceding round.

c. He illustrates this explanation by various examples of fire orders. He then requires one or more members of the group to give a fire order, calling on others to point out any errors made. The group is then divided into smaller groups and the exercise is continued under group instructors.

d. When the groups have become proficient in the issuance of oral fire orders, the instructor explains that because of noises, distances, and other factors, arm-and-hand signals are frequently necessary to transmit firing data. The signals are first demonstrated by two trained assistants; group instructors then conduct the practical instruction.

■ 63. BINOCULAR M3 (fig. 25).—*a. Description.*—(1) This is the standard binocular used for observation and approximate measurement of small angles. It has six-power magnification and an objective pupil diameter of 30 mm. (The binocular, type EE (fig. 26) is a field glass with characteristics basically the same as those of the binocular M3.)

(2) The binocular M3 consists of two compact prismatic telescopes pivoted about a hinge which provides adjustment for interpupillary distances varying between 56 and 74 mm. The left telescope contains the reticle.

(3) The reticle (fig. 27) has a horizontal mil scale graduated at intervals and numbered from 50 mils right to 50 mils left of the center of the field of view. Above the horizontal line are two series of reference marks. These marks are spaced 5 mils apart for convenience in observing fire. The vertical scale, graduated in hundreds of yards, with the 1,800-yard indication in line with the horizontal mil scale, is used by infantry organizations in indirect firing at long ranges and at indistinct field targets. Although this scale has no general application to mortar firing, it may be of value under certain conditions as stated in *b*(4) (*b*) below.

(4) The neck strap secured to the strap loops of the instrument prevents accidental dropping and keeps the instru-

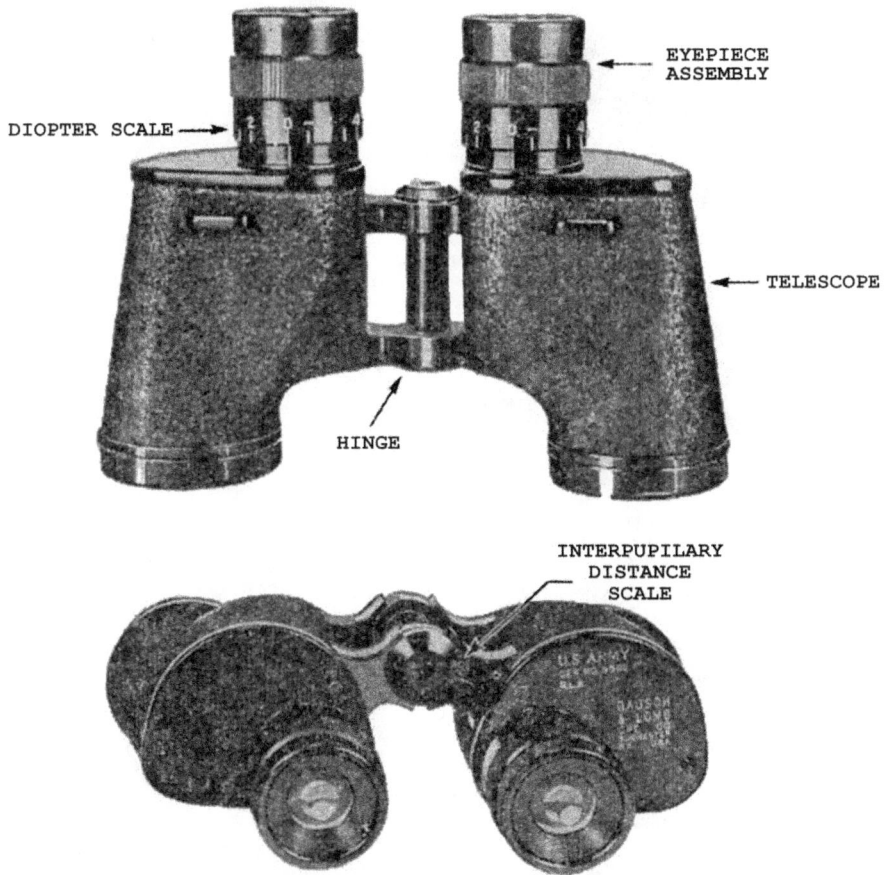

DIOPTER SCALE

EYEPIECE ASSEMBLY

TELESCOPE

HINGE

INTERPUPILARY DISTANCE SCALE

FIGURE 25.—Binocular M3.

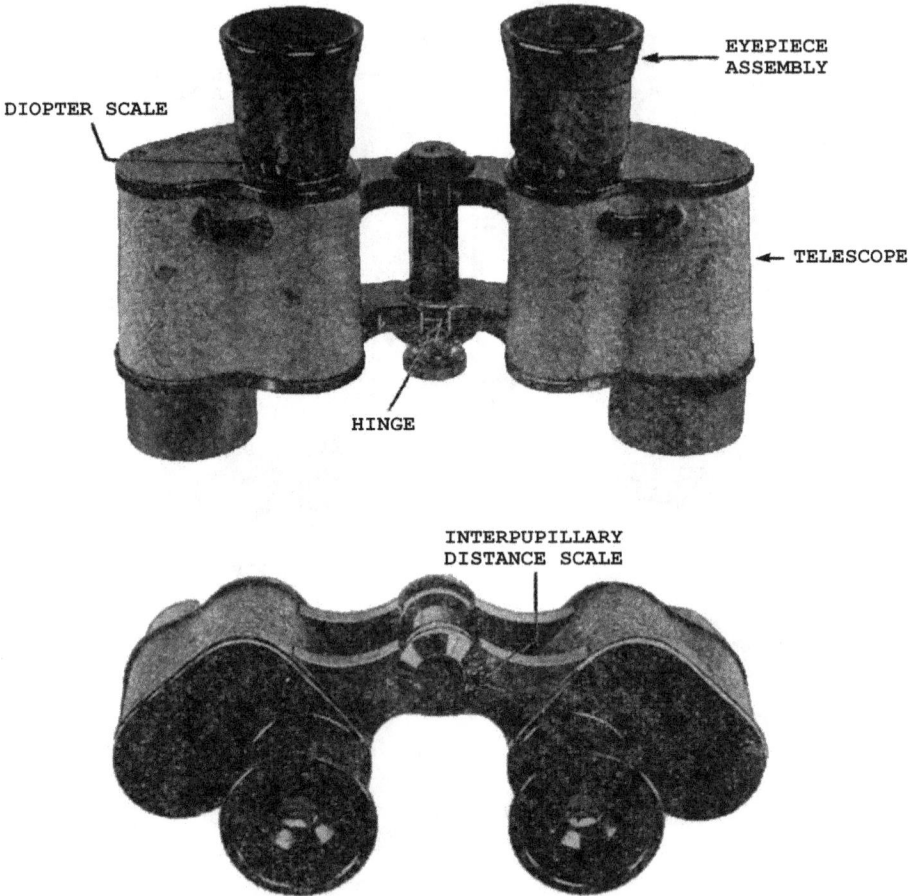

FIGURE 26.—Binocular, type EE.

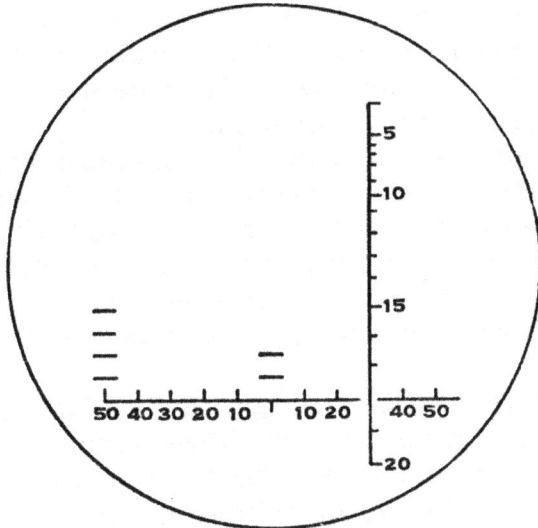

① Binocular M3.

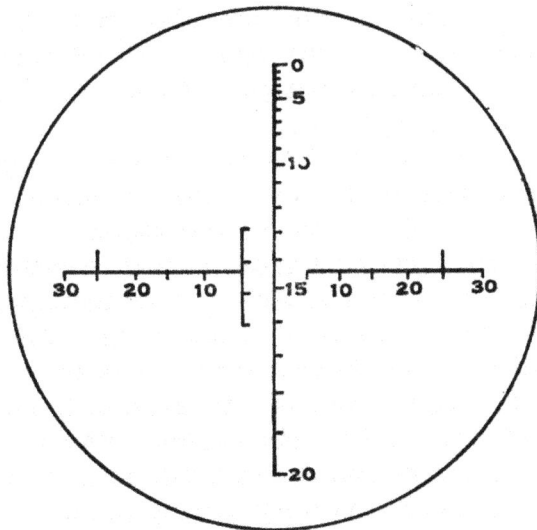

② Field glass, type EE.

FIGURE 27.—Reticle patterns.

ment within easy reach.   A russet leather carrying case with a carrying loop and shoulder strap protects the instrument when it is not in use.   The instrument is carried in the case with the objective end up.   When replacing the binocular in the case, the diopter scale setting need not be disturbed but the hinge may need adjusting.

b. *Operation.*—(1) *Setting interpupillary distances.*—To set the binocular so that the eyepieces are the same distance apart as the observer's eyes, first look through the glass at some fairly distant object; then open or close the glasses at the hinge until the field of view ceases to be separate or overlapping circles and appears to be one sharply defined circle.

(2) *Focusing.*—Look through the eyepieces, both eyes open, at a fairly distant object.   Place a hand over the front of one telescope and screw the focusing nut of the other in or out until the object is sharply defined.   Repeat for the other eye.   Then note the diopter scale reading on each eyepiece.   A similar setting on the eyepieces of any other field glass will accommodate the observer's eyes.   Avoid touching the objective lens.

(3) *Observing.*—Hold the binocular in both hands, eyepieces pressed lightly to the eyes to avoid transmission of body tremors to the instrument.   When possible, use a rest for the binocular or elbows.

(4) *Use of reticle.*—(a) The mil scales are seen superimposed on the observed objects.   The horizontal and vertical angles may be read between the mil scales.

(b) The stadia (vertical) scale is used to secure range settings on sharply defined auxiliary aiming points when the target is not clear enough for direct aiming.   The target must be visible and its range known for the observer to determine these range settings.   In use, the graduation marking the known range is laid on the true target.   Any sharply defined object which coincides with a graduation on the vertical scale may be selected as an auxiliary aiming point.

c. *Care and preservation.*—(1) The binocular is rugged in construction but should not be subjected to rough handling.

(2) The instrument is not to be disassembled by the using

arm. Repairs involving disassembly or painting are to be referred to ordnance maintenance personnel.

(3) The instrument should be carefully wiped dry immediately after use in wet weather and returned to the carrying case. Optical surfaces are to be carefully wiped with lens tissue paper.

(4) The binocular should not be lubricated by the using arm.

■ 64. IMPROVISED ALIDADE AND MIL SCALE.— a. This device is a field expedient which may be used to assist the observer in obtaining initial direction of fire (par. 59) and also to measure horizontal angles in the event the binocular M3 is not available. The general construction of the device is shown in figure 28. A scale placed on the alidade with $\frac{11}{60}$-inch graduations will measure 10 mils between markings when held 18 inches from the eye. A total of 400 mils may be measured with this scale.

b. A hook at each end or two small holes drilled through the alidade are necessary for fastening a cord. These holes should be 2 inches apart, with the 200 mil graduation halfway between the holes. This cord is inserted through the hooks or holes and tied, and is of such length that when the cord is looped around the neck and drawn taut, the scale will be 18 inches from the eye. When measuring a horizontal angle, the zero of the scale is placed on the burst or target, whichever is farthest to the left.

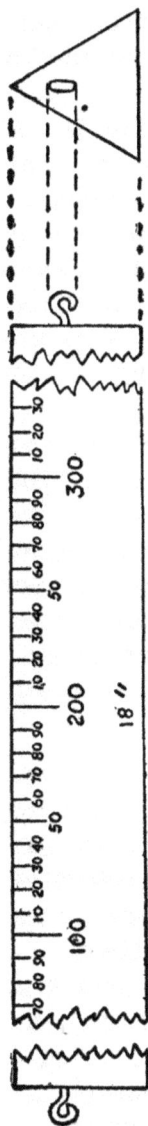

FIGURE 28.—Improvised alidade and mil scale.

SECTION II

SQUAD CONDUCT OF FIRE

■ 65. GENERAL.—a. Conduct of fire implies the ability of the observer to open fire when he desires, to adjust fire, to determine the distribution of fire upon the target, to shift fire from one target to another, and to regulate the kind and amount of ammunition expended.

b. Fire may be conducted either by squad, section, or platoon. The squad is the normal fire unit. Fire is conducted by the platoon as hereafter described for the section (pars. 108 to 111, incl.). Usually the observer conducts the fire of the squad from an observation post which is on or near the line mortar–target and close enough to the mortar position to enable him to transmit fire orders to the mortar crew by voice or arm-and-hand signals. When auxiliary means of communicaion are available, such as the sound-powered telephone or radio, the distance observer–mortar may be increased when necessary to obtain good observation of the target.

c. Only by experience and a practical knowledge of the dispersion of the mortar under various conditions can the observer accurately and promptly adjust the fire of a mortar and accomplish the tactical mission assigned to his squad. To acquire this experience, his squad must fire the weapon with combat ammunition. There are training aids which are of value in preparing the squad and observer for this training, but none is a satisfactory substitute for combat firing.

■ 66. DISPERSION.—*a. General.*—A great number of conditions affect mortar fire, and the obtaining of identical trajectories in firing is improbable. If a number of rounds are fired from a mortar laid each time at the same elevation and deflection, the rounds will not fall on the same point. This dispersion is caused by the conditions listed below.

(1) *Conditions affecting ammunition.*—Muzzle velocity is affected by variations in the weight of the shells and the amount of powder put in the propellant increments. Variations in the bourrelet, which is machined to fit closely the diameter of the bore, may permit the escape of a portion of the powder gases when the propellant increments are ignited, thereby reducing the muzzle velocity. Exposure of the propellant increments to moisture prior to firing may result in incomplete ignition of the powder and a consequent lower muzzle velocity.

(2) *Bore.*—A bore fouled by powder residue, particularly in wet weather, will reduce muzzle velocity to a certain degree.

(3) *Mount.*—Elevation and direction are affected by play in the mechanism of the mount and the degree of accuracy of the sight. The settling of the base plate while the first few rounds are fired may cause the rounds to fall slightly short of the true range at which the mortar is laid.

(4) *During flight.*—Trajectories are affected by air density and temperature, and irregular movements of the air in the form of head, rear, cross, or oblique winds. Gusty winds are an important factor.

b. *Dispersion.*—(1) When firing under apparently identical conditions, trajectories differ because of the foregoing conditions. This difference causes a scattering of rounds, called dispersion. The area covered by a number of rounds fired from a single mortar with fixed firing data is assumed to be rectangular, the long axis being along the line of fire. The area is called the rectangle of dispersion.

(2) An elementary knowledge of dispersion is essential for the observer, particularly when he determines the center of impact, in order that fire for effect will be more effective. A study of the table below indicates that it is desirable to reduce the time of flight so that adverse atmospheric conditions have less time to affect rounds fired, thereby reducing dispersion to a minimum.

DISPERSION TABLE

Range (yards)	Elevation (degree)	Charge	Time of flight (seconds)	Rectangle of dispersion (yards)
500	55¾	0	11.9	64 x 8
500	75½	1	19.3	80 x 32
1,000	49¼	1	15.1	96 x 24
1,000	69¼	2	23.3	112 x 56
1,500	46¼	2	17.9	128 x 40
1,500	66½	3	26.6	152 x 72
2,000	51	3	22.6	168 x 64
2,000	63½	4	29.1	192 x 88

(3) It is apparent from this table that the gunner should select the lower charge whenever possible (par. 32).

■ 67. SENSING.—*a.* Sensing is the determination, from observation of the burst of a shell, whether the point of strike is right or left, over or short of the target. If the burst is visible, but its location with respect to the target is not sufficiently definite for the observer to be sure that it is over or short, it is sensed as DOUBTFUL FOR RANGE. For example, where the initial round fired in adjustment bursts too far to the left or right of the target to permit accurate sensing for range, the observer should sense the round as doubtful for range. In such a case, the observer orders a correction for deflection (the distance of the burst in mils from the line mortar–target) and orders the next round fired at the same range as the previous round.

b. The observer studies the terrain around the target so as to locate any hidden hollows or ravines. He notes any woods, or other cover near the target location which might hide the burst of a round. If a round bursts in a hollow or ravine (the location of which, with respect to the target has already been noted by the observer), the round is sensed as DOUBTFUL FOR DEFLECTION in order to save time and eliminate probable erroneous sensing due to drifting of smoke before it rises into view. The observer immediately senses for range and makes his deflection sensing on the next round. A round is said to be *lost* when the observer sees no indication of the burst.

c. The observer should base his sensing on what he sees and not on what he remembers. Therefore, his sensing should be prompt except when a short delay is to his advantage, such as the sensing of a range by drifting smoke. He should locate the burst first with the naked eye and then apply the binocular. The principal reason for this is that the burst may be outside the field of view of the binocular and may cause the observer to sense the round as *lost*. Another reason is that eye fatigue will be reduced to a minimum.

■ 68. SENSING OF OBSERVER.—*a. Sensing when observer is on line mortar–target.*—(1) *General.*—The best location for the observer, in theory, is at the mortar position where his deflection sensing and the deflection correction to be made on the sight are the same. The tactical employment of the mortar, however, makes it necessary for the observer to place himself in a position other than at the mortar. If he places himself on the line mortar–target, the two methods described below are sufficiently accurate to enable him to direct the fire upon a target.

(2) *Observer 100 yards or less from mortar position.*—If the observer takes a position in front or in rear of the mortar position, and within 100 yards of the mortar, the errors in deflection can be measured from the target to the burst by means of the mil scale in the binocular M3 (fig. 29). For example, if the observer from a position in front or in rear of

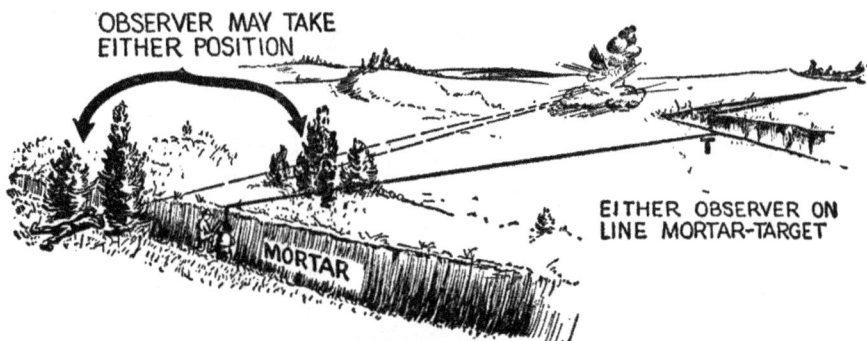

FIGURE 29.—Observer less than 100 yards from mortar.

the mortar location observes the burst to be left of the target and reads 30 mils on the mil scale of his binocular, he senses for deflection 30 left and orders a correction RIGHT 30.

(3) *Observer more than 100 yards from mortar position.*— Whenever the observation post is more than 100 yards from the mortar, the deflection sensing of the observer is not exactly the same as the deflection to be set off on the mortar sight. If the observer is in front of the mortar, the deflection sensing is greater than the deflection to be set off on the mortar. If he is in rear of the mortar, the deflection sensing is less than the deflection to be set off on the mortar. For example, if he is halfway between the mortar and the target, his deflection sensing is twice the correction to be made on the sight; if the mortar is halfway between the observer and

BASIC FIELD MANUAL

$$\frac{OT}{MT} = \frac{600}{800} = \frac{3}{4}$$

$$\frac{3}{4} \times 40 = 30 \text{ mils deflection}$$

600 YDS.

200 YDS.

40

?

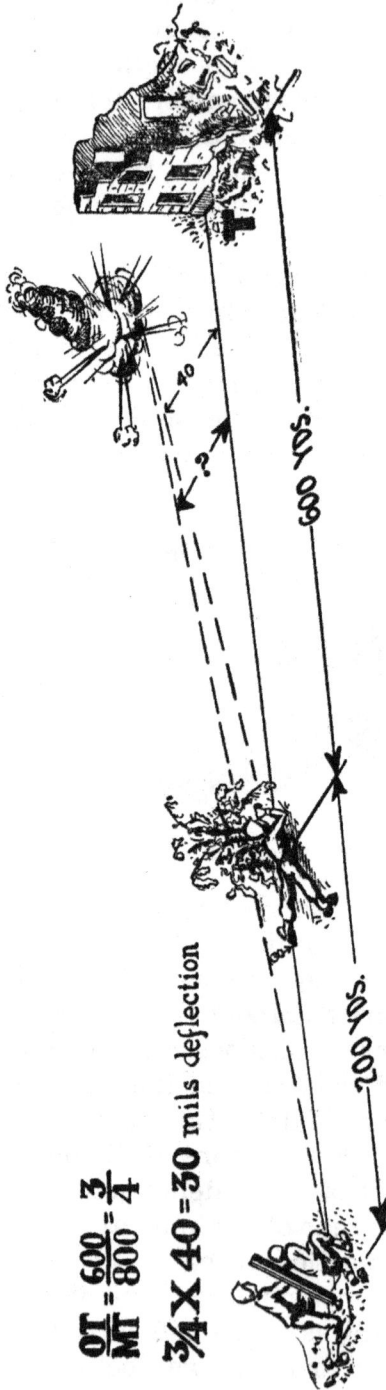

FIGURE 30.—Observer more than 100 yards from mortar.

the target, his deflection sensing is half the correction to be made on the sight. Since other distances give other ratios, it is necessary to apply a correction factor to the number of mils sensed before ordering a deflection change. This factor is a fraction, the numerator of which is the distance observer-target and the denominator of which is the distance mortar-target; that is

$$\frac{\text{Distance observer–target}}{\text{Distance mortar–target}}$$

For example, if the distance observer–target is 600 yards, the distance mortar–target is 800 yards, and the deflection read by the observer is 40 mils (fig. 30), the correction ordered is

$$\frac{600}{800} \text{ (or } \tfrac{3}{4}) \times 40 \text{ mils} = 30 \text{ mils}$$

In applying this factor, simplicity and speed should be sought. Therefore, distances used should be to the nearest even 100 yards.

b. Sensing when observer is off line mortar–target.—(1) It may be necessary for the observer to take a position to the flank, to the flank and forward, or to the flank and rear of the mortar position. In each of these situations, an additional error is introduced because the deflection sensing varies as the observer moves to right or left; that is, the positions of the target and the point of impact with relation to each other seem to change as the observer changes his position.

Example: In figure 31, the observer at *A* (the mortar position) reads the actual deflection which should be set off on the sight. If he moves to *B*, he sees the burst as if it were directly in line with the target. If he moves to *C*, he reads a deflection that is much greater than the correction to be set off on the sight. Since the distances an observer will move off the line mortar–target vary according to terrain and tactical situations, two general methods of sensing for deflection when the observer is to the flank are described below.

(2) Where the shortest distance between observation post and line mortar–target is *less than one-tenth* the distance observation post–target errors in deflection are measured from the target to the burst by means of the mil scale in the

binocular M3. Errors in deflection thus measured are not great enough to require specific corrective measures (fig. 32).

(3) Where the shortest distance between the observation post and the line mortar–target is *greater than one-tenth* the

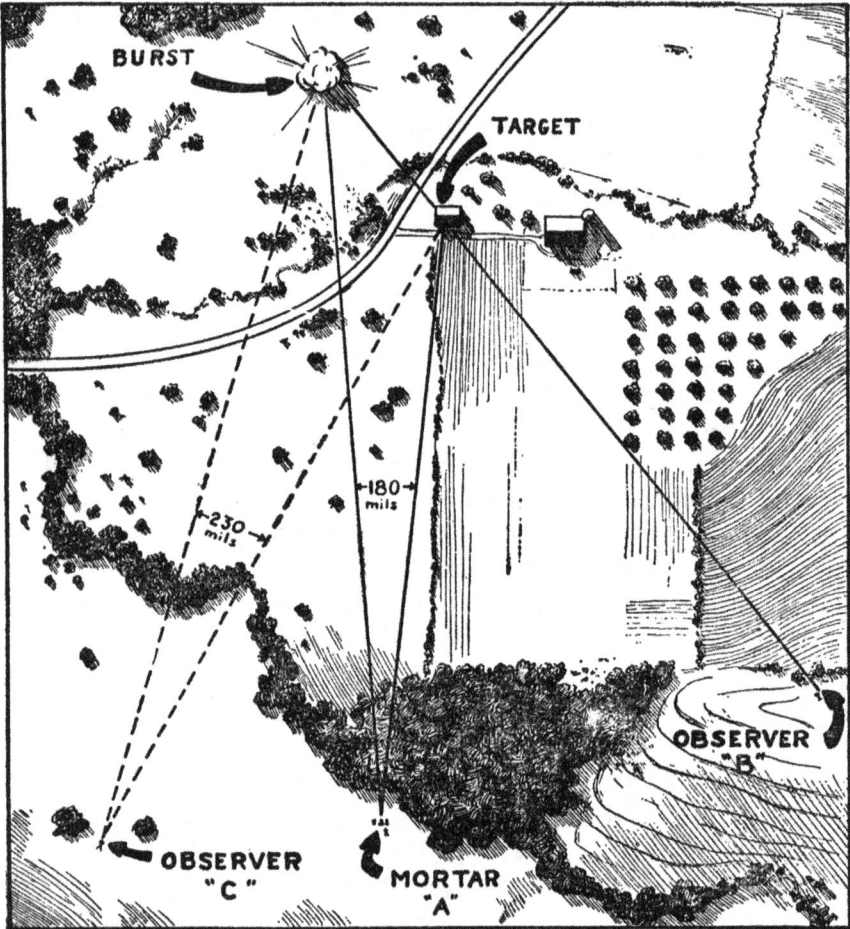

FIGURE 31.—Deflection sensings from flank positions.

distance observation post–target, the observer first determines *on the ground by inspection* what he believes to be the line mortar–target. Deflection sensings are then made *in yards* with reference to this line.

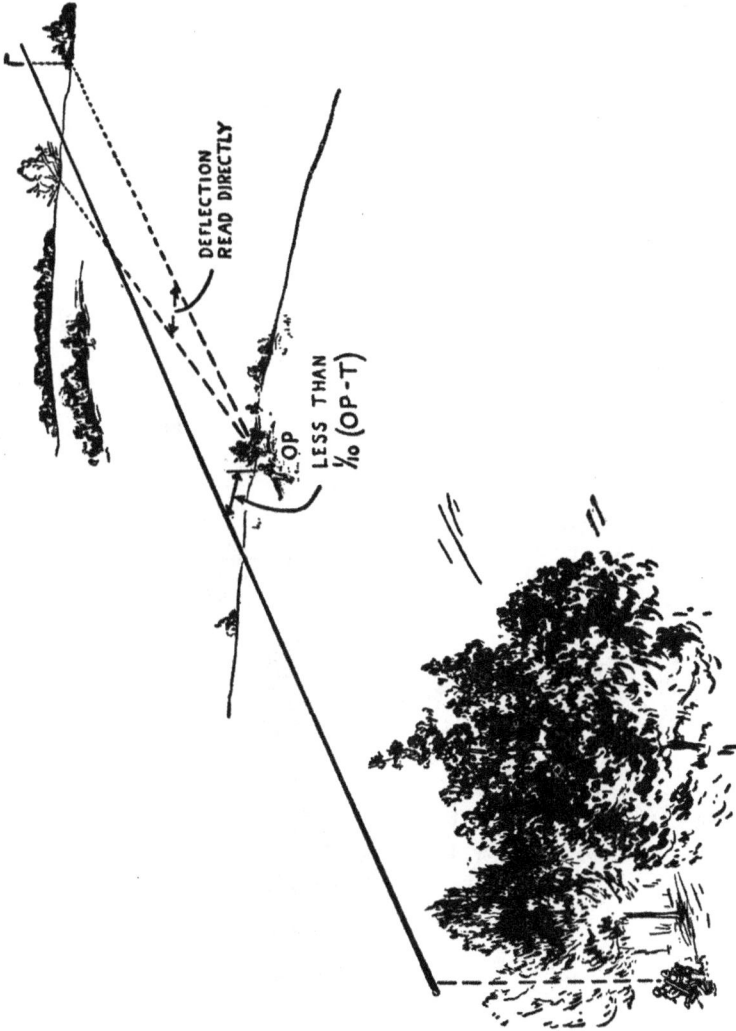

DEFLECTION READ DIRECTLY

LESS THAN $\frac{1}{10}$ (OP–T)

OP

FIGURE 32.—Sensing when distance from OP to line mortar–target is less than one-tenth distance OP–target.

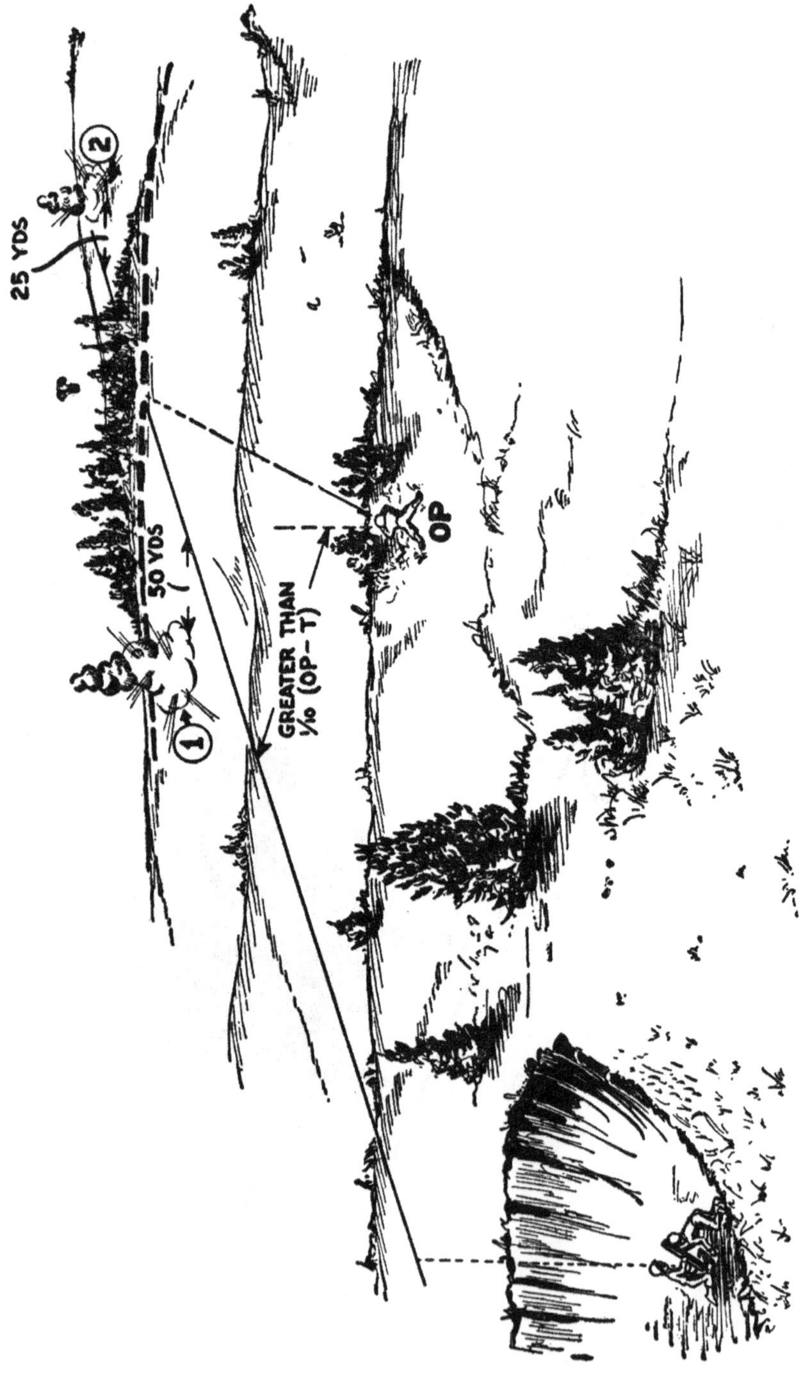

25 YDS

50 YDS

GREATER THAN
$\frac{1}{10}$ (OP–T)

OP

FIGURE 33.—Sensing when distance from OP to line mortar–target is greater than one-tenth distance OP–target.

Example: In figure 33, it will be assumed that the observer has transmitted by sound-powered telephone, voice, arm-and-hand signals, or other means an initial fire order to the gunner at the mortar position as follows:

HE, LIGHT

ZERO

STAKE

800

ONE ROUND

The first round is fired, and the observer senses that it is 50 yards left of the mortar-target and short. In order to convert deflection in yards to mils, he examines the deflection-conversion table (app. I) under the column headed 50, at a range of 800 yards and finds that the number of mils is 64. To correct the errors in deflection and range, his subsequent fire order will be:

RIGHT 65

900

ONE ROUND

The second round is fired, and the observer senses that it is 25 yards right of the line mortar–target and over. Again looking at the deflection-conversion table, he interpolates (takes the average) between figures listed in column 20 and 30 at a range of 900 (range at which the round was fired) and computes 28 mils. His next fire order will be:

LEFT 30

850

ONE ROUND

Subsequent errors in deflection and range are corrected by the procedure described above until the observer is satisfied with fire for adjustment.

■ 69. FIRE FOR ADJUSTMENT.—*a. General.*—The object of fire for adjustment is to determine, from the observed positions of the bursts and the target, the firing data to begin fire for effect. During fire for adjustment, the necessary corrections for range and deflection are made in order to place the center of impact on or near the target.

b. Adjustment for range.—(1) *Bracketing method.*—(a) The bracketing method is a system of range changes based on observation whereby fire is adjusted on a target. When a round is fired at the estimated range to the target, the observer determines whether the round is over or short of the target. He then makes an initial range change to establish a bracket. A target is said to be bracketed when one short and one over have been obtained. The amount of the initial range change will vary with the range. As a general rule, for all ranges under 1,000 yards the initial range change should be 100 yards; for ranges of 1,000 yards and over, the change should be 200 yards. The principal reason for this rule is that, at the shorter ranges, more favorable observation of the target and the relative position of the burst can be obtained. At the greater ranges, sensing and target observation are more difficult, especially under combat conditions.

(b) The range to the target is estimated as accurately as possible, and the initial round is fired at the elevation corresponding to the range. If the burst is observed to be an over, the range setting is decreased 100 yards for ranges under 1,000 yards and another round is fired with this new setting. If this round is a short, the third round is fired with a range setting which is the mean or average of the two previous range settings. Subsequent rounds are fired with range settings which are the mean of the last short and the last over. If the first burst is a short, the range setting is increased 100 yards, and another round is fired in order to establish the bracket. After the bracket is obtained, the range is increased or decreased in steps of 50 and 25 yards, according to the desired size of the final bracket. Where the range is over 1,000 yards, the initial bracket of 200 yards is used, with subsequent ranges increasing or decreasing in steps of 100, 50, and 25 yards.

(c) Experience has proved that the bracketing method is the most economical in the matter of ammunition expenditure and except where time is the governing factor the most effective under normal combat conditions. Attempts to estimate the distance between a burst and the target are seldom successful because of the inability of observers to estimate accurately the distance between two points of the line mortar-target. The bracketing method eliminates the necessity for doing this. The observer merely determines whether a burst is a short or an over. The method is applicable to practically all situations. Even when firing at a target on the crest of a hill, the shorts can be observed and all unobserved bursts are treated as overs.

(d) The following example illustrates the procedure in fire for adjustment as described in (b) above.

Example: The range to the target is estimated to be 800 yards and the first round is fired with this setting. The burst is sensed a short. The range setting is increased 100 yards, and the next round is fired with a setting of 900 yards. The burst is sensed an over. The bracket is now established. The range setting for the third round is the mean of the short (800) and over (900) and is fired with a setting of 850 yards. The third round is fired and sensed as over. Since the target is between the ranges of 800 and 850, adjustment of fire and fire for effect should be combined, and three rounds should be fired at the range of 825. The effective bursting radius of the shell (25 yards) and the dispersion of the rounds will cover the target.

(e) Where a round fired in adjustment on a point target is so nearly correct for range that the observer is uncertain that the target is beyond the effective bursting radius of the shell, he makes a deflection change where necessary and commands: THREE ROUNDS. If these three rounds fail to cover the target adequately, the observer should give the necessary change in range (within the bracket) and again commands: THREE ROUNDS. Where a round is sensed as slightly short or over for range so that it appears to be near the outer limit of the bursting radius, a small change in elevation is given before fire for effect is ordered, such as, DOWN ONE TURN (UP ONE TURN), THREE ROUNDS. A change of one-half turn, or of two turns may be indicated. The total change should amount to less than 25 yards. (Exception: When the *first* round is fired, causing the base plate to settle, and the round is a near, short, or a hit, the next round will usually be over for range. Hence, if the tactical situation permits, a confirming round should be fired and a more positive sensing made. If this confirming round includes the target within the effective bursting radius of the shell, fire for effect can proceed without delay; otherwise the observer will use a 50-yard bracket to adjust fire. Where the tactical situation requires speedy fire for effect and where the first round fired falls about 25 yards short for range, the base plate not being settled, the command: THREE ROUNDS is given. (Usually, these rounds will fall about 25 yards farther than the first.) If the three rounds fail to cover the target, the necessary change in turns is given and three more rounds are fired.)

(*f*) When the first round is obviously nearer the target than the amount of initial change in range which the observer would normally give in his subsequent fire order to obtain a bracket (100 or 200 yards), the observer should use the next smaller bracket (50 or 100 yards). Then, if he obtains a bracket with the second round, one round is conserved. If he fails to obtain a bracket with the second round, he should make the same change in range between the second and third rounds as he made between the first and second. He would then obtain a final bracket with the same expenditure of ammunition as would occur by following the general rule in *b*(1)(*a*) above. (In rare cases where a second round fails to establish a bracket but is fairly close to the target, it may be regarded as being the first round, and the smallest initial range change to obtain a bracket may be selected.)

(*g*) When a bracket has been established but a subsequent round is obviously erratic because of faulty ammunition or other causes, another round should be fired with the same elevation to prevent erroneous sensing. The order in this instance is simply ONE ROUND.

(2) *Creeping method.*—(*a*) When a target is close to friendly troops, firing should be opened with a range which is manifestly over. Subsequent changes in range should be such that the shells do not burst so short of the target that friendly troops are endangered. Therefore, the bracketing method cannot always be used. The method employed when the target is dangerously close to friendly troops and when the mortar is relatively far behind the front line is called the creeping method. (Should the observer be certain that the nearest round for adjustment by any other method will fall at least 200 yards ahead of the friendly troops, that method may be used instead of the creeping method.) For the

creeping method, the observer uses a combination of the principles of adjustment without sights (par. 71) and of searching fire (par. 72).

(b) The following illustrates the procedure: The observer estimates the range to the target (assume 600 yards), adds 200 yards for safety, and issues an initial fire order:

> HE, LIGHT
>
> 72° (800 YARDS)
>
> CHARGE 1
>
> ONE ROUND

The gunner lays the mortar and commands: FIRE. The observer *immediately* commands: UP EIGHT TURNS (the difference in degrees between elevation for 800 and 600 yards) and makes a mental note that, since eight turns represent 100 yards at this range, a 50-yard change can be made with four turns, or a 25-yard change with two turns. He meanwhile awaits the fall of the first round. If the observer's initial estimate of range was reasonably accurate, the round should fall over the target anywhere between 100 and 200 yards. The observer merely determines whether the round is at least 100 yards over and, if so, reads the deflection (assume left 30 mils) and completes his fire order:

> RIGHT TWO TURNS
>
> 1 ROUND

NOTE.—The observer, after ordering the mortar to be elevated eight turns, expects the second round to land 100 yards shorter than the first round. Each succeeding order is modified so as to take but one-half of the turns of the elevating crank ordered for the preceding round. When this second round is fired, the observer immediately commands: UP FOUR TURNS, and awaits the fall of the second round. Again he determines whether this round is at least 50 yards over the target and, if so, orders any necessary deflection correction and commands: ONE ROUND. He then commands: UP TWO TURNS and awaits the fall of the third round. Based on the fall of this round, the observer decides whether it will be safe to fire three rounds for effect at the elevation then placed on the mortar or whether the mortar should be depressed a turn or a fraction of a turn before firing for effect.

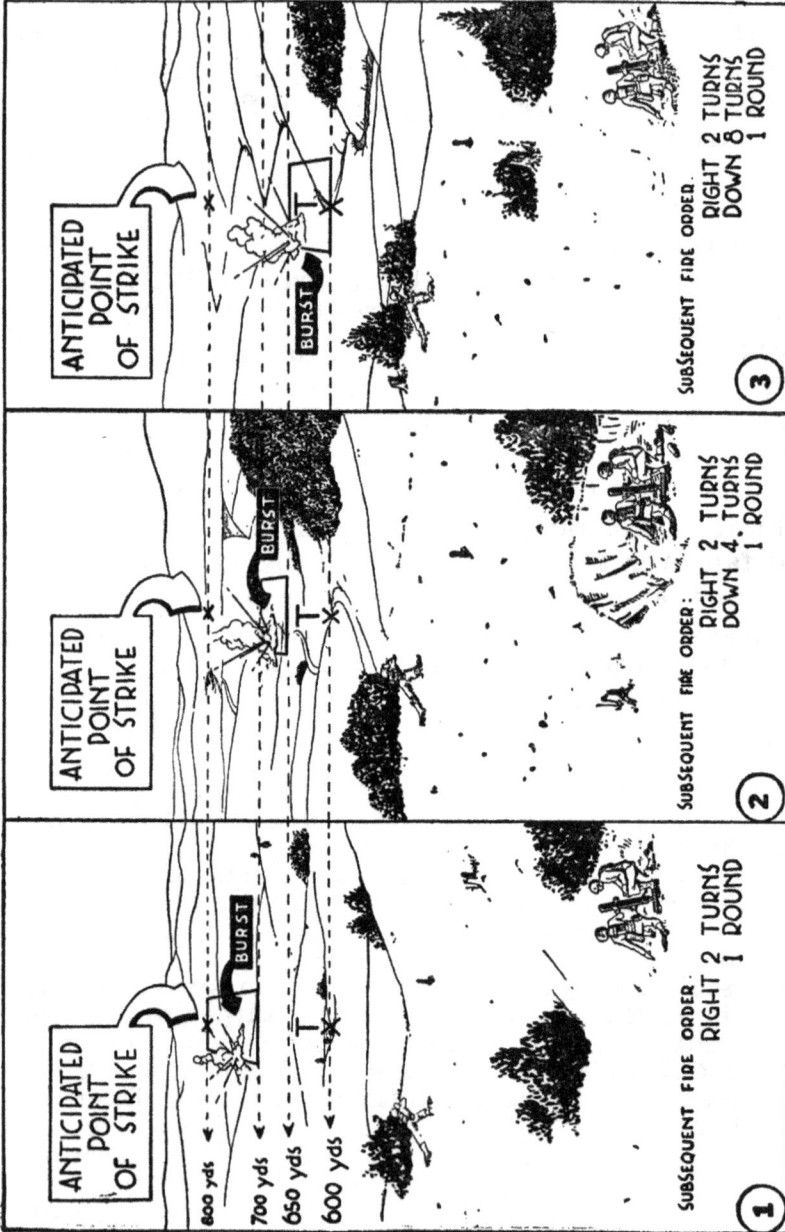

FIGURE 34.—Creeping method, sensing first burst. (Note that the terrain shown in ①, ②, and ③ is not identical and that each sketch is for a separate problem.)

(c) As a general rule, if a round falls short of the expected overage, the observer orders the mortar to be depressed exactly one-half of the preceding number of turns, before firing the next round, in order to minimize the chance of obtaining a round short of the target. The following figure illustrates three principles to be applied when the first round falls as indicated in this discussion. In figure 34①, since the first round had landed about 150 yards over the target, the observer is correct in giving the subsequent fire order shown. Suppose, however, that the first round, fired in pursuance to an initial order as given in (2) (b) above, bursts as indicated in figure 34②, since the round has not fallen with at least a 100-yard clearance beyond the target, the observer must order the mortar depressed one-half of the original number of turns taken on the elevating crank in order to avoid a short on the second round. In figure 34③, since the round has fallen only slightly beyond the target, the observer must modify his order so as to bring the mortar back to the sight setting at which the last round was fired. Having done this, he fires a confirming round with the sight setting as for the last round fired.

(d) *General safety rule.*—81-mm mortar fire should be at least 200 yards from friendly troops. Where our own troops are within 400 yards of the target, the creeping method of adjustment will be used. (Exception: Where the range from the mortar to our front line is definitely known, the observer may safely use any method of adjustment so long as he never fires at a range less than the range from the mortar to the front line, plus 200 yards.) Where the target is at a range greater than 400 yards from our own troops, other methods of adjustment should be used.

(e) *Adjustment for deflection.*—Adjustment for deflection proceeds simultaneously with adjustment for range. The observer, in most situations, measures the horizontal angle between the target and the burst by means of the mil scale of the binocular. Other means of measuring this angle would be with an improvised mil scale or by the use of fingers (every observer should know the mil calibration of his fingers). Having applied the necessary corrections, he orders the deflection applied to the mortar in the proper direction.

NOTE.—Since the HE, heavy shell M56 constitutes only a small percentage of the ammunition available for the squad, and since it is necessary to make a very fine adjustment for range to obtain a direct hit, the following should be used as a guide:

a. First obtain a bracket with the HE, light, shell, M43A1, preferably with a range change of 100 yards. Then fire the intermediate ranges with the HE, heavy, shell to complete the adjustment.

b. Where a 200-yard range change is needed to establish a bracket, fire the first intermediate range (plus or minus 100 yards) with the HE, light shell and, after sensing the round, fire all subsequent rounds within the bracket with the HE, heavy shell.

■ 70. EXERCISE IN CONDUCT OF FIRE.—The best and most direct method of teaching the observer the conduct of fire is by firing combat ammunition. However, ammunition allowances and range limitations often restrict training by this method and it becomes necessary for the instructor to supplement such training by work on a miniature (1,000 inch) range, and by use of the training projectile M68 (par. 31). The observer should receive progressive instruction, first on the miniature range, next with the training projectile, and last in field training with combat ammunition. The following methods of instruction are suggested for miniature range work and firing of the training projectile:

a. Miniature range.—(1) Equipment.—The equipment is set up as shown in figure 35. Ranges in hundreds of yards are indicated by stakes numbered from 5 to 10. (On this range, since the distance from the observation post to the stake numbered 10 is 1,000 inches, the binocular M3 or other means should be used to measure deflection errors.) Bursts are represented by the instructor using a pointer with a ball of cotton or waste attached to the end of the pointer. Targets may be small stakes, sight cases, toy weapons, and like items. The red stake is the observation post for the observer. The mortar is mounted about 25 yards in rear of the red stake. One range should be provided for each mortar squad with trained assistants for each range. The training projectile M68 (or an improvised wooden replica), should be available to provide training in loading. No ignition cartridges will be used. Squares of leather or other material should be prepared to represent propellent increments.

(2) *Purpose.*—The purpose of these exercises is to provide training for the observer in computing initial direction of fire, sensing, the issuance of fire orders, and the adjustment of fire. They also serve to give the gunner additional training in sight setting and laying of the mortar and to train No. 2 in the proper method of loading the round. The sequence described below should first be demonstrated by trained personnel.

(3) *Procedure.*—(a) The instructor designates a target, directs the observer to obtain initial direction of fire by the direct alinement method, and announces that the bracketing method of fire adjustment is to be used. When the mortar has been mounted and the safety precautions checked, the observer issues an initial fire order as, for example:

HE, LIGHT

ZERO

STAKE

900

ONE ROUND

(Range indicators are used for the initial range estimates.) The gunner announces the charge, lays the mortar on the aiming stake, and checks for mask clearance. He then removes the sight, places his left foot on the base plate, and commands: FIRE. Nos. 2 and 3 follow the procedure indicated in paragraph 54 for preparing and loading the ammunition.

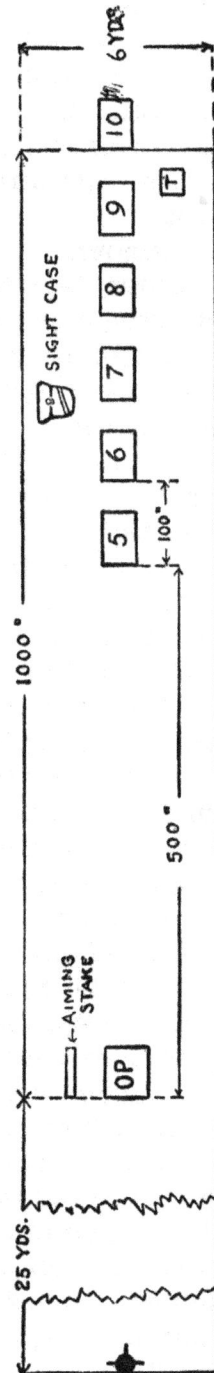

FIGURE 35.—Miniature range lay-out.

(b) When the round has been loaded, the instructor momentarily places his pointer over the target (it is unnecessary to place the pointer at the point on the range corresponding to the range given in the initial fire order). The observer in this instance sees that the burst is an over and issues his subsequent fire order:

    800

    ONE ROUND

The gunner lays the mortar and orders the second round fired. The instructor places his pointer in front of and to the right of the target; the observer reads the error in deflection, observes that the burst is a short, and issues his next fire order:

    LEFT 10

    850

    ONE ROUND

After this round is fired, the instructor places his pointer in front or in rear, right or left of the target, depending on the point he desires to bring out. Should the observer give an incorrect fire order, such as right deflection instead of left deflection, the instructor places the burst as called for in order to bring out the error in the instruction.

(c) After fire for effect has been ordered, the instructor should cause the base deflection to be marked, additional aiming stakes placed (the required procedure after marking base deflection), and then he should indicate a new target to the observer. Fire is adjusted on the second target in a manner similar to that just described. Instruction may be varied in the following manner: obtain initial direction of fire by the azimuth method; use an initial range change of 200 yards for the bracketing method; use the creeping method of adjustment; require a misfire to be removed during adjustment of fire; and similar problems.

(d) During inclement weather, conduct of fire may be taught on a sand table (par. 160) in much the same manner as that used on the miniature range.

b. *Training projectile M68.*—With a few exceptions, the training conducted on the miniature range can be applied to training with the projectile M68.

(1) *Range lay-out.*—The range indicators should be at

least one foot square. They should be placed at 100-foot intervals from the mortar position and should be numbered from 2 to 10. The impact area should be visible only to the observer, and the mortar should be placed in defilade. Since it is difficult to sense the fall of a round because of the inert construction of the projectile, bursts may be indicated by placing a small marker (flag, waste, etc.) at the point of strike immediately upon impact of the shell. An alternate method of indicating the burst is to sprinkle a heavy coating of ashes in a rectangle surrounding the target. A puff of dust from the ashes caused by the fall of the projectile will permit a brief sensing of the round for deflection and range.

(2) *Purpose and procedure.*—The purpose of this instruction is to train the squad in the application of principles learned and to apply these principles under conditions approximating those met with in the field. The procedure and sequence of instruction is very similar to that described for the miniature range. Although the range column of the firing table for this shell is graduated on the basis of feet, the observer should consider all ranges to be yards when issuing fire orders. Therefore, the range is scaled from 200 to 1,000 yards in order to simulate field conditions.

■ 71. ADJUSTMENT WITHOUT SIGHTS.—*a.* When the observer has established the initial direction of fire, he estimates the range to the target, determines the angle of elevation by reference to the firing table (par. 48), and issues his initial fire order, for example:

HE, LIGHT

69° (675 YARDS)

CHARGE 1

ONE ROUND

NOTE.—It is important that the charge zone selected will permit completion of fire for adjustment and fire for effect. Fractions of degrees should be disregarded in all calculations.

b. The first round falls 45 mils left of the line mortar–target and short. To correct for deflection, the observer mentally divides 45 mils by 15 mils (number of mils in one turn of the traversing handwheel) and obtains 3 turns. In order to bracket the target for range, the observer calculates the difference in degrees between the ranges of 675 and 775, multiplies the difference in degrees by 2 (one turn of the elevating crank equals ½ degree) to determine the equivalent number of turns for the elevating crank, and issues his subsequent fire order:

> RIGHT THREE TURNS
> DOWN EIGHT TURNS
> ONE ROUND

(The gunner should be given the deflection before the observer establishes the number of turns in elevation that are required. This procedure saves time in laying the mortar.) The second round is fired and falls 15 mils left of the line mortar–target and over. Still following the bracketing method for range, the observer's fire order would be:

> RIGHT ONE TURN
> UP FOUR TURNS
> ONE ROUND

The third round falls close to the target and, by issuing minor or fractional changes for deflection and range errors, the observer can complete fire for adjustment and order fire for effect.

c. Once a bracket has been established, for all subsequent changes in elevation, the observer should take one-half of the number of turns used for the last round, in the required direction. Fractional degrees of elevations should be disregarded when the initial number of turns of the elevating crank is being figured.

■ 72. FIRE FOR EFFECT.—a. *Definition.*—Fire for effect is that fire delivered on a target to accomplish a desired tactical result. Mortar fire must first be adjusted for deflection and range. The final bracket for range adjustment need not always be fired before fire for effect is delivered. The observer may, therefore, combine fire for adjustment with fire for effect, particularly where speed in destroying or neutralizing a target is essential. Fire for effect is delivered by firing a number of rounds, each round being fired at the command of the gunner as rapidly as accuracy in laying the mortar permits.

b. *Types.*—(1) *Fixed fire.*—A volley of three rounds is usually fired on a point target or a small area not to exceed 50 by 50 yards. Three rounds will normally accomplish the mission, provided the center of impact is on or near the target. If the observer judges that the rounds have not destroyed the target, because of inaccurate adjustment, he may order three additional rounds fired with slight adjustments made for range and/or deflection. Five rounds may be fired for effect on a target located at an extreme range where three would be ineffective because of dispersion factors. The gunner should check the lay of the mortar for elevation and deflection before firing each round.

(2) *Distributed fire.*—For distributed fire, the rounds are distributed laterally or in depth, or both, by—

Normal traversing fire

Alternate traversing fire

Searching fire

Traversing and searching fire

(a) *Normal traversing fire* (fig. 36).

1. Three rounds are distributed laterally across a target not over 100 yards wide. After each round, the gunner traverses the mortar the number of turns of the handwheel specified. The mortar should be cross-leveled before each succeeding round is fired. A fire order would be:

    1,100

    TRAVERSE LEFT THREE TURNS

    THREE ROUNDS

    (Range would not be repeated where there is no change from the previous round fired in adjustment.)

2. The number of turns of the traversing handwheel is determined by the observer, who measures the width of the target in mils with the binocular and divides by the constant 30. The result will be the number of turns between rounds. The turns calculated should be to the nearest half. (The constant 30 is used since there are 15 mils per turn of the traversing handwheel and there are two intervals between the three bursts. The

number of turns may be determined, using a longer process, by dividiing the width in mils by 15 and then dividing the result by 2. *Example:* Width of target in mils at a range of 1,100 yards for a width of 100 yards, equals 92 mils. 92÷30=3 turns, or 92÷15=6÷2=3 turns.)   (See Appendix II.)

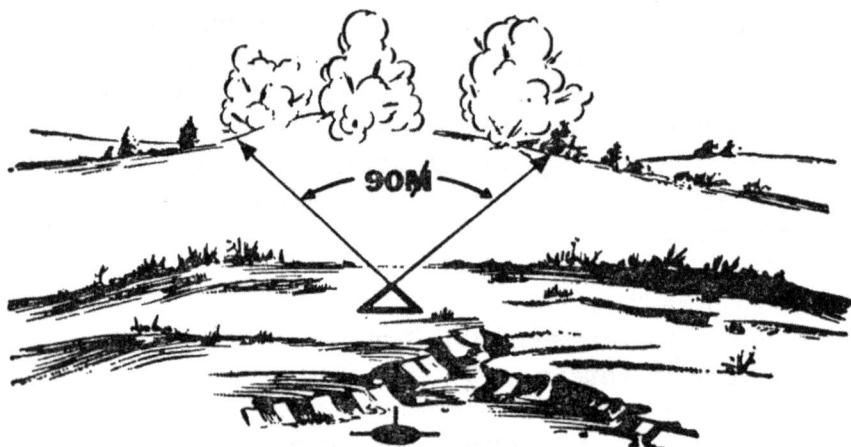

OBSERVER MEASURES WIDTH OF TARGET IN MILS AND THEN DIVIDES BY 30

$$\frac{90}{30} = \text{3 TURNS}$$

**FIRE ORDER
TRAVERSE RIGHT (LEFT) 3 TURNS, 3 ROUNDS**

FIGURE 36.—Normal traversing fire.

(b) *Alternate traversing fire.*—Another form of traversing fire may be used where a heavier concentration of fire is desired on a target, as, for example, on a primary target in a defensive situation (par. 78). The width of the target should not exceed 100 yards. The same technique is used as stated above, but a volley of three rounds instead of one is fired at each point.   The fire order for this type of fire is:

THREE ROUNDS

LEFT FIVE TURNS, THREE ROUNDS

LEFT FIVE TURNS, THREE ROUNDS

(The fire order may be given in its entirety or separately after each volley is fired.)

NOTE.—For all targets requiring lateral distribution of rounds, the observer must, during the adjustment of fire, inform the gunner as to the direction of eventual traverse.   In most cases, the traversing screw nut must be so positioned that the gunner can traverse twice the number of turns announced in the fire for effect order.   Having been forewarned as to the direction of traverse, the gunner determines by a glance at the traversing screw nut whether or not its position will allow the required manipulation.   If not, he turns the traversing screw off center, directs No. 2 to move the bipod, and lays accurately again on the stake.   For a right traverse, the traversing screw nut should be positioned on the right side of the yoke; for traverse to the left, the traversing screw nut should be positioned on the left side of the yoke.

(c) *Searching fire* (fig. 37).

1. Three rounds are distributed in depth over a target not over 100 yards deep by firing at three successive ranges.   After each round, the gunner depresses (or elevates) the mortar the number of turns he has calculated by reference to the firing table.   A fire order would be SEARCH 1,100–1,200, 3 ROUNDS.

2. The number of turns of the elevating crank for each range change of 50 yards is equal to the number of degrees of difference between the angles of elevation corresponding to the range limits of the target.   All rounds must be fired within the same charge zone.   The mortar should be cross-leveled between rounds.   For example, if the range limits are 1,100–1,200, the corresponding angles of elevation are $66\frac{1}{2}°$ and $63\frac{1}{2}°$, respectively.   The difference is 3° (disregard fractions in all calculations).   Therefore, the number of turns of the elevating crank to be taken between rounds is three. (One turn equals $\frac{1}{2}°$.) (See app. II.)

(d) *Traversing and searching fire* (fig. 38).

1. Nine rounds are distributed laterally and in depth over an area not exceeding 100 x 100 yards, by a combination of the methods used for traversing

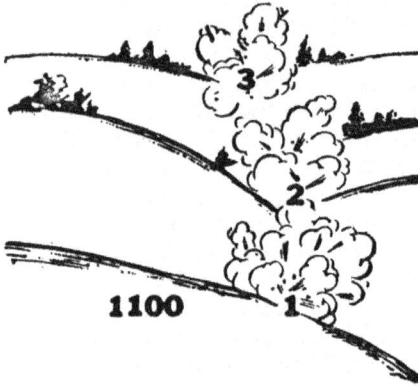

GUNNER RECEIVES
FIRE ORDER
SUBTRACTS ELEV.
OF LIMITING RANGES
1100   66 DEG.
1200   63 DEG.
DIFFERENCE = 3 DEG.

GUNNER TAKES NUMBER OF
TURNS OF ELEVATION CRANK
BETWEEN ROUNDS
EQUAL TO DIFFERENCE
IN DEGREES

FIRE ORDER
SEARCH 1100-1200
3 ROUNDS

FIGURE 37.—Searching fire.

and searching fires. The fire is adjusted on a convenient point as, for example, a corner near the edge of the target area. The gunner traverses as described in (a) above. When the third round has been fired, the gunner changes to the next elevation as described in (c) above, for searching fire, and traverses in the opposite direction. When the sixth round has been fired, the gunner changes to the next elevation and traverses in the initial direction. A fire order would be: SEARCH 1,100–1,200, TRAVERSE LEFT THREE TURNS, NINE ROUNDS. After covering the target, the gunner waits for a reasonable length of time while anticipating another order to cover the

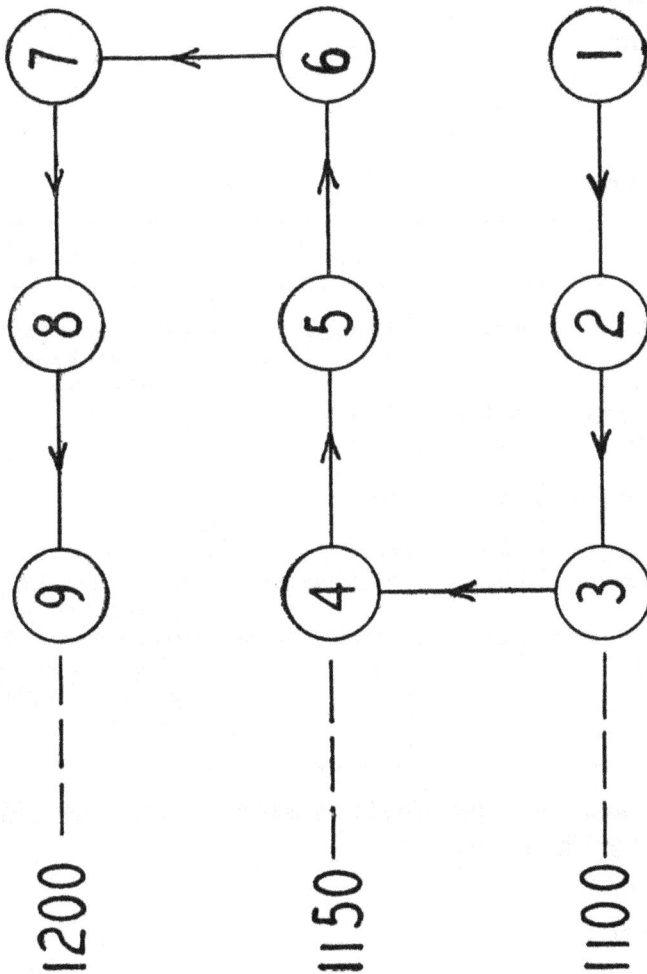

FIGURE 38.—Traversing and searching fire.

target again. If no order is given, he lays the mortar back on the base point.
2. Figure 38 indicates the manner in which the rounds should fall on the target. If the observer desires

to cover the area again, his fire order would be: SEARCH 1,200–1,100, TRAVERSE RIGHT THREE TURNS, NINE ROUNDS.

■ 73. TYPE PROBLEMS.—The following type problems illustrate the procedure in the conduct of fire of the squad:

a. *Fire on point target.*
Initial order:

> HE, LIGHT
> ZERO
> STAKE
> 1,000
> ONE ROUND

Order	Sensing		Remarks
See initial order_____	50 right____	Doubtful_____	Must bring burst closer to line observer–target to sense for range.
LEFT 50; ONE ROUND___	10 right____	Short_____	
LEFT 10; 1,200; ONE ROUND.	5 left_____	Over_____	
RIGHT 5; 1,100; ONE ROUND.	Line_____	Over_____	
1,050; ONE ROUND_____	Line_____	Over_____	
1,025; THREE ROUNDS___	Line_____	Slightly short____	Observer fires final bracket as part of fire for effect.
DOWN ONE TURN; THREE ROUNDS.	Line_____	Mission accomplished.	Fragmentation is more effective when center of impact is slightly over the target.

b. *Distributed fire by single mortar.*—Target is approximately 100 by 100 yards.
Initial order:

> HE, LIGHT
> ZERO
> STAKE
> 1,600
> ONE ROUND

Order	Sensing		Remarks
See initial order_____	20 right___	Short_____	The adjustment in this case is on the right, near edge of the target area.
LEFT 20; 1,800; ONE ROUND__	5 right____	Over_____	
LEFT 5; 1,700; ONE ROUND___	Line_____	Over_____	
1,650; ONE ROUND_____	Line_____	Short_____	Observer decides to fire final bracket as part of fire for effect. Speed in delivering fire makes it desirable to combine fire for adjustment with fire for effect.
SEARCH 1,675–1,775, TRAVERSE LEFT TWO TURNS, NINE ROUNDS.	_____	_____	Order for fire for effect.
SEARCH 1,775–1,675, TRAVERSE RIGHT TWO TURNS, NINE ROUNDS.	_____	_____	Observer desires to cover area again.

■ 74. EXERCISE IN DISTRIBUTED FIRE.—a. General.—Preliminary instruction and practical work in the technique of distributed fires should be conducted on the miniature range. When the observer and gunner have reached that stage of proficiency where an approximation of field conditions is desirable, the training projectile M68 should be used.

b. The miniature range.—(1) Equipment.—The same equipment as described in 70b should be used for this exercise.

(2) Purpose.—The primary purpose of this exercise is to train the observer in the technique of distributing fire laterally and in depth and to provide practice for the gunner in the manipulation of the traversing and elevating mechanisms, based on the fire orders issued by the observer. The secondary purpose of the exercise is to impress upon the squad members that teamwork is required to place fire upon a target from the time the target is designated to the observer to the command FIRE by the gunner for the last round for effect. The sequence described below should first be demonstrated by trained personnel.

(3) Procedure.—(a) The instructor designates a point on the range on which fire will be adjusted by the bracketing

method. The instructor informs the observer that he will place traversing fire on a target outlined by two stakes. The observer obtains data for initial direction of fire to either limit of the target area. When the mortar is mounted, the observer issues the necessary fire orders to adjust fire on the designated limit of the target area. The burst pointer is used to indicate the fall of the rounds. During adjustment of fire, the observer forewarns the gunner as to the direction of eventual traverse. The observer also measures the mil width of the target to determine the number of turns of the traversing handwheel to be taken between rounds for fire for effect. When the final 25-yard range change is reached, the observer combines fire for adjustment with fire for effect and issues his subsequent fire order, for example:

925
TRAVERSE RIGHT (LEFT) THREE AND ONE-HALF TURNS
THREE ROUNDS

(b) When the gunner has completed the required manipulation of the mortar, he is instructed to wait a reasonable length of time in order to permit the observer to sense the rounds fired. If the observer desires to reverse the direction of fire and fire three additional rounds, he issues the necessary order, and the gunner can fire the rounds without delay. When the observer gives no subsequent order, the gunner automatically re-lays on the aiming point.

(c) When the traversing fire problem is completed, the observer commands: OUT OF ACTION. Successively, problems are worked involving the use of alternate traversing fire, searching fire, and traversing and searching fire. Practical work in these types of fire should be progressive. To insure maximum efficiency in combat, every member of the squad should be thoroughly acquainted with the principles and technique involved in each type of fire. Frequent rotation of duties is not only desirable but necessary to insure complete understanding of the technique of fire.

c. The training projectile, M68.—Essentially the same type of training as indicated in (b)3 above, can be conducted with the training projectile. Terrain selected for this type of firing should contain small irregularities to simulate in miniature as much as possible areas where hostile weapons would normally be located. The actual target area may be invisible to the observer; in such a case a clearly defined reference point should be available for adjustment of fire. For example, a traversing target might be designated as follows:

LEFT FRONT
REFERENCE: BLACK STUMP ON RIDGE
LEFT, 35
TARGET: MACHINE GUNS IN DEFILADE JUST OVER RIDGE, EX-
   TENDING RIGHT, 90
LAY NORMAL TRAVERSING FIRE ON AREA INDICATED

This type of designation will require the observer to adjust fire on some observable point and will necessitate a change in data to place fire for effect on the target area.

SECTION III

COMBAT EXPEDIENTS—RAPID ADJUSTMENT OF FIRE

■ 75. FOR THE SQUAD LEADER.—Now that you, corporal, have a basic knowledge of the principles of fire for adjustment and have trained the various members of your squad to act as a team, you should be told about some short-cuts in technique which can be used in battle. As you well realize, a most important factor in adjustment of fire is the time interval between the fall of the first round for adjustment and the first round for effect. The enemy will know, before many rounds have fallen, that he is the object of your adjustment and will attempt to move out of range before your fire for effect falls on him. You must surprise him by speedy adjustment. To attain this end, some "combat expedients" will be described which you and your squad should be familiar with and practice before you ever reach the combat areas.

a. You are well acquainted with the principles of the bracketing method. Take a few minutes, however, and review paragraphs 48 and 71 (firing and adjustment without sights), as we are going to combine bracketing principles with some of the principles laid down for adjustment without sights. We call this expedient the "bracketing method, modified."

(1) First of all, your gunner will have a sight mounted on the mortar. To determine initial direction of fire, use any of the methods described in paragraph 59. While the mortar is being mounted, you estimate the range to the target to be, say, 700 yards. When your gunner is ready, you issue the following initial fire order:

HE, LIGHT
68°
CHARGE 1
ONE ROUND

Suppose this round falls over the target and you read it to be 15 mils to the left of the line mortar–target. By observation of the bursts and its relation to the target, you feel that a decrease of 100 yards in range will establish a bracket on the target. This is entirely a matter of judgment. (In some cases, you may use a 50-yard range change at the shorter ranges, or you may be forced to use a 200-yard range change at the longer ranges.) Having established this distance in your mind, all you have to do is to refer to your firing table, multiply the difference in degrees between the ranges of 700 and 600 yards (4°) by two, and give your subsequent fire order:

RIGHT ONE TURN
UP EIGHT TURNS
ONE ROUND

This round should be short of the target. Once you have established a bracket, the only thing to remember for range adjustment is to take one-half of the number of turns used for the preceding round and order the correction in the proper direction (down or up). Adjustments for deflection should be made simultaneously with the correction for range.

(2) You can readily see that with this method the gunner can lay the mortar quickly, since he does not need to set elevation and deflection angles on the sight and then place the corresponding angle on the mortar. Only after the first round (which causes the base plate to settle) does he center his longitudinal bubble and cross-levels before going up eight turns. Thereafter, he only cross-levels as he makes each change. He does not take up time looking at the firing table

for angles of elevation; you tell the gunner exactly what to do from your observations.

(3) Now, assemble your squad, inform them about the bracketing method, modified, and practice on the miniature range what you have just been taught. Rotate the duties so that any member of your squad can take over your duties in the event that you become a casualty.

b. Here is another expedient for rapid adjustment of fire. Imagine a giant ladder with the rungs of the ladder 50 yards apart resting on the ground between the mortar position and the target. It would be easy to figure the exact range to the target if you knew the range to one of the rungs near the target, and if it were possible to count the number from that rung to the target. Instead of rungs on a ladder, substitute shell bursts placed in the vicinity of the target at 50-yard range intervals. Three rounds fired at 50-yard range intervals would make rungs of a huge ladder on the ground, provided they fell a few seconds apart so that all bursts could be observed at the same time. Apply these thoughts to another combat expedient for rapid adjustment of fire. This will be called the "ladder method."

(1) For a few minutes, review that part of paragraph 72 which pertains to searching fire. For this expedient searching fire technique will be used to place a ladder on the ground in the vicinity of the target. Assume that you have obtained initial direction of fire by any of the prescribed methods (par. 59), that your mortar is ready to fire, and that you have estimated the range to the target to be 650 yards. Since your estimate is just as likely to be over as short, you would give your fire order in such a manner that the second round will be fired at the estimated range. The first round should consequently be fired at 700 yards and the third round at 600 yards. Your initial fire order to engage the target would be only slightly different from the normal searching fire order:

HE, LIGHT
SEARCH 700–600
CHARGE 1
THREE ROUNDS

(The charge zone is given to the gunner, since the number of turns of the elevating crank used by the gunner must be the same as the number you have estimated by reference to the firing table.) Your gunner will select the angle of elevation for the first range announced in charge 1 zone and will follow the technique prescribed for searching fire. From your firing table, determine how many turns of the elevating crank the gunner must take between rounds. Within

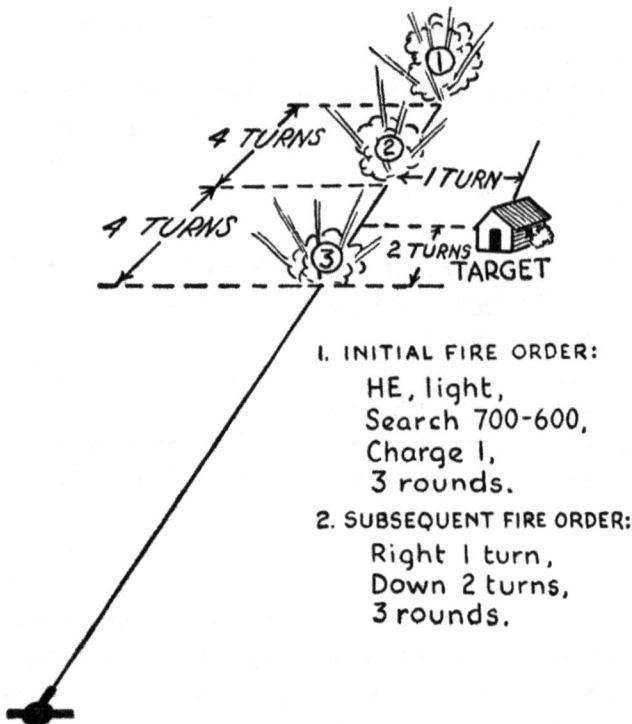

1. INITIAL FIRE ORDER:
   HE, light,
   Search 700-600,
   Charge 1,
   3 rounds.
2. SUBSEQUENT FIRE ORDER:
   Right 1 turn,
   Down 2 turns,
   3 rounds.

FIGURE 39.—Ladder method.

8 seconds, the gunner should be able to place three rounds in the air that will land at 50-yard range intervals (fig. 39). After firing the first round, he has only to relevel his longitudinal bubble, cross-level, and come up four turns; after this second round, he only comes up four turns and cross-levels. He does not re-lay on this aiming point after the initial lay.

(2) Keep in mind the number of turns that the gunner

had to take between rounds (four turns in this case) and await the bursts. Suppose that the first round is over, the second round is over, and the third round is short. Your target is bracketed half-way between the second and third bursts. Suppose that you measure the error in deflection for the last burst to be 15 mils to the left of the line mortar-target. You immediately give your subsequent fire order:

RIGHT ONE TURN
DOWN TWO TURNS
THREE ROUNDS

This should bring the three rounds squarely on the target. If the center of impact of this volley is off in range or deflection, you can order minor corrections and have three additional rounds fired.

(3) If you and your squad work as a team, you can attain maximum speed and efficiency by use of this method, which requires not more than 60 seconds from the fall of the first round for adjustment to the last round for effect. Using this method, firing missions may be completed in considerably less time if the technique has been perfected with practice. The method can be used at any range requiring the use of charge 3 or less.

c. Assuming that you are proficient in the ladder method, let us examine a modification of the method. It is called the "modified ladder." In this method we fire only one round initially and, after the round bursts, order necessary corrections before firing the last two rounds of the ladder.

(1) The initial direction of fire is obtained in the usual manner. The range to the target is estimated as accurately as possible. We refer to the firing table, select the angle of elevation for the estimated range (assume 750 yards), and issue an initial fire order:

HE, LIGHT
66°
CHARGE 1
ONE ROUND

The gunner lays the mortar for these data and orders the first round fired. After it is fired, he centers his longitudinal level bubble, and cross-levels without re-laying on his aiming point. This round falls short and 30 mils to the right of the line mortar–target. We next determine whether we want to fire the remaining two rounds of the ladder at 25-, 50-, or 100-yard intervals. In other words, we are going to select the smallest initial range change to bracket our target. Assume that our judgment tells us in this case that we should fire the next two rounds so that they will fall 50 yards apart. We judge that one of the rounds will fall over, to establish the bracket.

(2) We refer to the firing table, read the difference in elevation between the ranges of 750 and 850 yards to be 4°, and give our subsequent fire order:

    LEFT TWO TURNS
    DOWN FOUR TURNS
    ONE ROUND

The gunner makes only the change in turns as ordered, cross-levels, and commands: FIRE. As soon as this round has left the muzzle of the mortar, we IMMEDIATELY give this order.

    DOWN FOUR TURNS
    ONE ROUND

The gunner has only to go down four turns, cross-level, and fire. Suppose that the second round happens to fall correct for range and deflection and that the third round is over. By the time the third round is fired, the gunner will have placed eight turns on the mortar. To place fire for effect on the target, our fire order is:

    UP FOUR TURNS
    THREE ROUNDS

The gunner merely comes up four turns, cross-levels, and commands: FIRE. He cross-levels after the first round and commands: FIRE, then cross-levels again and once again commands: FIRE. He ignores the aiming point throughout, after laying the mortar for the first round.

d. On unfamiliar terrain, we advise the use of the modified ladder because you have a choice of the range intervals (rungs) which may be placed out in the vicinity of the target. Where you have been on the same terrain for some time and know the approximate ranges to certain landmarks, the ladder method can be used with tremendous surprise effect. The main point to keep in mind is that we always want to bracket the target, if possible, with two of the three rounds fired in order to place effective fire on the target with the next round. If none of the three rounds bracket the target but all are over or short, you will have to estimate the number of turns needed before delivering fire for effect. In such a situation, however, you see the ground pattern of a 50-yard (sometimes 25 or 100) range change, and by projecting this yardstick (rung) to the target, you can reasonably estimate the number of additional turns needed.

e. Whenever you use the ladder or modified ladder, it is advisable to have the base plate fully seated if you wish to obtain accurate results. To seat a base plate, where the tactical situation permits, fire one round in the general direction of the enemy at a range requiring the use of charge 5 or 6. This round is wasted, as far as calculated casualty effect is concerned, but it has served a useful purpose.

SECTION IV

PREARRANGED FIRES

■ 76. GENERAL.—Prearranged fires are supporting fires for which the firing data have been prepared in advance and which are delivered on call or prearranged signal. Prearranged fires are frequently distributed fires, since the targets selected are areas which the enemy is most likely to occupy. Prearranged fires are nearly always used in defensive situations, since time for securing data is usually available in the defense. In the attack, each 81-mm mortar may fire on suitable point targets or areas requiring distributed fires. In the defense, each 81-mm mortar is assigned a sector of fire and must be prepared to fire on any target which may appear within its sector. Computation of fire data consumes time which may be limited at the moment the fire is needed. Hence, in either attack or defense, the securing of fire data *in advance* is a continuous process, limited only by the time and opportunities available. In the attack the observer, whenever the situation permits, continually selects possible targets (key localities), and computes and records data for them. This is imperative, if he is to deliver immediate fire on surprise targets.

■ 77. TARGET AREAS IN DEFENSE.—One or more target areas within the sector of fire will be assigned to the squad leader through the chain of command. Examples of such areas are gaps in the final protective fires, defiladed areas of departure for small units, and critical avenues of approach or communication. This is particularly important during periods of low visibility. Target areas are assigned orally (by ground designation) or, at times, by overlays, aerial photographs, or maps. Each mortar is assigned one primary target and, depending on the time available and the tactical requirements of the situation, one or more secondary targets. (See FM 7–15, pars. 178 to 187 incl.) The primary target is the principal fire mission of the squad, and the mortar must be ready at all times to fire on this target. A base stake should be placed to mark the direction to this target. If time is available, and provided friendly troops are not situated in the target areas, fire should be adjusted on the primary target (base point), and data for ranges and deflections to secondary targets should be estimated and measured from the base point.

■ 78. METHODS OF PREPARING DATA IN DEFENSE.—Having been assigned a sector of fire, a primary target, and one or more numbered secondary target areas, the squad leader prepares firing data for his mission by range estimation and the use of instruments on the ground. In rare cases, these data are prepared from a map or aerial photograph (par. 122b). For ground data, the range to the target is obtained by adjustment, if possible by estimation, or by use of the range finder or aiming circle. Direction to the primary target may be obtained by means of a compass. For secondary targets, ranges will be estimated and deflections calculated from the base point (par. 123). Upon occasion, it will be practicable to determine data by reconnaissance and actual measurement on the ground. When reconnaissance of the foreground is possible, this may be done by pacing and compass direction. For map or aerial photograph data, ranges and azimuths are obtained after accurately plotting the mortar position and the various target areas.

■ 79. RANGE CARDS.—*a*. The prepared data should be recorded on a range card, which should include not only the data for setting the scales of the sight but also data for the manipulation of the mortar. Primary target areas are designated by the letter M (mortar squad) followed by the numerical designation of the squad, as for example M2, which indicates the primary target area of the second squad. Secondary targets are designated by numbers only and are numbered serially from right to left. Times for firing or signals for fires are included under the column "Description." The "Remarks" column should indicate the type of fire to be employed and the required manipulations of the mortar. Normally, a type of traversing fire is used in firing on the primary target. Secondary target areas are engaged with the type of fire best suited for each particular target. It may be fixed fire or any of the types of distributed fire. A copy of the range card prepared by each squad leader is given to the platoon leader (fig. 40).

b. Range cards should be prepared by squad leaders immediately upon assignment of target areas. Since the range cards form a part of the record turned over to the relieving mortar crews and are considered a part of the special orders for a position, they should be prepared as soon as possible for alternate and supplementary positions. It greatly facilitates the preparation of the cards in the field if some basic form such as that shown in figure 40 is made up beforehand and issued to squad leaders.

RANGE CARD, 81-MM MORTAR

Location 200 yds. south of Reynolds Hill

Date May 18, 19--

RANGE	AZIMUTH	NO.	DESCRIPTION	DEF.	ELEV.	CH.	REMARKS
600	1,650	M2	Ravine (white star parachute).	0	72	[1] 1	0—base stake—3 rounds; Right 5½ turns, 3 rounds; Right 5½ turns, 3 rounds (repeat to left).
700	1,830	1	Clump of woods	R180	68½	1	R30—first right stake—traverse right 5 turns, search down 4 turns, 9 rounds.
750	1,490	2	Road junction	L160	66½	1	L10—first left stake—3 rounds.
1,400	1,390	3	Road cut	L260	55½	2	R40 [2]—second left stake—1 round; down 9 turns, 1 round; down 9 turns, 1 round (repeat up).

[1] For a primary target, where there is a choice between two charge zones, the higher charge should be selected in order to obtain more effective distribution.
[2] Deflection taken from the nearest stake.

FIGURE 40.—Range card.

■ 80. Procedure After Preparing Data.—Upon receipt of all range cards, the platoon leader prepares a sketch (overlay, where a map has been used) showing the areas 'which will by covered by mortar fire. A copy is sent to the heavy weap-

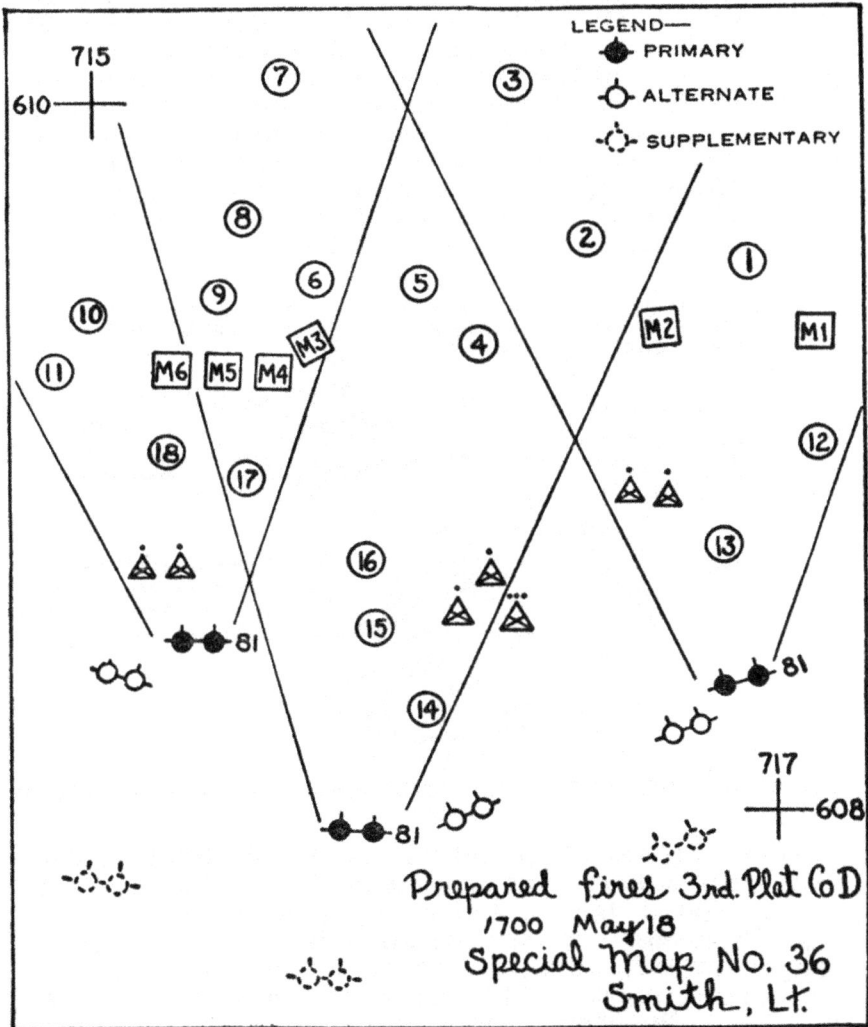

Figure 41.—Platoon leader's overlay.

ons company commander (see par. 185, FM 7–15). The platoon leader's copy should include any technical details which will assist him in delivering fire with speed whenever the call or signal is received for fire on a particular target area (fig. 41).

NOTE.—In many cases, the observation available to a mortar section will not lie to the immediate front of its firing position. This will necessitate assignment of a sector of fire extending to the left front or right front of that section. For example, in the above diagram, it might be necessary to assign the right section the central sector of fire and the center section the right sector of fire. This would involve a change in the numbers given primary target areas, since each is given the number of the squad to which it is assigned. Hence, in this example, M1 and M2 would become M3 and M4, respectively; M3 and M4 would become M1 and M2, respectively. No change would be made in M5 and M6.

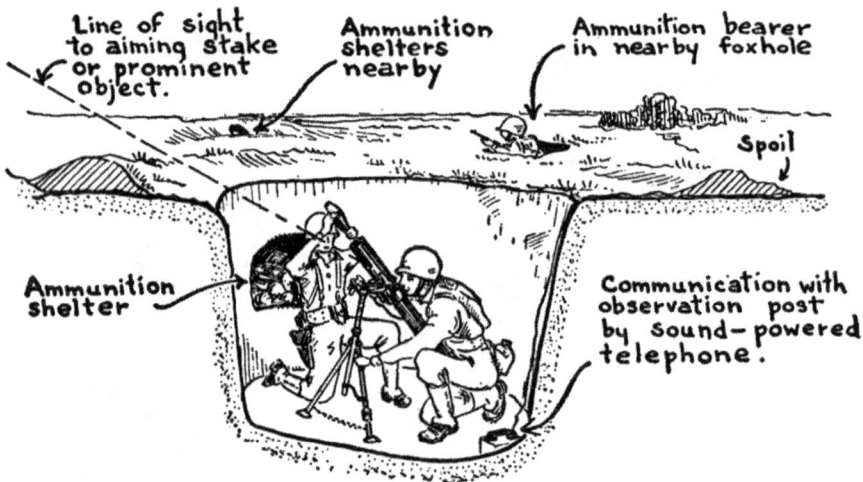

FIGURE 42.—Sketch of 81-mm mortar emplacement with crew in action.

NOTES.—1. Size of the pit will vary with different size men, but the dimensions are roughly 5 feet wide by 6 feet long at ground level, and about 4½ feet in depth.

2. The gunner and his assistant will each require space roughly 3 feet in diameter to permit accurate manipulation of the mortar. This space will also permit some shifting of the bipod to right or left when it is necessary to change direction of fire.

3. Spoil from the pit is camouflaged to match natural growth in the area, or is hidden.

4. Fox holes for members of the mortar squad and additional ammunition shelters are prepared near the emplacement.

■ 81. Mortar Emplacement.—*a. General.*—In a defensive situation, when the squad leader has been assigned the location for his mortar and has designated his mortar position, the squad members will immediately construct a mortar emplacement. Simultaneously, other members of the squad prepare slit trenches or fox holes. Camouflaging the position should be undertaken as soon as time permits.

b. Construction.—(1) The emplacement for the 81-mm mortar consists of a pit which is large enough to receive the mortar, the gunner, and the assistant gunner (fig. 42).

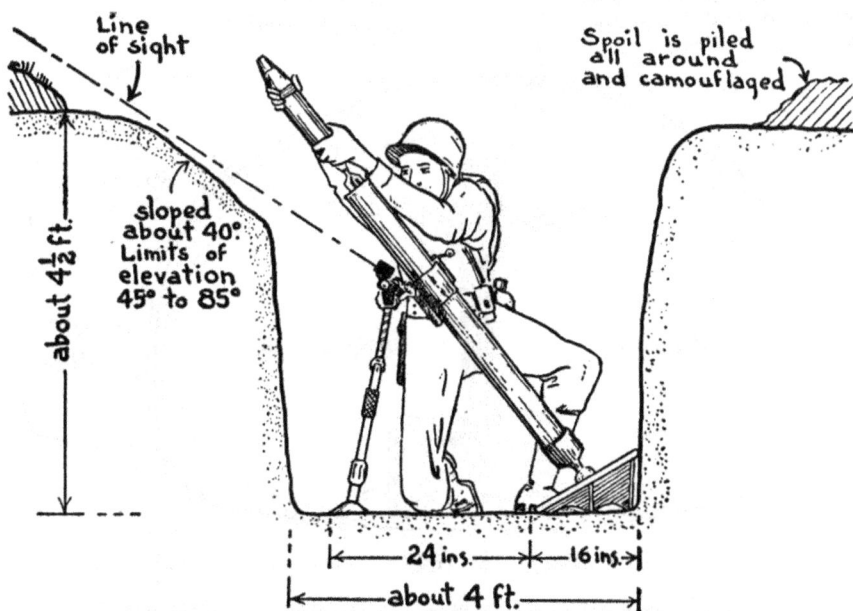

FIGURE 43.—Profile of 81-mm mortar emplacement.

Note.—Maximum width at ground level is about 5 feet. Length of emplacement is about 6 feet.

The emplacement is small enough at ground level to afford protection against machine-gun fire from hostile airplanes and the burst of air bombs and artillery shells. At the same time it allows room for the manipulation of the mortar and provides space for some ammunition. Additional ammunition is placed in nearby ammunition shelters. The front edge is sloped so as neither to interfere with the sighting of the mortar nor with the trajectory of the shell.

(2) A profile of the 81-mm mortar emplacement, with No. 2 loading the mortar, is shown in figure 43.

(3) A top view of the mortar pit is shown in figure 44.

■ 82. EXERCISE IN PREPARATION OF RANGE CARDS.—*a*. The purpose of this exercise is to teach the observer the correct method of preparing range cards.

b. The instructor assembles the groups on suitable terrain where he explains the method of preparing range cards

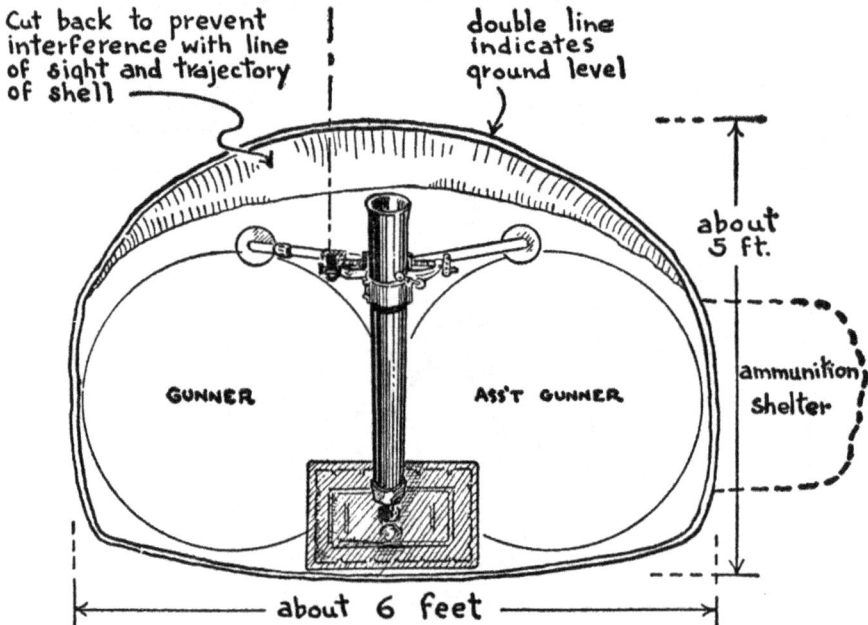

FIGURE 44.—81-mm mortar emplacement, top view.

described in paragraph 79. A set-up similar to the one indicated in figure 46 may be used as a guide for the instructor. Group instructors then supervise the practical work of their groups, pointing out any mistakes and requiring their immediate correction. The men are then required to make a range card without the help of the instructor. The instructor collects these cards, points out any mistakes made, and requires the men to correct them. This exercise is repeated until the men are considered proficient.

CHAPTER 5

MARKSMANSHIP

                                                      Paragraphs
SECTION I. Preparatory instruction_____ 83–86
        II. Examination _____ 87–90
       III. Qualification course, gunner's test_____ 91–98
        IV. Qualification course, expert's test_____ 99–104
         V. Targets, ranges, and range precautions_____ 105–107

SECTION I

PREPARATORY INSTRUCTION

■ 83. OBJECT AND SCOPE.—The purpose of preparatory instruction is to teach the individual soldier to perform accurately the duties of gunner and squad leader in the delivery of fire. The instruction consists of a series of exercises which require the soldier to perform in a prescribed manner each of the duties of gunner and squad leader.

■ 84. METHOD OF INSTRUCTION.—a. The applicatory method of instruction is used throughout. The conditions and requirements of each subject of the qualification course are first explained and demonstrated to the men undergoing instruction. Each man is then given practical work in the subject under supervision of the group instructors. Accuracy is stressed at first; speed is attained through repetition.

b. The officer in charge of the instruction should detail such assistants as he requires. The squad leaders usually act as group instructors.

c. Upon completion of the explanation and demonstration of each of the instruction exercises, the groups return to their squad equipment where the assigned squad instructors conduct the practical work.

■ 85. PRIOR TRAINING.—Before receiving instruction in mortar marksmanship, the soldier should be proficient in mechanical training (ch. 1), the training of the gunner (ch. 2), the appropriate portions of training for placing the mortar in action (ch. 3), and the training of the observer (ch. 4).

■ 86. PREPARATORY EXERCISES.—*a*. The preparatory exercises of the mortar marksmanship course consist of training in the various subjects of the qualification course as prescribed in sections III and IV. The soldier will first perform the exercises without regard to time. Once the habit of exactness is attained, he will practice for speed until he is able to perform each test with the required accuracy in the allotted time.

b. If desired, examination in the subjects of the gunner's test may be started immediately after preparatory instruction in those subjects is completed, following which the preparatory exercises of the expert's test may be given. Those initially failing the gunner's test will continue their training until they qualify on a subsequent test. Upon completion of the latter exercises, examination in the ex-

PROGRESS CHART, 81-MM MORTAR PREPARATORY EXERCISES

Names	Mounting mortar	Laying mortar with initial fire data	Relaying mortar for changes in fire data	Laying mortar on aiming stake	Establishing direction by azimuth	Manipulation of mortar for traversing and searching fire	Preparation of range cards	Computation of firing data	Individual field firing

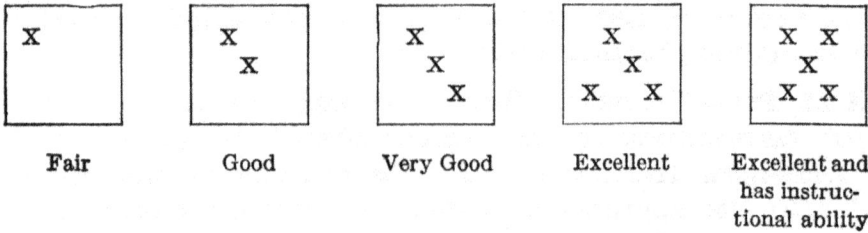

X	X X	X X X	X X X X	X X X X X
Fair	Good	Very Good	Excellent	Excellent and has instructional ability

FIGURE 45.—Progress chart, 81-mm mortar marksmanship.

pert's test may be given. Instruction for the expert's test will be continued for those failing to qualify until they have attained proficiency in the subject matter of this test.

c. The progress of each soldier in the preparatory instruction is noted by the instructor on the progress chart as shown in figure 45.

SECTION II

EXAMINATION

■ 87. GRADES AND BASIS OF QUALIFICATION.—The proficiency of individual soldiers with the mortar is indicated by classifying them as expert gunner, first-class gunner, second-class gunner, and unqualified. The unqualified class includes those men of an organization who have been examined and who have failed to qualify as second-class gunner or better, and all others who for any reason have not been examined. Examinations will be held as required to determine the proficiency and qualification of personnel undergoing instruction.

■ 88. EXAMINING BOARDS; APPOINTMENT AND CONSTITUTION.— The examination is conducted by a board of three or more officers not more than one of whom is a member of the same company as the man being tested. Boards are appointed by the commanders having authority to issue qualification orders.

■ 89. SUBJECTS OF EXAMINATION.

   a. *Gunner's test.*   *Value*

(1) Mounting mortar_____ 40

(2) Laying mortar with initial fire data_____ 30

(3) Re-laying the mortar for changes in fire data____ 30

(4) Laying the mortar on aiming stakes_____ 30

(5) Establishing direction by azimuth_____ 30

(6) Manipulation of mortar for traversing and searching fire_____ 40

   b. *Expert's test.*

(1) Preparation of range cards_____ 100

(2) Computation of firing data_____ 100

(3) Individual field firing_____ 100

■ **90. General Rules Governing Examining Boards.**—The following rules govern examining boards:

a. The conditions of the examination will be made as nearly uniform as possible for all candidates. The board will be responsible that no data obtained by a candidate during a particular test are transmitted to any other candidate who is to take that test under identical conditions; also, that no candidate receives the benefit of any sight setting or laying of the weapons, as left by a previously tested candidate.

b. Only ranges that are listed in the firing table available to the candidate will be ordered.

c. Should any candidate fail in any trial through the fault of an examiner or any assistant, or because of the failure or malfunction of the sight or other instrument used, that trial will be disregarded and the candidate will immediately be given another trial of the same nature.

d. The candidate may select the authorized assistants.

e. Each candidate will be given the tests in the order in which they are described herein.

f. In any test requiring the candidate to lay for elevation or to cross-level the mortar, the board will consider the position of the bubble in either the longitudinal or cross-level vial to be correct if the bubble is more than half inside the two short center lines on the glass tube.

g. When because of a loose condition the mortar has failed to maintain the lay after the candidate has called "Ready" or "Fire," a member of the board will twist the mortar until the vertical line of the collimator is again alined on the stake. If the cross-level bubble is centered at this point, the candidate will be given full credit for the trial of the test, provided the other conditions are correctly fulfilled.

h. The board will see to it that no unauthorized assistance is given the gunner during the examination. The gunner has been trained for combat performance of his duties and should be tested with this thought in mind.

SECTION III

QUALIFICATION COURSE, GUNNER'S TEST

■ **91. Scope.**—This section prescribes the requirements of the gunner's test. The gunner's test is divided into six subjects as listed in paragraph 89.

■ 92. MOUNTING THE MORTAR.—*a. Equipment.*—(1) *For candidate.*—Mortar, complete, and two aiming stakes.

(2) *For board.*—Stop watch and score card.

b. Conditions.—(1) Two stakes will be driven about 25 yards apart, one of which will be designated as the base plate stake and one as the aiming stake.

(2) The base plate, bipod, and mortar will be laid out on the ground about 15 yards from the base plate stake.

(3) Each candidate will have two trials in this subject.

(4) Each candidate will be allowed two assistants to perform the duties of Nos. 2 and 3, as described in paragraph 5.

c. Procedure.—(1) The sight, in a latched case, is placed 2 feet to the left of the base plate stake by a member of the board. When the candidate is ready to receive orders for mounting the mortar at the base plate stake, a member of the board will give the command for mounting the mortar, for example, TO YOUR FRONT, ACTION.

(2) At this command, the mortar will be mounted and laid on the line established by the aiming stakes as prescribed in paragraph 5, the candidate performing the duties of the gunner (No. 1).

(3) As soon as the mortar is mounted and laid as prescribed in paragraph 5, the candidate will call "Ready."

(4) Time will be taken from the announcement of the command by the board to the announcement of "Ready" by the candidate.

d. Scoring.—(1) *No credit will be given if the—*

(*a*) Time exceeds 80 seconds.

(*b*) Sight is not set correctly for deflection (zero) and elevation (62°).

(*c*) Mortar is not correctly laid for elevation.

(*d*) Mortar is not cross-leveled.

(*e*) Vertical line of the collimator is more than 3 mils off the left edge of the aiming stake.

(*f*) Traversing screw is more than two turns to the left or right of the center position.

(2) If the mortar is found to be correctly laid within the limits prescribed, credit will be given as follows:

Time in seconds exactly or less than_____	60–65–70–75–80
Credits_____	20–18–16–14–12
Total score possible (two trials) _____	40

■ 93. LAYING MORTAR WITH INITIAL FIRE DATA.—*a. Equipment.*—(1) *For candidate.*—Mortar, complete, one aiming stake, and firing table (for shell, HE, M43A1).

(2) *For board.*—Stop watch and score card.

b. Conditions.—(1) The mortar will be mounted as described in paragraph 5 with an aiming stake set at a convenient distance. The mortar will be laid on the stake with the sight set at zero deflection and the traversing screw approximately centered. The elevation scale will be set at 62°, and the longitudinal and cross-level bubbles will be centered.

(2) The amount of deflection given must not exceed 60 mils; that is, it must not require a movement of the bipod. The range must not be more than 2,500 or less than 700 yards.

(3) Each candidate will have two trials in this subject.

(4) For each trial the candidate will take the gunner's position on the left of the mortar and check to see that it is properly set up and laid as described in (1) above. The candidate may start this test with his left hand on the deflection knob of the sight if he so desires.

c. Procedure.—(1) When the candidate is ready to receive the order, an initial fire order will be announced by a member of the board, for example:

HE, LIGHT

LEFT 40

STAKE

1,600

ONE ROUND

The candidate will repeat each element of the order, set the sight with the data as ordered, announce the correct charge, and re-lay on the left edge of the aiming stake, cross-leveling simultaneously. As soon as the mortar is laid, he will command: FIRE.

(2) Time will be taken from the announcement of the first element of the order by the board to the command FIRE by the candidate.

d. Scoring.—(1) No credit will be given if the—

(*a*) Time exceeds 35 seconds.

(*b*) Charge announced is incorrect.

(*c*) Sight is set incorrectly for elevation or deflection.

(*d*) Mortar is not correctly laid for elevation.

(*e*) Mortar is not cross-leveled.

(*f*) Vertical line of the collimator is more than 3 mils off the left edge of the aiming stake.

(2) If the mortar is found to be correctly laid within the limits prescribed above, credit will be given as follows:

Time in seconds exactly or less than	20–22–25–28–32–35
Credits	15–13–11–9–7–5
Total score possible (two trials)	30

■ **94. Re-laying Mortar for Changes in Fire Data.**—*a. Equipment.*—(1) *For candidate.*—Mortar, complete, one aiming stake, and firing table.

(2) *For board.*—Stop watch and score card.

b. Conditions.—(1) A mortar is mounted as described in paragraph 5, with an aiming stake set at a convenient distance. The mortar will be laid on the stake with a deflection set off on the sight and the traversing screw approximately centered. The elevation scale will be set at 62°, and the longitudinal and cross-level bubbles will be centered. The conditions set forth above will be checked by the candidate before his first trial is begun. The second trial may begin with the mortar as laid by the candidate at the end of the preceding trial.

(2) The amount of deflection given must not exceed 60 mils; that is, it must not require a movement of the bipod. The range must not be more than 2,500 yards or less than 700 yards.

(3) Each candidate will have two trials in this subject.

(4) The candidate will take the gunner's position on the

left of the mortar and note the elevation and deflection recorded on the sight. He may start this test with his left hand on the deflection knob of the sight, if he so desires.

c. Procedure.—(1) When the candidate is ready to receive a fire order, a new range and a deflection change will be announced, for example:

RIGHT 50

1,800

ONE ROUND

(2) The candidate will repeat each element of the order, set the sight with the data as ordered, announce the charge, and re-lay on the left edge of the aiming stake, cross-leveling simultaneously. When the mortar is laid, he will command: FIRE.

(3) Time will be taken from the announcement of the first element of the order by the board to the command FIRE by the candidate.

d. Scoring.—(1) No credit will be given if the—

(*a*) Time exceeds 35 seconds.

(*b*) Charge announced is incorrect.

(*c*) Sight is set incorrectly for elevation or deflection.

(*d*) Mortar is not correctly laid for elevation.

(*e*) Mortar is not cross-leveled.

(*f*) Vertical line of the collimator is more than 3 mils off the left edge of the aiming stake.

(2) If the mortar is found to be correctly laid within the limits prescribed above, credit will be given as follows:

Time in seconds exactly or less than_____	20–22–25–28–32–35
Credits_____	15–13–11–9–7–5
Total score possible (two trials) _____	30

■ 95. LAYING MORTAR ON AIMING STAKES.—*a. Equipment.*—(1) *For candidate.*—Mortar, complete, three aiming stakes, and firing table.

(2) *For board.*—Stop watch and score card.

b. Conditions.—(1) Three aiming stakes will be set out in such a manner that the angular distance between each stake, measured at the mortar position, is 150 mils. The stakes will be designated as base stake, left stake, and right stake.

(2) The mortar will be mounted with the elevation scale set at 62°, and the longitudinal and cross-level bubbles will be centered. The deflection scale will be set at zero, and the traversing screw will be approximately centered. The mortar will be initially laid on the base stake, as described above, and will be checked by the candidate before each trial is begun.

(3) The candidate will be allowed to choose one assistant whose duty during the test will be to move the legs of the bipod.

(4) Each candidate will have two trials in this subject.

c. *Procedure.*—(1) With the candidate in the gunner's position on the left of the mortar and his left hand on the deflection knob of the sight, a member of the board will give the fire order for laying the mortar on either of the other two stakes, for example:

HE, LIGHT

LEFT 25

RIGHT STAKE

1,000

ONE ROUND

(2) The candidate will repeat each element of the fire order, set the sight with the data as ordered, announce the correct charge, direct the movement of the bipod, and re-lay on the left edge of the designated stake with the announced deflection and elevation. As soon as the mortar is laid, the candidate will command: FIRE.

(3) Time will be taken from the announcement of the first element of the fire order by the board to the command FIRE by the candidate.

(4) For the second trial, the mortar will be re-laid on the base stake as in *b*(2) above. A different range, deflection, and aiming stake will be ordered.

d. *Scoring.*—(1) No credit will be given if the—

(a) Time exceeds 55 seconds.

(b) Charge announced is incorrect.

(c) Sight is set incorrectly for elevation or deflection.

(d) Mortar is not correctly laid for elevation.

(e) Mortar is not cross-leveled.

(*f*) Vertical line of the collimator is more than 3 mils off the left edge of the proper aiming stake.

(*g*) Traversing screw is more than 2 turns off the center position.

(2) If the mortar is found to be correctly laid within the limits prescribed, credit will be given as follows:

Time in seconds exactly or less than	35–38–42–46–50–55
Credits	15–13–11–9–7–5
Total score possible (two trials)	30

■ 96. ESTABLISHING DIRECTION BY AZIMUTH.—*a. Equipment.*— (1) *For candidate.*—Lensatic compass, two aiming stakes, and entrenching ax.

(2) *For board.*—Stop watch and score card.

b. Conditions.—(1) A stake is driven to mark the position of the base plate.

(2) Each candidate will have two trials in this subject.

(3) Each candidate will be allowed one assistant for the sole purpose of placing and driving the stake.

c. Procedure.—(1) When the candidate is ready to receive orders, a member of the board will announce an azimuth as, for example, "Magnetic azimuth 2,200."

(2) The candidate will direct his assistant to move out about 25 yards in the approximate direction of the azimuth ordered. He will then place his compass on the stake which marks the position of the base plate, lay off the required azimuth, and direct the assistant to drive an aiming stake along the line of sight of the instrument. As soon as the candidate is satisfied with the line thus established, he will call "Ready."

(3) Time will be taken from the announcement of the magnetic azimuth by the member of the board to the announcement of "Ready" by the candidate.

(4) The board will then check the azimuth from the base plate stake to the aiming stake. The candidate's compass will be used.

d. Scoring.—(1) No credit will be given if the line established by the two stakes is more than 40 mils off the correct azimuth.

(2) If the line is established within the allowable errors described in (1) above, credit will be given as follows:

Time in seconds exactly or less than	55–60–65–70–75
Credits:	
Error of 0–20 mils	15–13–11–9–7
Error of 21–40 mils	11–9–7–3–1
Total score possible (two trials)	30

■ 97. MANIPULATION OF MORTAR FOR TRAVERSING AND SEARCHING FIRE.—a. *Equipment.*—(1) *For candidate.*—Mortar, complete, and firing table.

(2) *For board.*—Stop watch and score card.

b. *Conditions.*—(1) The mortar will be mounted as prescribed in paragraph 5 with an aiming stake set at a convenient distance. The mortar will be laid on the stake with the deflection scale set at zero and the traversing screw approximately centered. The elevation scale will be set at 62°, and the longitudinal and cross-level bubbles will be centered.

(2) Ranges announced must not be less than 700 yards nor more than 1,200 yards. (Requires gunner to position traversing screw right or left center so that he can traverse twice the number of turns announced in the fire order. Ranges given should be even hundreds of yards.)

(3) The candidate will be allowed to choose one assistant whose duty during the test will be to move the legs of the bipod.

(4) Each candidate will be given two trials.

c. *Procedure.*—(1) When the candidate is ready, a fire order will be announced by a member of the board, for example:

SEARCH 1,000–1,100

TRAVERSE RIGHT THREE TURNS

NINE ROUNDS (TARGET WIDTHS ASSUMED TO BE 100 YARDS)

(2) Time will be taken from the announcement of the first element of the order by the board to the command FIRE for the ninth round by the candidate.

(3) The candidate will determine the initial elevation and announce the charge and number of turns for the elevating

crank (fractions of turns should be disregarded). He will direct his assistant in the movement of the bipod legs for the initial laying of the mortar with the new data announced.

d. Scoring.—(1) No credit will be given if the—

(*a*) Time exceeds 2½ minutes.

(*b*) Elevation scale is not set initially at the proper elevation and the longitudinal level bubble is not centered.

(*c*) Candidate fails to give the correct charge.

(*d*) The candidate fails to order FIRE for each round.

(*e*) The difference in elevation measured on the sight at the end of the ninth round varies by more than 1½° from the elevation prescribed in the firing table opposite the limit set by the fire order. (*Example:* The limiting range for the sample fire order being 1,100 yards, the elevation should be 66° (whole number) and by turning the elevation knob of the sight until the longitudinal bubble is centered, the tolerance of 1½° from 66° can be measured.)

(*f*) The number of mils necessary to bring the vertical line of the collimator back on the left edge of the aiming stake at the end of the ninth round, with the mortar cross-leveled, is greater than 20 mils added to or subtracted from the product of the multiplication of the number of turns of the traversing handwheel by the constant 30. (*Example:* In the sample fire order, the number of turns announced was three. This three is multiplied by 30 to obtain the basis from which to determine the limits of tolerance of 20 mils. The limits would be 70–110.)

(2) If the task is found to be correct within the limits prescribed, credit will be given as follows:

Error in mils exactly or less than	10–15–20
Credits:	
Time less than 1½ minutes	20–16–12
Time between 1½ and 2 minutes	16–12–10
Time between 2 and 2½ minutes	12–8–6
Total score possible (two trials)	40

■ 98. Maximum Credits for Gunner's Test.

Mounting the mortar	40
Laying the mortar with initial fire data	30
Re-laying mortar for changes in fire data	30
Laying mortar on aiming stakes	30
Establishing direction by azimuth	30
Manipulation of mortar for traversing and searching fire	40
Total possible credit for gunner's test	200

Section IV

QUALIFICATION COURSE, EXPERT'S TEST

■ 99. Scope.—This test is divided into three subjects as follows:

  a. Subject No. 1.—Preparation of range cards.

  b. Subject No. 2.—Computation of firing data.

  c. Subject No. 3.—Individual field firing.

■ 100. Selection of Terrain.—The examining board selects the terrain upon which the tests in subjects Nos. 1 and 2 are to be conducted so that the various ranges used are not familiar to the candidates.

■ 101. Preparation of Range Cards.—*a. Equipment.*—(1) *For candidate.*—Firing table, binocular, pencil, and blank range card (fig. 40).

  (2) *For board.*—Lensatic compass, range card ruled as illustrated in figure 40, stop watch, firing table.

  b. Conditions.—(1) The candidate will be tested in the preparation of a range card for a defensive position, as prescribed in section IV, chapter 4.

  (2) The position and sector will be selected by the examining board. The lay-out for the test and some of the requirements thereof are as indicated graphically in figure 46.

  (3) The board will prepare a correct solution, using the same compass the candidate will use. Ranges and magnetic azimuths will be determined to a particular point in each target area, which point will be announced to the candidate.

  (4) The same stake positions and target areas will be used for all candidates examined on any one day. If practicable,

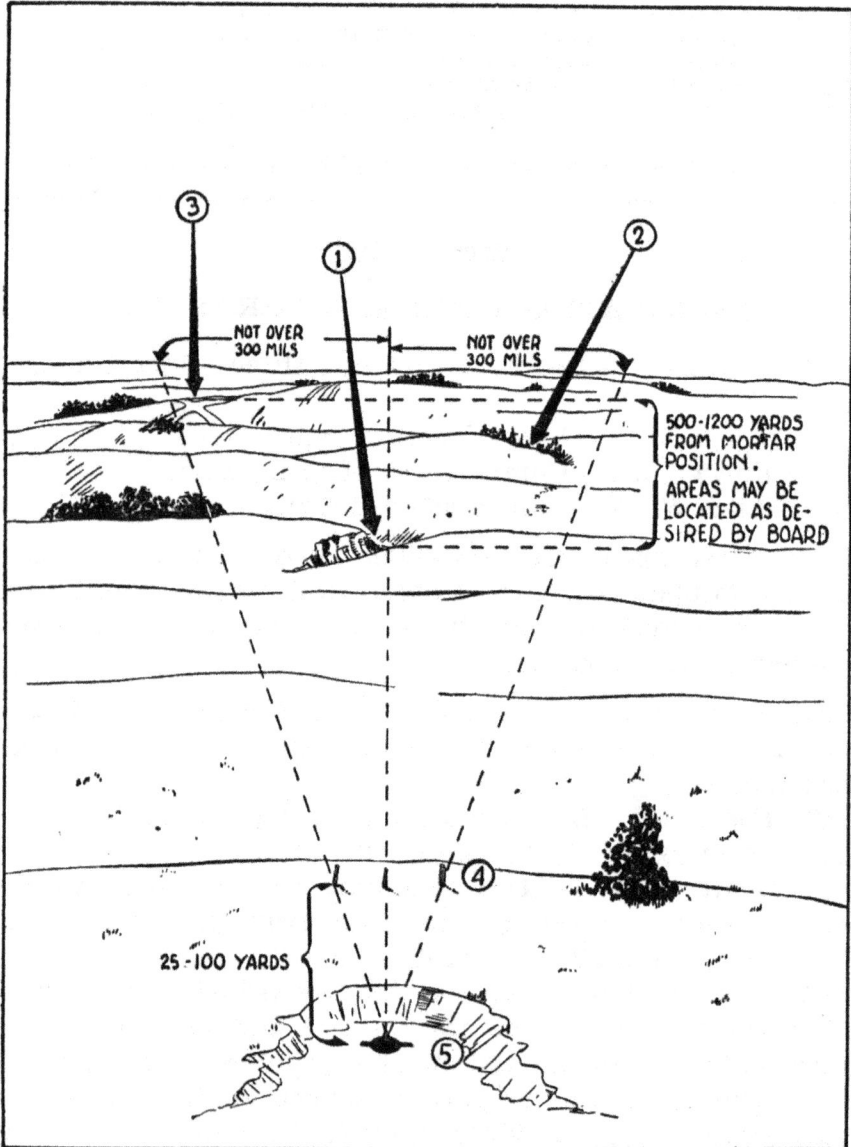

FIGURE 46.—Lay-out for range card examination.

all candidates serving at the same post or in the same regiment will be examined in this subject on the same day.

Notes.—1. Traversing fire target, 75 to 100 yards wide, the primary target.

2. Traversing and searching fire target, not over 100 by 100 yards, a secondary target.

3. Fixed fire target, less than 50 by 50 yards, a secondary target.

4. Observation post for candidate. Targets must be visible from this point. Compass support stakes driven on approximate line mortar–target.

5. Mortar position indicated by a mortar properly mounted.

c. *Procedure.*—(1) A member of the board will furnish the candidate with a compass, point out the location of the target areas and designate the primary target area, indicating the point in each target area to which ranges and azimuths will be taken. He will inform the candidate that a stake has been driven on the line mortar–target for the three target areas and that azimuth readings will be taken from these stakes. He will also point out the mortar position in rear of the points from which azimuths will be read. When the candidate states that he identifies all targets and understands the procedure involved, the board will call "Time."

(2) The candidate will read the azimuths, estimate the ranges to all targets, and enter these in their appropriate places on the card. He will fill out the column "Description" for each target. He will then compute and enter the deflection (deflection for the primary target is always zero). From the firing table the candidate will then record the correct elevation and charge for each range that he has estimated. The "Remarks" column will be completed in the manner outlined in paragraph 79, to include all the firing data necessary to engage the particular targets designated.

(3) The board will require the candidate to submit his range card within 20 minutes.

d. *Scoring.*—(1) No credit will be given if the range card is not submitted within 20 minutes.

(2) If the candidate's range card is submitted within the prescribed limit, credit will be given as follows:

(a) Percentage of error in range for each target—
Exactly or less than_____ 15–20–30
    Credit _____ 5–4–2
Total score possible (three targets) _____ 15
(b) Error in azimuth for each target—
Exactly or less than (mils) _____ 10–20–30
    Credit_____ 5–4–2
Total score possible (three targets) _____ 15
(c) For recording, computation, and legibility of each of the following on the range card:

	Each	Score possible
1. Numbering of primary target_____	4	4
2. Numbering of secondary targets_____	2	4
3. Suitable "description" of targets_____	2	6
4. Correct deflection_____	3	9
5. Correct elevation (based on the ranges actually estimated by the candidate)_	3	9
6. Correct charge_____	2	6
Total score possible (three targets)_____		38

(d) For computation of firing data in "Remarks" column, as follows:

	Each	Score possible
1. Deflection (no deduction will be made if a deflection is listed for which a prior deduction was made in (c)4 above)__	3	9
2. Aiming point_____	2	6
3. Turns of the traversing handwheel or elevating crank to distribute fire properly (within one turn of the solution determined by board)_____	4	8
4. Number of rounds_____	2	6
5. Correct sequence_____	1	3
Total score possible (three targets)_ __		32

(e) Total possible for range card_____ __ 100

■ 102. COMPUTATION OF FIRING DATA.—*a. Equipment.*—(1) *For candidate.*—Lensatic compass, binocular, pencil and paper, and deflection-conversion table.

(2) *For board.*—Stop watch and score card.

b. Conditions.—(1) The board will select an observation post from which the target and the mortar position are both visible. The observation post must be between 100 and 200 yards from the mortar position and at least 100 yards to one flank of the line mortar–target. The target and mortar positions will be designated to the candidate from the observation post, and he will not be allowed to move from this post.

(2) The correct data will be determined beforehand by the board, using each of the compasses to be used by the candidates. The solution and compass number for each compass will be recorded by the board. These data will be used to check the candidate's solution.

c. Procedure.—(1) The candidate will determine and record the following:

(*a*) Range (mortar to target).

(*b*) Magnetic azimuth of line mortar–target.

(2) Time will be taken from the announcement of "Time" by a member of the board. When three minutes have elapsed, "Time" will be announced again, and the candidate will be required to cease work and turn in his solution.

d. Scoring.—(1) No credit will be given for any data not submitted within 3 minutes.

(2) Data submitted within the prescribed limit will be graded as follows:

(*a*) Magnetic azimuth, line mortar–target.

Error in mils exactly or less than_____ 20–25–30–35
    Credits_____50–45–40–35

(*b*) Range, mortar to target.

Percentage of error in range exactly or less
    than_____ 15–20–25–30
    Credits_____50–45–40–35

■ 103. INDIVIDUAL FIELD FIRING.—*a. Personnel and equipment.*—(1) *For candidate.*—Mortar crew; mortar, complete for firing; binocular; and individual ammunition allowance as prescribed in AR 775–10.

(2) *For board.*—Record form for individual field firing (see sample form in *d* below), binocular, and score card.

b. Conditions.—Individual field firing will be conducted by the bracketing method on a point target as described in paragraph 69 and under the following conditions for each problem:

(1) The candidate will compute the initial firing data and give the gunner the necessary orders to enable him to lay the mortar and open fire upon the target.

(2) After firing has commenced, the candidate will order the proper corrections until fire is adjusted upon the target or his ammunition allowance is expended. If adjustment is completed, fire for effect will be ordered by the candidate, but the fire will not be delivered.

(3) The actual range to the target must be not less than 500 yards nor greater than 1,500 yards.

(4) The authorized individual ammunition allowances must not be exceeded.

(5) The target will be clearly designated to the candidate but must not be visible from the mortar position.

(6) The observation post must be not more than 50 yards from the mortar position.

(7) If practicable, all members of the platoon except those who are yet to take this test will be permitted to witness the firing.

(8) No person will correct or coach the candidate at any time during firing, and no one except an official conducting the examination will communicate or in any way interfere with any person connected with the firing.

c. Procedure.—When the target has been clearly designated to the candidate by a member of the board, the candidate will give his initial fire order to the mortar crew. Thereafter he will give the necessary fire orders to correct the errors sensed. When fire has been adjusted to the point where the last 25-yard range change would be included in the candidate's next fire order, he will combine adjustment of fire with fire for effect. His fire order will include the element of THREE ROUNDS. Since fire for effect will not be delivered, the board will terminate the problem when he has progressed this far.

d. Scoring.—If the problem is fired without error, the candidate will receive a credit of 100 points. If errors are made, his score will be the difference between 100 points and the number of points deducted by reason of the following errors:

Error	Deduction points
Initial fire order:	
Type of ammunition incorrect or failure to indicate_____	1
Deflection incorrect or failure to indicate_____	3
Aiming point, failure to indicate_____	1
Range, failure to indicate_____	3
Range, error in range for each 100 yards greater than 200 yards_____	5
Number of rounds incorrect or failure to indicate_____	2
Subsequent fire orders:	
Each correction ordered more than ½ minute following a burst_____	3
Each deflection correction ordered which is in error more than 10 mils_____	3
Each failure to order correct range_____	10
Each failure to order number of rounds_____	2
Each repetition of unnecessary elements_____	1

EXPERT'S TEST, FIELD FIRING PROBLEM, 81-MM MORTAR

Problem No. _____ Date _____ Candidate_____
Organization _____

Initial fire order

Elements	Candidate's order	Deductions
Type of shell_____	_____	_____
Deflection_____	_____	_____
Aiming point_____	_____	_____
Range_____	_____	_____
No. of rounds_____	_____	_____
	Deductions, initial fire order_____	

Round No.	Candidate's fire order			Board's fire order			Deductions
	Deflection	Range	Number of rounds	Deflection	Range	Number of rounds	
1	(See above.)						
2							
3							
4							
5							
6							

Deductions, subsequent orders_____

Deductions, initial fire order_____

Initial credit_____ 100

Total deductions_____

Credit_____

----------------------------,
President.

----------------------------,
Recorder.

■ 104. MAXIMUM CREDITS FOR EXPERT'S TEST.

 a. Subject No. 1.—Preparation of range cards_____ 100

 b. Subject No. 2.—Computation of firing data_____ 100

 c. Subject No. 3.—Individual field firing_____ 100

 Total score possible for expert's test_____ 300

SECTION V

TARGETS, RANGES, AND RANGE PRECAUTIONS

■ 105. TARGETS.—Targets for 81-mm mortar firing are natural features of the terrain. Artificial targets, such as panels and silhouettes, should be used only when the terrain available for firing is not varied enough to furnish reference points or targets.

■ 106. RANGES AND RANGE PRECAUTIONS.—Range areas and safety precautions for 81-mm mortar firing must conform to the instructions set forth in AR 750–10.

■ 107. ADDITIONAL SAFETY PRECAUTIONS.—Individual safety precautions to be observed by the mortar crew are described in paragraph 53.

CHAPTER 6

ADVANCED TRAINING

Paragraphs
SECTION I. Section conduct of fire_____ 108–111
II. Employment of smoke_____ 112–119
III. Fire control instruments_____ 120–121
IV. Use of fire control instruments_____ 122–123

SECTION I

SECTION CONDUCT OF FIRE

■ 108. GENERAL.—*a.* The conduct of fire by section includes all situations in which the fire of one or both mortars is initiated and controlled by the section leader. The normal method used by the section leader in engaging one or more targets is to assign each target as a separate mission to a squad, so that the squad leaders may conduct their own fire. Exceptionally, lack of observation in the vicinity of the mortar positions may make it impossible to use this method and it may be necessary for the section leader to control the fire of both mortars. Usually the requirements of cover and the necessity for providing mortar support at different places in the battalion zone make platoon concentrations impracticable. Mortars are not usually emplaced in battery to perform artillery missions.

b. The conduct of fire by the section includes the same elements as described for the squad; that is, preparation of initial data, fire orders, sensing, fire for adjustment, and fire for effect. These elements, as described in this section, contain only the points wherein they differ from the squad. The preparation of initial data and sensing are the same as for the squad.

■ 109. FIRE ORDERS.—*a.* Fire orders differ chiefly in the necessity for conducting the fire of two mortars instead of one.

b. Origin and transmission.—Fire orders originate with the section leader who transmits them to the squad leaders. The squad leaders repeat the orders to the mortar squads by voice, converting elements, when necessary, into proper orders for their particular squad.

c. *Following orders.*—A fire order is followed by both mortars, unless it includes the element: NO. (SO AND SO). This may be given as the first element of a fire order for the purpose of requiring the mortar not specified to remain on its particular mission, and the one specified to follow subsequent orders. When firing both mortars, a change for an individual mortar is preceded by the order: NO. 1 (OR NO. 2) (SO AND SO). Subsequent elements of the fire order which apply to both mortars are preceded by the command SECTION. To fire the mortars successively, the command is: SECTION RIGHT (LEFT). From the mortar position, the mortar which is mounted on the flank corresponding to the direction designated in the order is the first to fire. The base mortar, usually, fires first.

Examples:

> NO. 1, RIGHT 20; NO. 2, RIGHT 35 (both mortars set different deflections).
> SECTION, 850 (both mortars use same range).
> ONE ROUND (each mortar fires when ready).
> SECTION, RIGHT 25 (both mortars use same deflection).
> NO. 1, 850; NO. 2, 800 (each mortar uses different range).
> SECTION RIGHT, ONE ROUND (mortars fire successively from the right at 5-second intervals).

■ 110. FIRE FOR ADJUSTMENT.—Fire for adjustment by section is begun with a single mortar, the base mortar. When a bracket has been established by the base mortar, the range thus found is corrected by any difference in depth between the two mortars and applied to the second mortar.

a. Both mortars are usually laid for initial direction by means of a base azimuth; that is, they are laid parallel. It is rarely necessary to fire both mortars on a point target. For an area which is large enough to require the fire of both mortars, No. 2 mortar may be adjusted directly on that portion of the target on which it is desired to begin fire for effect.

b. Any deflection correction found by firing No. 1 mortar should be applied to No. 2 in firing its initial round, in addition to a correction for the interval between mortars. The initial round fired from the No. 2 mortar, using the data obtained from the base mortar, as described above, should be fairly accurate, and only a small adjustment in range and deflection should be necessary. The section leader may, therefore, establish a 50-yard bracket at once, instead of the 100- or 200-yard bracket prescribed for a single mortar. If it is desired to assign a section to fire on an area too large for a single mortar (more than 100 by 100 yards), the section leader may divide the area and assign one mortar to cover each half. Each mortar is adjusted on a corresponding point in its own half of the area before beginning fire for effect. For example, No. 1 may be adjusted on the near left corner and No. 2 on the center of the near edge. Any deflection correction for the interval between mortars may be quickly determined by the section leader by referring to the deflection-conversion table.

■ 111. FIRE FOR EFFECT.—a. The mortars having been properly adjusted to begin for effect, the procedure for each mortar is the same as described for the squad. Each mortar fires on the target, or its portion of the target, as if it were firing on an individual target.

b. Example: Distributed fire (see fig. 47).—(1) Both mortars are mounted on an azimuth of 3,200 mils to place the fire of No. 1 mortar on the right corner. No. 2 mortar is 50 yards to the left and 25 yards in the rear of No. 1 mortar.

(2) The initial fire order of the section leader is:

SECTION

HE, LIGHT

ZERO

STAKE

1,425

NO. 1

ONE ROUND

Mortars Nos. 1 and 2 lay for elevation and direction but only No. 1 mortar fires the initial round. (The mortar which is to fire is always designated before the number of rounds is given.) The section leader senses the round to be an "over" and left of the line mortar–target. His subsequent fire order might be:

SECTION

RIGHT 20

1,225

NO. 1

ONE ROUND

Again the same data are applied to both mortars, but only No. 1 fires the second round. The section leader senses this round to be a "short" and on the line mortar–target. Since a bracket has now been established, No. 2 mortar can be adjusted almost simultaneously with No. 1. The next fire order would be:

NO. 1

1,325

NO. 2

LEFT 20

1,350 (25-YARD DIFFERENCE IN DEPTH)

SECTION RIGHT

ONE ROUND

(The deflection for No. 2 mortar is calculated as follows: The section leader has measured the width of the target to be 110 mils, or 55 mils for one-half of the target width. Since No. 2 mortar is laid parallel and at an interval of 50 yards to the left of No. 1, the section leader can determine the number of additional mils necessary to place the initial round of No. 2 in the center of the near edge of the target by means of the deflection-conversion table; that is, a width of 50 yards at a range of 1,400 yards is equivalent to 36 mils. The figure 35 is used to make the process easier. Since the interval measures 35 mils, 20 additional mils will place the first round more or less in the center of the near edge of the target.)

(3) The words, "Section right," indicate that No. 2 mortar fires a round 5 seconds later than No. 1 to permit the section leader to sense each round. In adjusting No. 2 mortar, an initial bracket of 50 yards may be used in view of the previous adjustment for range made by No. 1 mortar. The

final bracket would be obtained in the manner described above, and the section leader would then be ready to combine fire for adjustment with fire for effect.

(4) Fire for effect is accomplished by the following fire order:

NO. 1, SEARCH 1,375–1,475

NO. 2, SEARCH 1,400–1,500

SECTION

TRAVERSE LEFT TWO AND ONE-HALF TURNS

NINE ROUNDS

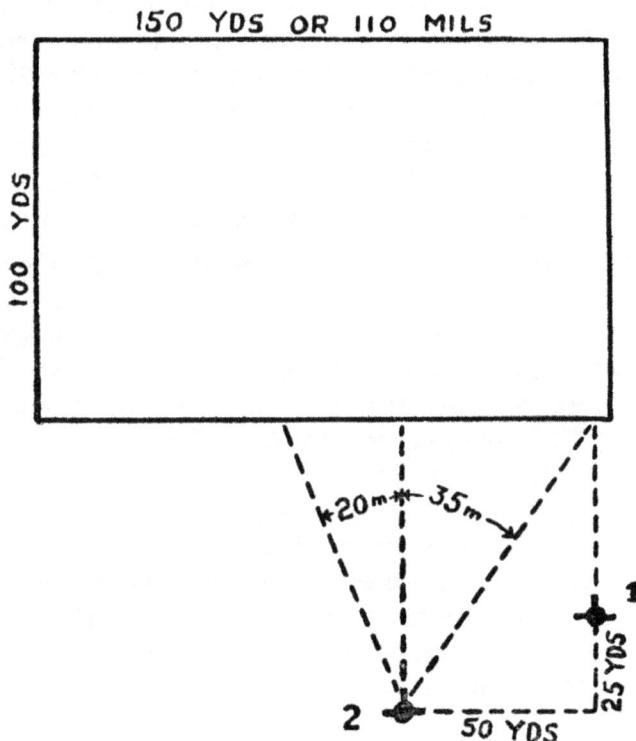

FIGURE 47.—Initial laying and adjustment by section.

SECTION II

EMPLOYMENT OF SMOKE

■ 112. IMPORTANCE.—Smoke is of great importance for the purpose of blinding enemy observation, thus preventing him from observing tactical movements and delivering aimed fire on advancing friendly troops. It may also be used to screen an advance, to protect an exposed flank, to screen a withdrawal, or to support a counter attack. (For details see FM 3–5.) As smoke will attract hostile attention, it may be desirable to lay down smoke, in several places simultaneously, in order to deceive the enemy as to the location of the actual attack. In the employment of smoke, observation is desirable for accurate placement and maintenance of the screen. The location of forward elements of friendly troops should at least be known at the time smoke is being placed on hostile positions. By the correct use of smoke, nighttime conditions are imposed upon hostile elements while friendly troops retain daytime maneuverability. The basic consideration in the use of smoke is that it must accomplish the mission for which it is intended without impeding the action of friendly troops or interfering with the elements of command.

■ 113. MATÉRIEL.—The smoke shell WP, M57 comprises a relatively small per cent of the total ammunition normally carried with the 81-mm mortar. This shell weighs 11.36 pounds and is filled with white phosphorus. When the shell is exploded by its bursting charge, the solid phosphorus is shattered and broken into small fragments. These fragments are scattered into the air and, upon coming in contact with the air, ignite due to the chemical action of the air on the phosphorus. The burning phosphorus particles produce the smoke cloud. In addition to its smoke-producing effect, phosphorus causes serious burns if the particles come in contact with the human body. For this reason, the shell M57 is classed as casualty producing. It also serves as an incendiary.

■ 114. INFLUENCE OF WEATHER AND TERRAIN.—*a. Weather.*— Favorable weather conditions for the employment of smoke include the following:

(1) High humidity.
(2) Cool temperature.
(3) Cloudy skies.
(4) Steady winds of less than 10 miles per hour velocity.

b. Terrain.—Smooth open terrain is most favorable for the

use of smoke. Deep valleys and sharp ridges tend to cause wind variations which dissipate the smoke cloud.

■ 115. CHARACTERISTICS OF THE SMOKE CLOUD.—Smoke moves with the wind, becoming diluted as it travels from its source (see fig. 48). For this reason, to maintain a smoke cloud on a given line, continued production of smoke on the desired line is necessary. The movement of a smoke cloud is characterized by lateral spread, vertical rise, drag effect, and settling out. Under average conditions, the lateral spread of the cloud is about 20 percent of the distance traveled. Vertical rise depends upon temperature and ground conditions. The drag effect is caused by the motion of the upper cloud which is more rapid than the part nearest the ground. This motion is caused by wind action. The drag is greater on terrain covered with vegetation than on open ground. For this reason, where there is a choice between placing a smoke screen slightly in rear or slightly in front of the edge of woods, the shells should be placed slightly in rear of the woods line. The drag effect on the cloud, caused by trees and underbrush, is considerable and increases the persistency of the smoke. As the smoke cloud moves along, the smoke particles also gradually settle out on the ground and vegetation. The result of all of these factors is that the cloud produced from a single shell becomes too thin to be effective after it has traveled about 200 yards. Therefore, for a wind parallel to the front to be screened, 200 yards is the maximum frontage which can be screened from a fixed point.

■ 116. POSITION OF SCREEN.—The smoke screen is placed, as nearly as possible, directly on the hostile position so as to envelop it in the forming cloud. The purpose of this is to prevent enemy observation and to prohibit him from delivering aimed fire. Those shells which fall directly among the enemy troops will cause casualties, confusion, and disorganization. In the absence of good natural cover along the entire front of the enemy position, it is desirable that screens be laid beyond the actual flanks so that hostile forces are prevented from observing the terrain from those directions. By placing smoke upon an enemy firing line, our troops are given a fire superiority of approximately four to one.

■ 117. GENERAL TECHNIQUE.—Since so many variables, such as wind, temperature, terrain, and extent of the target, affect smoke operations, the technique described below should be

MIST

SCREENING SMOKE

HEAVY CONCENTRATION

BURST

WIND

FIGURE 48.—Smoke diffusion.

used as a guide and general source of information only and not as one demanding strict adherence.

a. The initial screen.—It is advisable before attempting to lay a screen to fire one smoke round in the general vicinity of the area to be smoked in order to sense for wind direction and speed, and to correct for range errors. (Since preparations for firing smoke on a large scale are usually deliberate, the range finder should be used to obtain the range to some point near the area to be screened.) Despite the fact that a certain type of wind prevails around the observation post, it is difficult to predict wind conditions near targets which

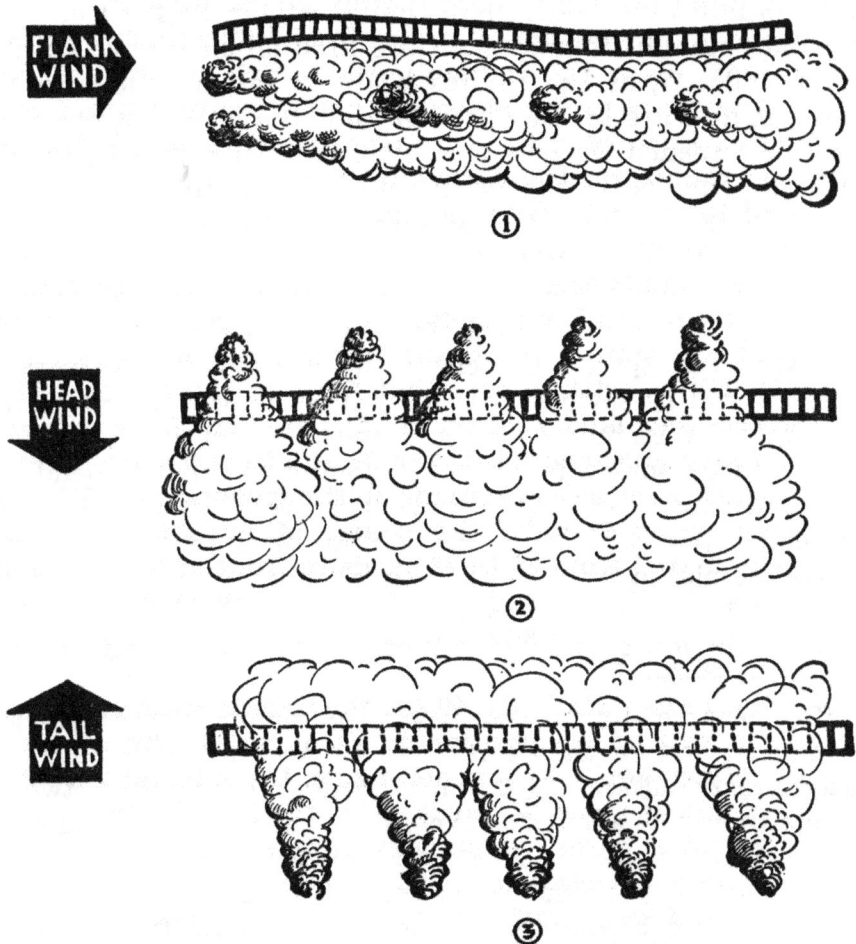

FIGURE 49.—Smoke screen placement.

are situated in terrain broken by irregularities such as ravines, draws, and gullies. Some of the elements of surprise delivery of smoke will be lost by firing this "spotting" round, but the chances for more accurate placement of the screen

are increased, and the chances of wasting a number of smoke
rounds before a satisfactory initial screen is laid are mini-
mized.   When the observer has had an opportunity to note
the dispersion of the smoke cloud, he places succeeding
rounds on the terrain after consideration of the following
factors:

(1) For a flank wind (see fig. 49①) with a velocity of less
than 15 miles per hour, more rounds should be fired on the
upwind points of impact than are fired on successive points
downwind.   If, as the rounds begin to fall on the upwind
flank, it appears to the observer that the entire target will
soon be screened because of a favorable wind, it is better to
place no rounds on the downwind half (or third, with less
wind) of the target.   The ammunition thus conserved may
be used to maintain the concentration on the upwind flank.
The initial rounds fired on the upwind flank should be placed
far enough upwind from the flank of the target so that when
the wind has spread the cloud the heaviest concentration
(fig. 48) will be settling over that flank of the target.   The
interval between bursts for the rounds fired on the downwind
side will vary somewhere between 25 and 50 yards, depending
on the sensing the observer made on the spotting round.   For
screening purposes only, the center of impact for range
should be placed from 25 to 75 yards in front of the position
to be smoked.   For screening and casualty effect, a considerable proportion of the shells must be placed directly on the
hostile position.

(2) For a head wind (fig. 49②), the rounds must be placed
rapidly in *rear* of the position to be screened with an even
lateral distribution.   As a general rule, the interval between
bursts should be about 25 yards, since the lateral spread of a
smoke round is about 20 percent of the distance traveled.
For screening purposes only, the center of impact for the
rounds should be placed not more than 75 yards in rear of
the position to be smoked. For screening and casualty
effect, a majority of the shells must be placed directly on the
hostile position.

(3) For a tail wind (fig. 49③), the rounds must be placed
in *front* of the position to be screened in the same manner
as for a head wind.

b. Maintenance of the screen.—(1) Since it is difficult to predict the action of a smoke screen, even after the initial round has been fired, any attempt to compute the effect of the smoke laying in advance of the firing, as to exact method of laying and of maintaining it, is a waste of time. The observer must study the screen carefully after he has established it in order to decide when, where, and how many additional rounds need to be fired. If there is no cross wind, he may space the next rounds at the same interval as for the first laying. If there is a strong cross wind, he may place many rounds near the upwind flank of the target, a few in the center, and none at all on the downwind half. With a more gentle wind, his action will lie somewhere between these extremes. He may have to increase or decrease his range, because of head or tail winds springing up after the screen is built. As a painter is free to place daubs of paint on a canvas in any place he desires, the observer must be able to daub the terrain with smoke shells as the situation requires. To be able to do this, he controls the fire, round by round. He avoids giving orders for traversing fire, since the net effect would be to place the rounds haphazardly on the ground. He observes for that part of the screen which appears to need reinforcement. He determines the change in turns necessary to lay his mortars (or, occasionally only one mortar) in the direction necessary to increase the smoke density at the required location and gives the necessary orders to have the rounds fired at that spot. He pays particular attention to the upwind flank and orders two or three rounds fired at a time on the extreme flank when the smoke begins to thin out.

(2) In some cases, the maximum screening effect of the initial cloud may persist for as much as five minutes, with favorable terrain, low wind velocity, or high humidity, before reinforcement is necessary. In other situations, the initial screen must be reinforced, in whole or in part, one or two minutes after it has been laid. Where the screen needs partial reinforcement only, the observer may double the initial interval between bursts. For example, where the initial rounds were placed 25 yards apart, rounds for maintenance may be placed 50 yards apart.

(3) The length of time the screen is maintained will be governed by the amount of ammunition available for the mission and the tactical requirements imposed by higher authority. Generally, more ammunition is required for a mission involving a head or tail wind, and less where a cross wind is prevailing.

c. Unit to fire.—Ordinarily, a section of mortars is assigned a smoke mission. However, a single mortar may be assigned a special mission of screening an isolated point, or a front of 250 yards or less. A section of mortars can effectively screen an area of 500-yard frontage.

d. Ammunition supply.—The combat load of ammunition is small; therefore, its use requires pooling or prearranged supply.

■ 118. TECHNIQUE OF FIRING SMOKE.—Since the actions of the observer and the gunner(s) must be well coordinated, the procedure for manipulating the mortar should be simple and readily understood by all concerned. Two methods are indicated. Other methods may be devised to meet special situations, but complicated ones are to be discouraged, particularly where they tend to nullify the element of fire control by the observer.

a. Method 1.—(1) *Situation.*—Firing unit: a section. (Assume that it is impracticable to have each mortar fire independently with its own squad leader as observer.)

Range: 800 yards
Target width: 400 yards
Wind: light, apparently from 3 o'clock
Time: screen is to be maintained 5 minutes, beginning at 0530
Effect: screening only

(2) *Planning and initial actions of the leaders.*—(a) The section leader directs the squad leaders to obtain initial direction of fire for their mortars to designated points in the target area (fig. 50). While initial direction of fire is being obtained by the squad leaders, the section leader calculates the total number of turns of the traversing handwheel that each mortar must traverse to cover separate halves of the target area.

1. Since the target area at a range of 800 yards measures about 470 mils (the section leader can obtain this angle with the binocular, by an improvised mil scale, or by reference to the deflection-conversion table), each mortar must cover 235 mils. The section leader knows that the total

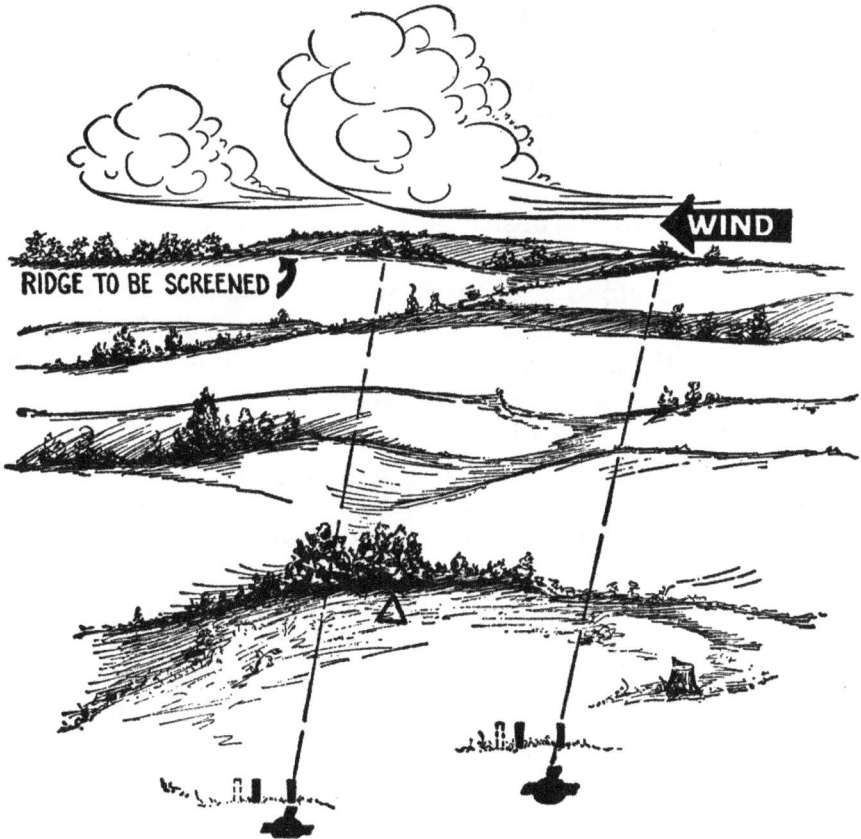

FIGURE 50.—Initial alinement to lay smoke.

number of mils traverse on the entire traversing screw is about 180 mils. Subtracting 180 from 235, he obtains 55 additional mils for each mortar to traverse. He decides tentatively to space the smoke shells at intervals of 50 yards.

2. By reference to his deflection-conversion table, the section leader finds that a width of 50 yards measures **64 mils** at a range of **800 yards**. He divides **64** by **15** (number of mils for one turn of the traversing handwheel) and obtains four turns. He knows that there are a total of twelve turns on the traversing screw (exactly 11¾, but, for ease of calculation, twelve turns are used as a basis). Twelve turns on the traversing screw cover an interval of **180 mils**. Since 64 mils, or four turns, must still be covered, an additional stake must be placed by the gunner.

(b) When the mortars are mounted, the squad leaders are told to supervise the placing of the additional aiming stake as follows:

1. The gunner positions the traversing screw nut on the left side of the yoke and directs No. 2 to move the bipod legs until the vertical line of the collimator is laid on the left edge of the *base stake,* with the mortar cross-leveled. The gunner then traverses the entire width of the screw, cross-levels, and directs No. 3 to place a *left stake* on the line of sight of the collimator.

2. When this has been done, the gunner again positions the traversing screw nut on the left side of the yoke, directs No. 2 to move the bipod, and lays accurately on the *base stake.* The ammunition loader and the ammunition handler for each mortar prepare the ammunition in advance of firing, since the laying of the initial screen requires rapid loading.

(c) The section leader now informs the squad leaders about his plans for creating the initial screen. He also informs them of an alternate plan for placing the initial screen in the event the wind direction shifts before firing is begun. After the initial rounds are fired, he explains that he *may* delegate maintenance of the screen to each squad observer. One reason for this might be that, because of a favorable wind the fire of both mortars need only be concentrated on the upwind flank of the target for maintenance of the screen. To avoid confusion, the squad leader of the mortar originally assigned the downwind half of the target would control the fire of his mortar. Another reason might be that, whereas one mortar may have laid a good screen in its half of the target, another mortar may need assistance in plugging gaps in the initial screen laid on its half of the target.

(3) *Firing phase.*—(a) At the proper time, the section leader issues the initial fire order as follows:

> SECTION
> SMOKE
> ZERO
> BASE STAKE
> 800
> ONE ROUND

Assume that when the rounds are fired the section leader senses that they are slightly short for range and believes that the wind direction and speed are such that he can lay the initial screen as planned. Immediately, he commands: SECTION, 850, TWO ROUNDS. (For about the first five rounds, the gunner must relevel the longitudinal bubble after each round is fired because of the settling of the base plate. The sight is removed for the first round only. The basis for this exception to the normal practice of removing the sight for the first three rounds lies in the fact that smoke must be laid without delay and also because one round of smoke settles the base plate as effectively as several rounds of HE, light (par. 54b(6))). As soon as the rounds are fired, he commands: LEFT FOUR TURNS, TWO ROUNDS. When these rounds are fired, he commands: LEFT FOUR TURNS, TWO ROUNDS, and after these rounds are fired, he orders: LEFT FOUR TURNS, ONE ROUND. When the rounds are fired, he commands: RIGHT FOUR TURNS, LAY ON LEFT STAKE. (Since four more turns must be taken to the left to cover the target, the gunner must turn the handwheel to the right, direct No. 2 to move the bipod until the vertical line of the collimator is laid on the left edge of the left stake, and relevel before the next order of the section leader can be executed.) When the mortars have been re-laid on the left stake, the section leader commands: LEFT FOUR TURNS, ONE ROUND. After the rounds are fired, he commands: RIGHT TWELVE TURNS, LAY ON BASE STAKE.

He is now ready to place more rounds on the windward flank and reinforce the screen where he deems necessary.

(b) Assuming that a satisfactory initial screen has been laid, the section leader starts to reinforce the screen when the smoke cloud begins to dissipate and thin out. His fire orders might be SECTION, TWO ROUNDS (it is usually necessary to place two rounds on the up wind flank each time the smoke is reinforced); LEFT FOUR TURNS, ONE ROUND; LEFT FOUR TURNS, ONE ROUND, etc. Upon completion of the laying requirements at the end of the order, the mortars are again laid on the base stake.

(c) It may happen that the section leader's decision to place smoke shells at 50-yard intervals is in error, as proved by the firing. To correct this, he reinforces and maintains the screen by reducing the interval to 25 yards and gives the following orders: SECTION, TWO ROUNDS; LEFT TWO TURNS, ONE ROUND; LEFT TWO TURNS, ONE ROUND, etc. When the target has been re-covered, the mortars are relaid on the base stake.

(d) Suppose that after the section leader has prepared the mortars for firing as described in (2) above, and, upon firing the spotting rounds, he discovers that the wind at the target is from 9:00 o'clock rather than from 3:00 o'clock. The initial screening of the area from left to right, rather than from right to left, is obtained in the following manner: The section leader commands: SECTION, LEFT FOUR TURNS, LAY ON LEFT STAKE, 850, TWO ROUNDS. When the rounds are fired, he commands: LEFT EIGHT TURNS, LAY ON LEFT STAKE, TWO ROUNDS; after the rounds are fired, he orders: RIGHT FOUR TURNS, TWO ROUNDS; when the rounds are fired, he commands: RIGHT FOUR TURNS, ONE ROUND; and later, RIGHT FOUR TURNS, ONE ROUND. When the last rounds of the initial screen are fired, he commands: LEFT FOUR TURNS, LAY ON LEFT STAKE and is ready to reinforce the screen.

b. *Method 2.*—(1) *Situation.*—Same as in a(1) above.

(2) *Planning and initial actions of the leaders.*—(a) The section leader calculates the total number of turns of the traversing handwheel in the same manner as for method 1.

However, for this situation, two additional aiming stakes must be placed by each gunner (fig. 50).

(b) When the mortars are mounted, the squad leaders are told to supervise the placing of additional aiming stakes as follows:

1. The gunner positions the traversing screw nut on the left side of the yoke and directs No. 2 to move the bipod legs until the vertical line of the collimator is laid on the left edge of the aiming stake, with the mortar cross-leveled. The gunner then traverses the entire width of the traversing screw, cross-levels, and directs No. 3 to place a *first left stake* on the line of sight of the collimator. He next turns the traversing handwheel at least five turns to the right, directs No. 2 to move the bipod until the vertical line of the collimator is approximately on the left edge of this stake, and lays accurately with the traversing handwheel, cross-leveling simultaneously. He then rotates the traversing handwheel four turns to the left, and directs No. 3 to drive a *second left stake* on the line of sight. (According to the requirements of the situation, a number of extra stakes may be placed at fixed intervals by following the procedure indicated above.)

2. When this has been done, the gunner again positions the traversing screw nut on the left side of the yoke, directs No. 2 to move the bipod, and re-lays accurately on the *base stake*.

(3) *Firing phase.*—(a) The initial rounds are fired in exactly the same manner as in Method 1. When the gunner reaches the end of the traversing screw, the section leader commands: LAY ON SECOND LEFT STAKE, ONE ROUND. The gunner directs No. 2 to shift the bipod in order to place the vertical line of the collimator on this stake, levels the longitudinal bubble, and commands: FIRE. The section leader then commands: RIGHT TWELVE TURNS, LAY ON BASE STAKE. This is done preparatory to reinforcing the screen.

(b) Where the initial interval between bursts is reduced

from 4 to 2 turns and the gunner has reached the end of the traversing screw, the section leader commands: LAY BE-TWEEN STAKES, ONE ROUND. The gunner directs No. 2 to move the bipod legs until the vertical line of the collimator is halfway between the first left and second left stake, checks the lay for elevation, and commands: FIRE. The section leader then commands: LAY ON SECOND LEFT STAKE, ONE ROUND. After the round is fired, the section leader orders: RIGHT TWELVE TURNS, LAY ON BASE STAKE.

(c) Where the initial screening must take place from left to right, rather than from right to left as originally planned, the section leader commands: SECTION, LEFT TWELVE TURNS, LAY ON SECOND LEFT STAKE, 850, TWO ROUNDS. When the rounds are fired, he commands: LAY ON FIRST LEFT STAKE, TWO ROUNDS; subsequently, he commands: RIGHT FOUR TURNS, TWO ROUNDS; RIGHT FOUR TURNS, ONE ROUND; RIGHT FOUR TURNS, ONE ROUND; and LEFT TWELVE TURNS, LAY ON SECOND LEFT STAKE.

c. (1) It has been found that the section leader exercises more control over the section and can place the smoke shells where he desires if he gives separate commands for all movements of the traversing handwheel. If this system of fire orders is followed, the section leader knows at any given moment the exact position of the traversing screw nut and can daub the terrain with a certain degree of flexibility.

(2) At ranges of 1,400 yards or over, additional aiming stakes need not be placed, since a 250-yard front for each mortar at that range measures 180 mils. For certain other ranges, where the target width for each mortar is less than 250 yards, additional aiming stakes are unnecessary for complete coverage of the target. Frequently the extra stakes will not be used after having been set out. After they are placed out and firing has begun, it may be found more satisfactory in a cross wind of more than 10 miles per hour to cover the upwind two-thirds of the target and to allow the wind to carry smoke over the remaining third. At ranges where they might be needed, however, additional stakes should always be placed out in advance.

■ 119. EXAMPLES OF EMPLOYMENT.—*a. Small unit attacking isolated resistance.*—Platoon A (fig. 51) has been stopped by hostile fire from *X*. Smoke is placed on *X* to enable Platoon B to envelop the hostile position.

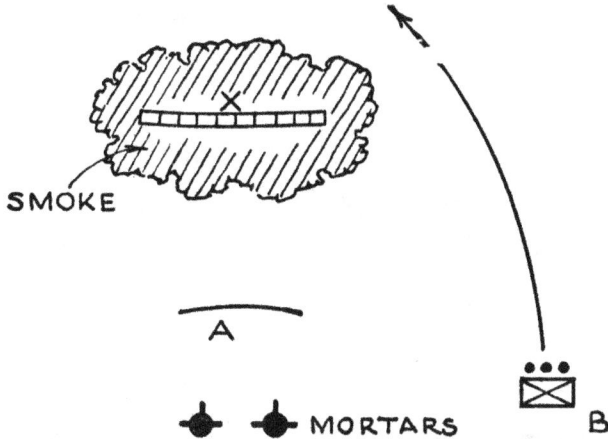

FIGURE 51.—Smoke assisting advance of rifle platoon.

b. Company in attack.—The right company (fig. 52) has a good covered route of approach. The left company must advance over open ground. Thus the objective of the left

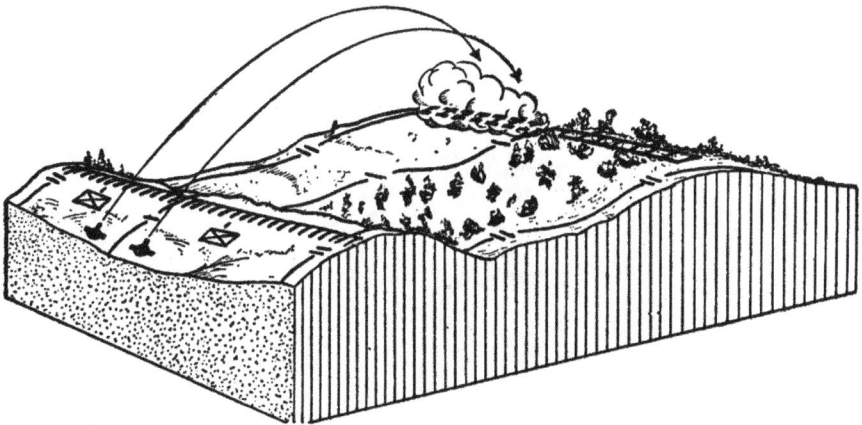

FIGURE 52.—Smoke assisting advance of rifle company.

company is smoked during its advance. The possibility of employing smoke for successive objectives is constantly considered.

c. Protection of exposed flank.—Company B (fig. 53) has advanced to the position indicated, while company A has been stopped as shown by the enemy in position at *X*, and is unable to advance. Company **B** is threatened by enfilade fire from the enemy at *X*. Smoke should be placed as indicated to blind this fire.

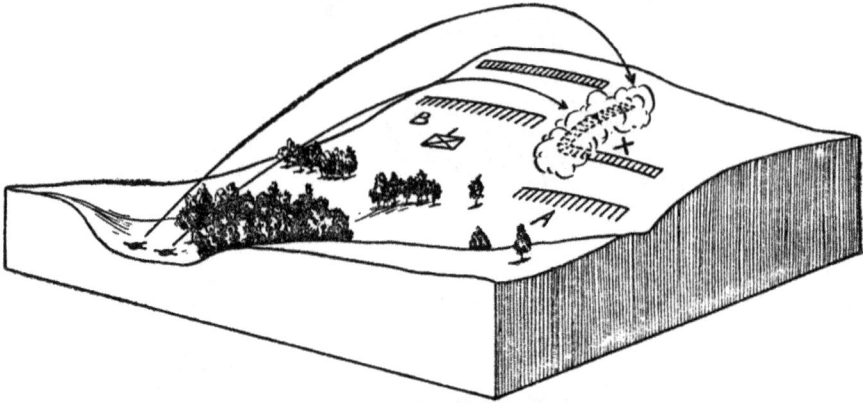

FIGURE 53.—Smoke protecting threatened flank.

d. Blind hostile observation.—Since the maximum screening effect rather than casualties is desired, smoke is placed

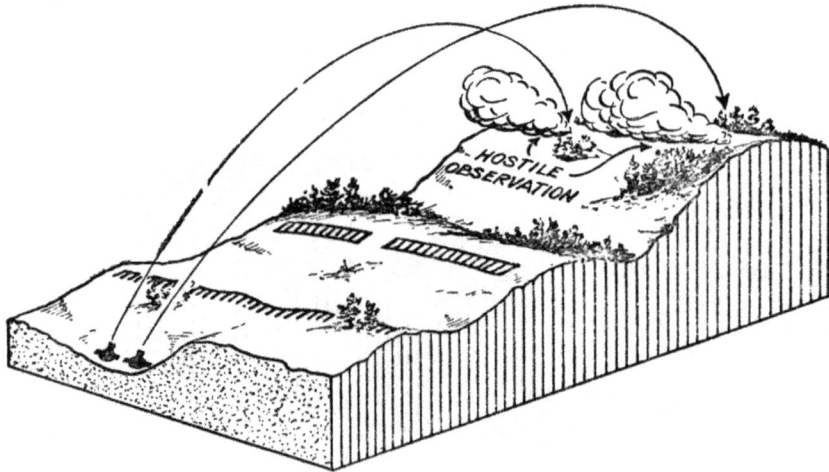

FIGURE 54.—Smoke preventing hostile observation.

immediately in front of the points to be screened (fig. **54**). Ordinarily the supply of smoke shells is strictly limited. Hence, to conserve ammunition, the screen should be placed only during critical periods of the action.

SECTION III

FIRE CONTROL INSTRUMENTS

■ 120. AIMING CIRCLES.—*a. General.*—The aiming circle is a small, compact surveying instrument. It is used for measuring azimuths, horizontal angles, angles of site, and vertical angles. The two types of aiming circles generally available for issue to mortar units are the M1916 and the M1. The

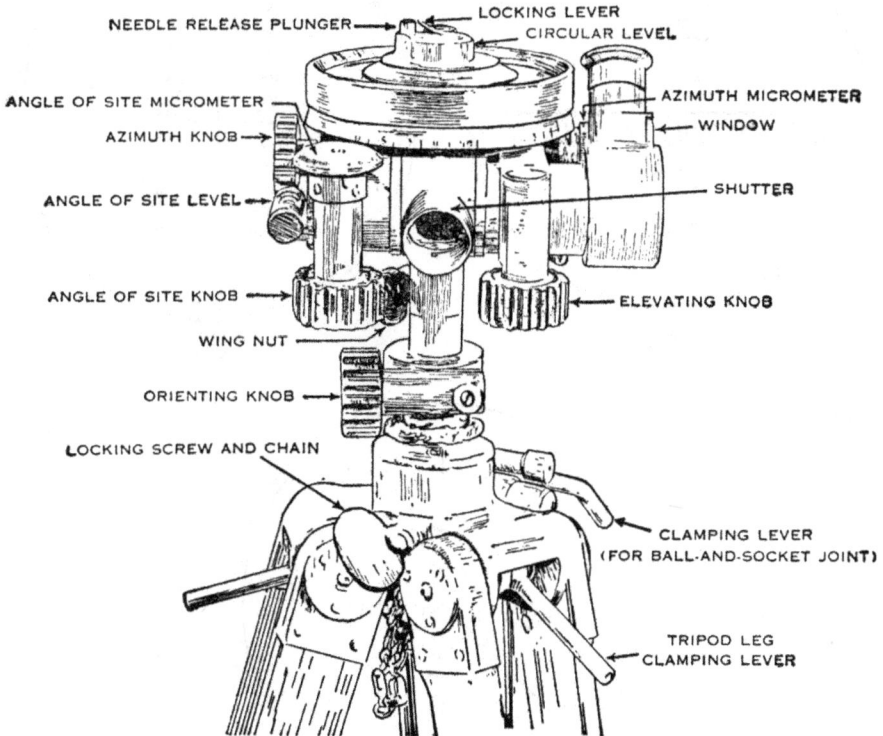

FIGURE 55.—Aiming circle, M1916.

functioning of these two instruments is essentially the same, except for the method used in obtaining the angle of site.

b. The aiming circle, M1916 (fig. 55).—(1) *General.*—The aiming circle complete consists of the instrument, tripod, and carrying case.

(2) *Instrument.*—The major components of the instrument are the telescope assembly and elevating mechanism, the angle of site mechanism, the cylindrical body or compass box, and the azimuth mechanism.

179

(a) The telescope assembly and elevating mechanism has the following characteristics:

1. The telescope is of the prismatic type, so arranged that the eyepiece is inclined normally at 60° from the horizontal. The telescope can be rotated ap-

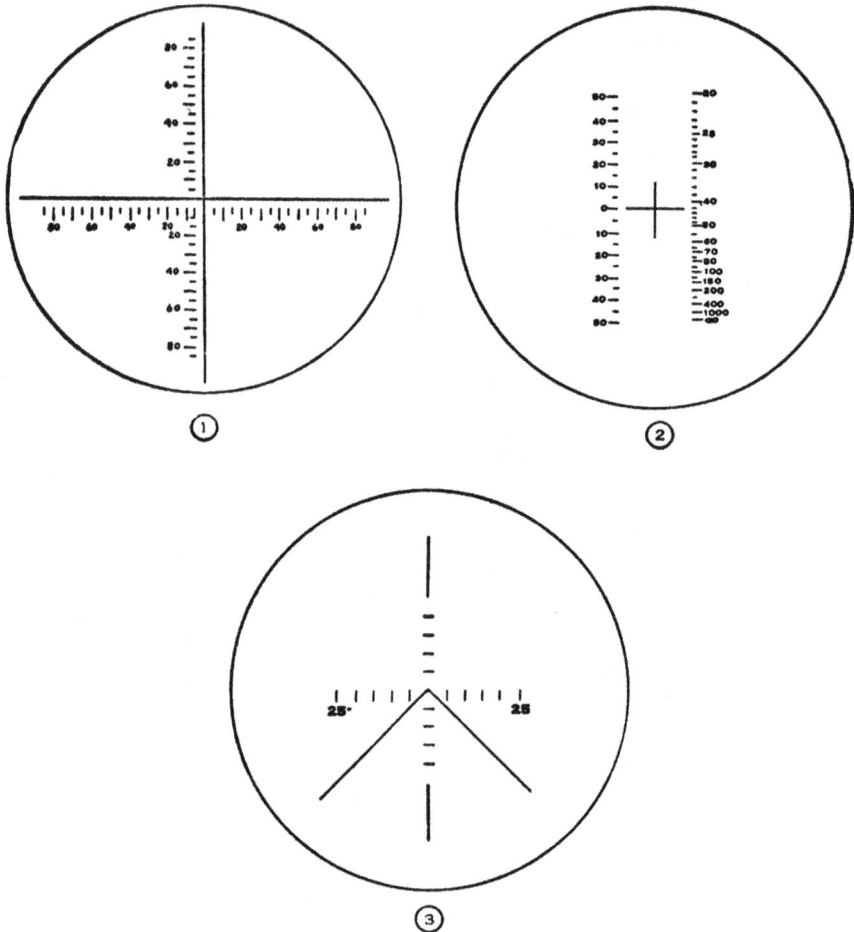

FIGURE 56.—Reticle patterns.

proximately 18°, or 320 mils, below and above the horizontal, by turning the elevating knob. The telescope has a magnifying power of 4.18 and a field of view of 10° or approximately 178 mils.

2. There are three types of reticles in use on the M1916

aiming circle (fig. 56). The optical center of the instrument is at the intersection of the cross hairs (fig. 56① and ②) or at the apex of the inverted "V" (fig. 56③). The eyepiece tube is fitted with a glass window opposite the reticle for illuminating it when used at night.

3. The objective prism is provided with a shutter which excludes dust and dirt when the instrument is not in use.

(b) The cylindrical body has the following characteristics:

1. The cylindrical body houses a magnetic needle. Arrow index lines indicating north and south are engraved on the inside portion of the body. The locking lever, when rotated over the needle release plunger, allows the needle to rotate freely within the confines of the needle stops.

2. A circular level housed in the raised portion of the needle release mechanism is used to place the instrument in a horizontal plane.

(c) The azimuth mechanism consists of the following:

1. The azimuth scale, graduated from 0 to 64. Each graduation represents 100 mils of horizontal angle. An auxiliary scale of 32 graduations which runs half around the compass box, above the azimuth scale, is provided for reading back azimuths.

2. The azimuth knob, used to turn the azimuth micrometer. The azimuth micrometer is graduated into 100 one-mil spaces and is numbered every 10 mils. One complete turn of the micrometer moves the azimuth index one space or 100 mils.

3. The throwout lever, by which the azimuth worm may be disengaged from the worm wheel. This permits motion of the index about the azimuth scale.

4. The orienting knob, used to rotate the spindle upon which the instrument is mounted. In orienting, fine adjustments are made by means of the orienting knob. For major adjustments, free rotation of the instrument is obtained by loosening the wing nut.

(3) *Tripod.*—The tripod, type **G** (fig. 57), is issued with the aiming circle, M1916. The lower portion of the vertical

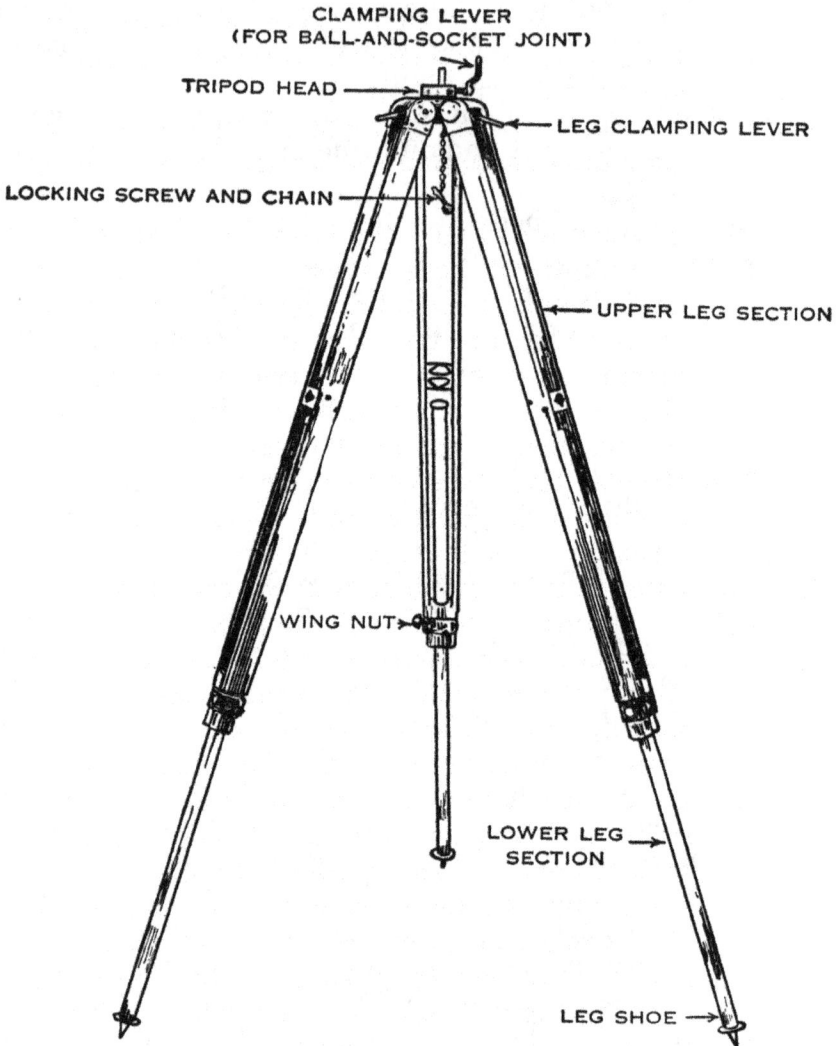

FIGURE 57.—Aiming circle tripod, type G.

spindle, seated in the tripod head, forms a ball-and-socket joint. To move this joint, it is necessary to loosen the clamping lever.

(4) *To set up the instrument.*—Extend the tripod legs to the desired height. Set the shoes firmly in the ground.

Place the aiming circle on the vertical spindle of the mount and clamp it by means of the wing nut. (See fig. 55). Move the ball-and-socket joint until the bubble in the circular level is centered; then tighten the clamping lever.

(5) *Operation.*—(a) *To orient on magnetic north.*—Rotate the locking lever so as to allow the needle to swing free. Set the azimuth micrometer and scale at zero. Loosen the wing nut and rotate the instrument until the north index of the body approximately coincides with the needle. Tighten the wing nut and rotate the orienting knob to bring the needle and index to coincide exactly. This orients the instrument; that is, the instrument is directed at magnetic north with an azimuth reading of zero.

(b) *To read the azimuth to an object.*—By use of the throwout lever, turn the telescope until the optical center of the reticle is approximately on the object. Bring the optical center exactly upon the object by rotating the azimuth knob and the elevating knob. The azimuth to the object is then indicated on the scale and the micrometer.

(c) *To declinate.*—Set up the aiming circle over a point from which several points of known map azimuth can be seen. These points should lie in different quadrants of the compass. Read the azimuth to each point selected. Check the readings a second time; if the second readings differ by more than one mil, the measurements are discarded and the readings repeated. Subtract the reading to each of the points from its known map azimuth (grid). The average of the differences of these readings is the declination constant of the instrument. A new declination constant must be determined for each new locality.

(d) *To orient on grid (Y) north.*—Orient the instrument on magnetic north (see (5) (a) above), then measure the angle to some auxiliary point. To this reading add the declination constant and place the resulting angle on the azimuth scale and micrometer. Then, by means of the orienting knob, bring the line of sight back on the auxiliary point. The zero on the azimuth scale is then oriented on grid (Y) north. (In order to orient on true north, the gisement or grid declination is added to the declination constant.)

(e) *To measure the horizontal angle between two points.*— Set the azimuth micrometer and scale at zero. Loosen the wing nut and rotate the instrument until the optical center of the telescope is approximately on the left-hand object. Tighten the wing nut and bring the optical center exactly on the object by rotating the orienting knob. By use of the throwout lever, turn the telescope in a clockwise direction until the optical center is approximately on the right hand object. Then, bring the optical center exactly on the object by turning the azimuth knob. The horizontal angle between the two objects can be read directly from the azimuth scale and micrometer.

(f) *To obtain the angle of site reading.*—The angle of site reading is not used in firing the mortar, and its employment need not be considered.

(6) *Adjustments.*—The aiming circle will be adjusted only in an ordnance shop.

(7) *Care and preservation.*—Before inserting the instrument in its carrying case, cover the objective prism by turning the shutter downward. Raise the compass needle from the pivot by rotating the locking lever. Avoid denting or marring the vertical spindle.

c. *Aiming circle, M1* (fig. 58).—(1) *General.*—The aiming circle, M1, consists of the instrument, tripod, lighting accessories, and carrying case.

(2) *Instrument.*—The major components of the instrument are the telescope assembly and elevating mechanism, the cylindrical body or compass box, and the azimuth mechanism.

(a) The telescope assembly and elevating mechanism has the following characteristics:

> *1.* The telescope is of the prismatic type, so arranged that the eyepiece is normally horizontal. It is provided with an eyepiece focusing sleeve. The telescope can be rotated approximately 8° or 142 mils, below and above the horizontal, by turning the elevating knob. The telescope has a magnifying power of 4 and a field of view of 10° or approximately 178 mils.

2. The eyepiece reticle (fig. 59) consists of a vertical and horizontal mil scale, intersecting at right angles, and graduated in units of 5 mils to a total of 85 mils from the point of intersection. Every 20 mils is numbered. The intersection of the hairlines marks the optical center of the instrument. The eyepiece tube contains a small window opposite the reticle for use in illuminating the reticle at night.

3. The angle of site level is set in the telescope body. When the bubble in the level is centered, the op-

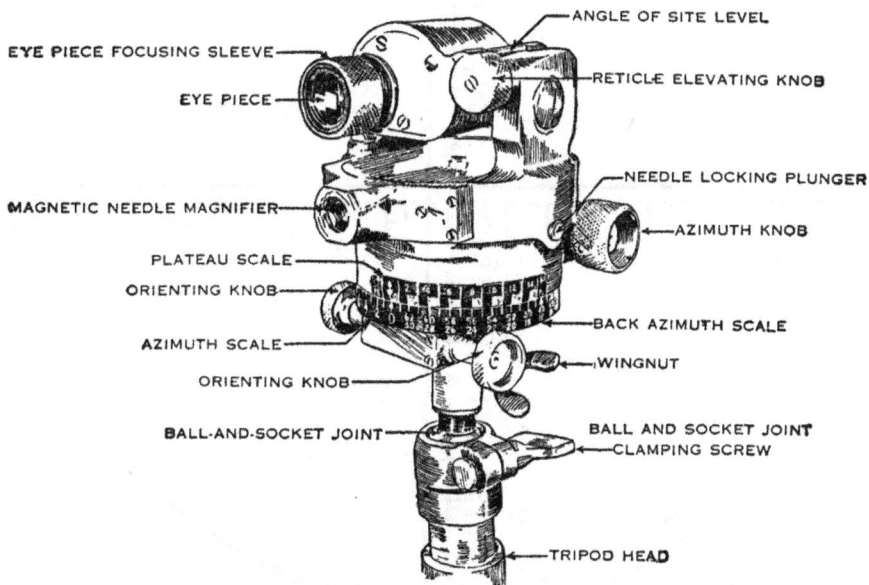

FIGURE 58.—Aiming circle M1

tical axis of the telescope is horizontal and the angle of site of an object within the field of view is indicated directly on the vertical mil scale of the reticle.

(b) The cylindrical body has the following characteristics:
1. The cylindrical body of the instrument contains a magnetic needle, which may be viewed through its magnifier for a very accurate orientation on magnetic north.

2. The needle release plunger (painted olive drab), when pressed in, allows the needle to rotate. The needle locking plunger (painted red), when pressed in, locks the needle and releases pressure on the needle jewel.

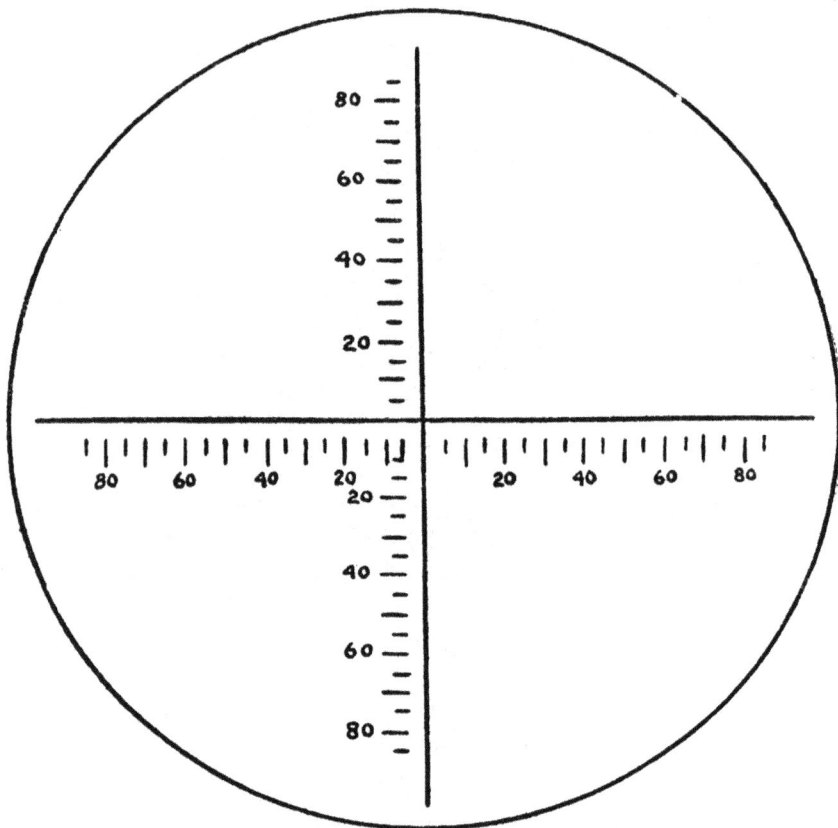

FIGURE 59.—Eyepiece reticle, aiming circle M1.

3. A circular level, located inside the compass box, is provided for leveling the instrument.
(c) The azimuth mechanism consists of the following:
1. The azimuth scale, engraved on the outer rim of the compass box, and graduated from 0 to 64. Each graduation represents 100 mils of horizontal angle.

2. A back azimuth scale, graduated from 0 to 32, which is below the 32 to 64 portion of the azimuth scale. This scale is not used by mortar units.

3. The plateau scale, just above the azimuth scale. This scale is not used by mortar units. The arrow under the 0 on the plateau scale is used as the index for the azimuth scale.

4. The azimuth knob, used to turn the azimuth micrometer and the plateau azimuth micrometer. The plateau azimuth micrometer is not used by mortar units. The azimuth micrometer is the outer scale and is graduated into 100 one-mil spaces, numbered every 10 mils. One complete turn of the micrometer moves the azimuth index one space, or 100 mils.

5. The throwout lever, which when depressed permits free motion of the index about the azimuth scale.

6. The orienting knob, used to rotate the instrument upon the spindle, upon which it is mounted. In orienting, fine adjustments are made by means of the orienting knob. For major adjustments, free rotation of the instrument is obtained by loosening the wing nut.

(3) *Tripod.*—The tripod, M5 (fig. 60) is issued with the aiming circle, M1. It is constructed of nonmagnetic material throughout.

(*a*) The sliding vertical support passes through the tripod head. It may be extended and clamped at the desired height by means of the clamping screw.

(*b*) The spindle, seated in the spindle socket assembly of the tripod support, forms a ball-and-socket joint. To move this joint, it is necessary to loosen the ball-and-socket joint clamping screw.

(4) *Lighting accessories.*—The instrument light, M2, provides the electrical illumination of the reticle of the telescope. This light includes a battery case which is connected by flexible cords to the reticle unit and to a hand light. When not in use, the hand light is held in place by a spring clip. The battery case may be clamped to a tripod leg. It has a

switch for controlling both lamps. The reticle unit fits in a dovetailed slot over the reticle window on the telescope.

(5) *Carrying case, M6A1.*—A lightweight, metal carrying case is provided (fig. 60). The aiming circle remains assem-

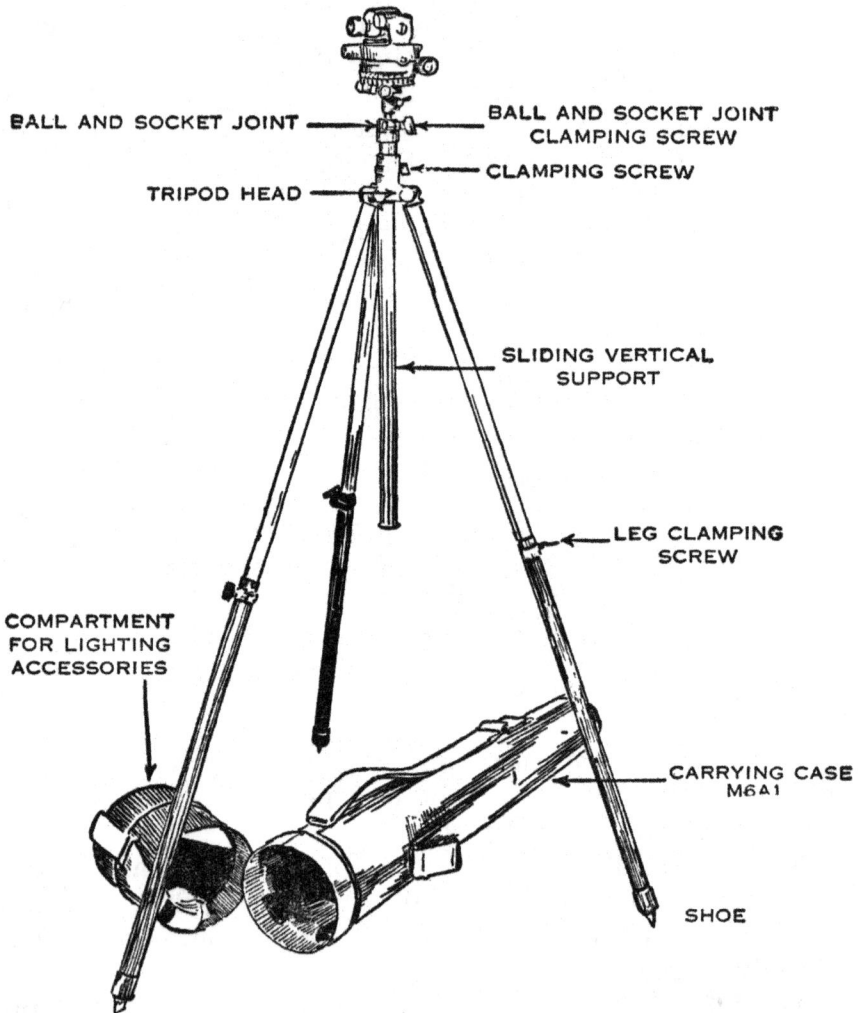

BALL AND SOCKET JOINT

BALL AND SOCKET JOINT CLAMPING SCREW

CLAMPING SCREW

TRIPOD HEAD

SLIDING VERTICAL SUPPORT

LEG CLAMPING SCREW

COMPARTMENT FOR LIGHTING ACCESSORIES

CARRYING CASE M6A1

SHOE

FIGURE 60.—Aiming circle M1, tripod M5, and carrying case M6X1.

bled to the tripod when placed in the case. In the head of the case a compartment is provided for the illuminating equipment.

(6) *To set up the instrument.*—Extend the tripod legs and clamp them at the desired height. Set the shoes firmly in the

ground. Level the instrument by means of the circular level and the ball-and-socket joint.

(7) *Operation.*—(*a*) *To orient by known azimuths.*—Set the azimuth scale and micrometer to indicate the known azimuth of a selected point. Loosen the wing nut and lay generally on the selected point. Place the optical center of the instrument accurately on the selected point by means of the orienting and elevating knobs. The instrument will then be oriented.

(*b*) *To orient on magnetic north.*—Set the azimuth micrometer and scale at zero. Release the needle by pressing in the needle release plunger. Loosen the wing nut and lay approximately on magnetic north. Tighten the wing nut and aline the needle accurately on the north index by means of the orienting knob. For a more accurate orientation, look through the magnetic needle magnifier and aline the south end of the needle exactly on the middle hairline by using the orienting knob.

(*c*) *Other operations.*—The following operations are performed with the aiming circle, M1, in the same manner as prescribed for the aiming circle, M1916:

1. To read the azimuth to an object (see par. 120 *b*(5)(*a*) and (*b*)).

2. To declinate (see par. 120 *b*(5)(*c*)).

3. To orient on grid (Y) north (see par. 120*b*(5)(*d*)).

4. To measure the horizontal angle between two points (see par. 120 *b*(5)(*e*)).

(8) *Adjustments.*—The aiming circle will be adjusted only in an ordnance shop.

(9) *Care and preservation.*—(*a*) When the tripod legs are collapsed preparatory to encasing the instrument, the leg clamping screws must be turned to the outside to avoid denting the sliding vertical support.

(*b*) The magnetic needle should always be locked except when in use.

(*c*) When setting the leg shoes in the ground, avoid putting undue pressure on the legs, as the hollow tubing bends easily.

(*d*) The aiming circle should be oiled by Ordnance personnel only.

(e) The ball-and-socket joint should be loosened slightly when placing the instrument in the case to avoid undue strain on the tripod.

■ **121. RANGE FINDERS.**—*a.* *General.*—(1) The range finder is an instrument used to measure distances. It operates on the principle that if one side and two angles of a triangle are known, the other angle and sides can be determined. The range finder is so constructed that when an operator looks through the single eyepiece, his vision is split into two channels so that he looks through two telescopes at the same time, cne at each end of the instrument (see fig. 61). In this way, when both telescopes are directed at the target, the instrument itself provides the triangle needed to determine a distance. The base of the triangle is formed by the instrument tube, using the distance between the two windows which serve as telescopes. Each line of vision forms a side of the triangle. The angles formed by the lines of vision with the base line supply the necessary "known angles," since they can be measured within the instrument. In principle, only one telescope moves; the other is fixed at a 90° angle to the base. The length of the base never changes. However, the angle between the movable telescope and the base does change; it is different for different ranges. Reference to figure 61 will show that, for targets nearer the instrument, this angle (ABT) is smaller; for targets farther from the instrument this angle (ABT') is larger. From this figure, it can also be seen that the angle (ABT) will always be the same for targets at the same range. Thus, for any range, there is a corresponding angle formed by the movable telescope. The scale of the range finder indicates changes in this angle for targets at different ranges. Instead of indicating the angular measurement in mils or degrees, however, it shows the range corresponding to that angle in yards.

(2) When both telescopes of the range finder are pointed directly at the target, thus completing the triangle, as shown in figure 61, a picture is formed in the field of view. In this picture, one telescope shows an upright image of the target while the other telescope presents an upside down or inverted image of the target. The two images of the target will ap-

pear to be alined as shown in figure 62. When this image is obtained, the range to the target may be read from the instrument, and described in *c*(3)(*a*) and *d*(2)(*b*) below. In making adjustments for this image, it is important that the most clear-cut line of one image be placed in exact prolongation of the same line on the other image.

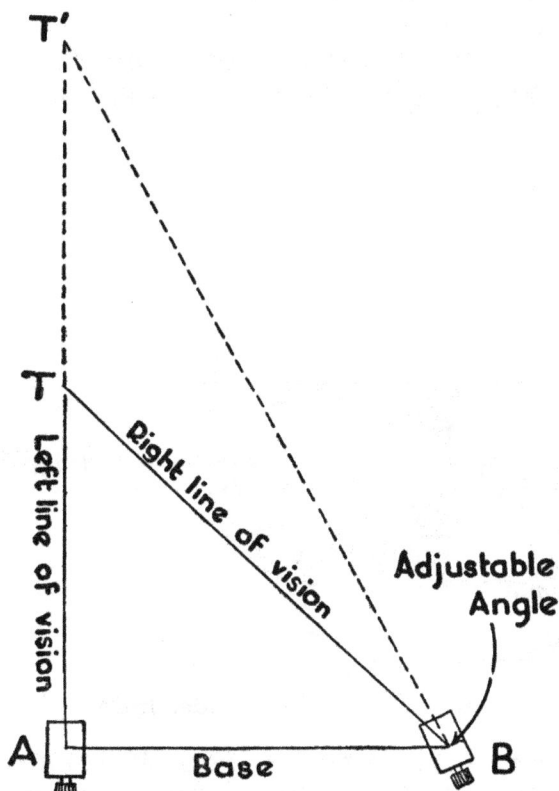

FIGURE 61.—Optical triangles in range finders.

(3) Under no circumstances will the range finder be focused on the sun, as the sun's rays may injure the instrument.

(4) A detailed explanation of the functioning of the range finder is beyond the scope of this manual. Only the necessary instructions for the adjustment and use of the various range finders used in the mortar platoon are given herein. For more detailed information concerning the range finder, see TM 9–1585.

b. Types of range finders.—There are six models of range finders carried by the Ordnance Department as available for use by mortar platoons. The standard for issue is the range finder, 80-centimeter base, M1914M1 (made by Bausch and Lomb). This is called the range roller type. The range finder, M1914, is the same in principle and operation, and differs only in that there is a slight variation in the optical arrangement. Four other models, all of the azimuth type, are in use as limited standard. The range finder, 80-centimeter base, M1917 (made by Bausch and Lomb) is typical of these.

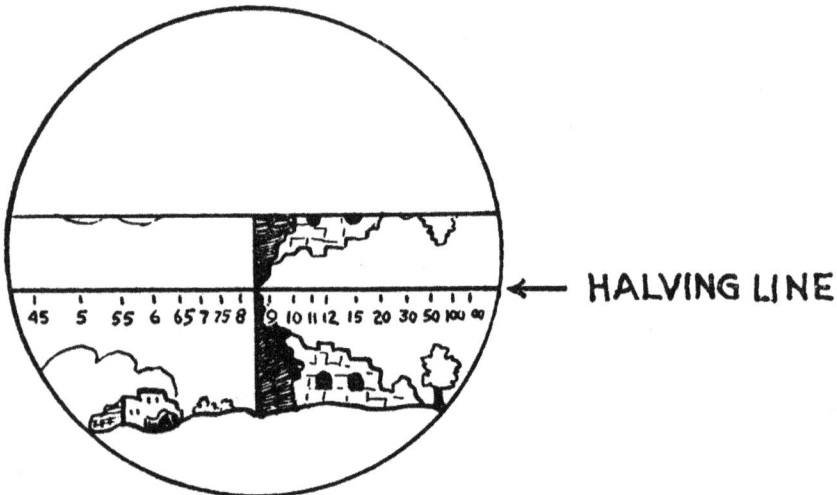

← HALVING LINE

FIGURE 62.—Range finder image.

c. Range finder, 80 centimeter base, M1914 and M1914M1. (Bausch and Lomb, range roller type).—(1) *Description.*—This instrument (see fig. 63) consists of the range finder, type R tripod (large), type S tripod (small), adjusting lath (type B), and two carrying cases (one case for the instrument and one for the type S tripod).

(a) There are two windows in the tube, one at each end facing to the front. Through them the operator may observe the target through the optical system. Revolving sleeves are provided for the windows so that the optical system may be protected against moisture and dust. The optical system has a magnifying power of 10.

(*b*) The single eyepiece is placed in the center of the tube. It is fitted with a rubber flange to protect the operator's eye. The eyepiece can be adjusted to suit the individual eye when focusing on the target. It is fitted with a diopter scale for quick adjustment.

(*c*) The field of view obtained through the instrument appears as in figure 66. It will be noted that this field is divided into two half-moon sections by a band running horizontally across the field. Objects appearing in the lower section are

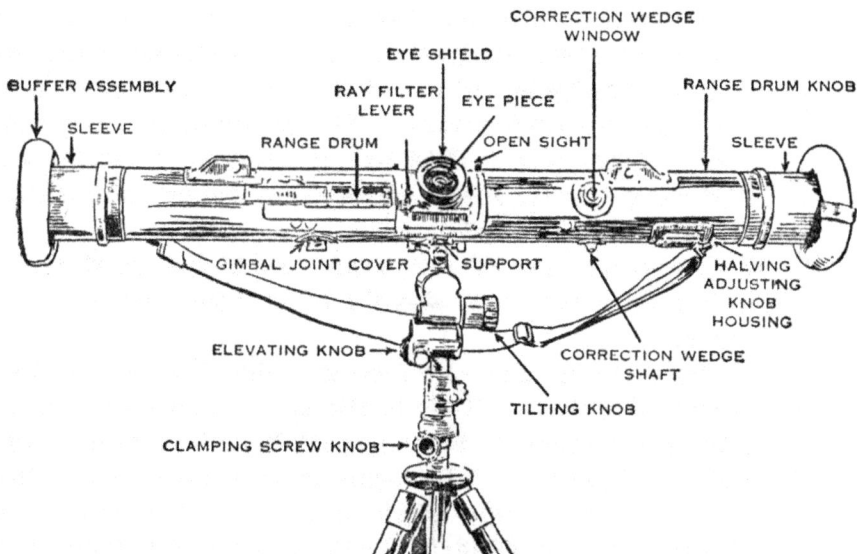

FIGURE 63.—Range finder, 80-centimeter base, M1914.

seen in their normal upright position. The part which extends above the dividing band may show a continuation of the lower upright image but should be disregarded. The dividing band is called the inverted field, and all objects seen in this field appear to be upside down. As the instrument is raised or lowered, objects seen in the inverted field will disappear as they reach the lines of demarcation of the lower or upper half-moon sections. The inverted (center) field and the upright (lower) field are cleanly divided by the lower edge of the inverted field. This dividing line is called the "halving line" (see fig. 62).

(*d*) Just to the left of and below the eyepiece is a small

lever that controls a ray filter holder. An amber and a smoked glass filter are provided for moderating exceptionally bright daylight or to cut down the glare of a searchlight or the reflection of the sun over water.

(e) Open sights mounted on the tube over the eyepiece permit rapid training of the instrument on the target.

(f) The yard scale, just to the left of the eyepiece, is covered by a sliding metal strip. The range is read from the column of figures nearest the index line. Although the yard scale runs from 400 to 10,000 yards, ranges above 5,000 yards may be considered only as approximate. This is because of the short base of the instrument. At the extreme right of the yard scale, infinity is indicated thus (00); this symbol is used in adjusting the instrument. The range drum on which the yard scale appears is turned by rotating the range drum knob. The range drum knob (actually a roller) is located near the right end of the tube.

(g) On the lower side of the tube, under the yard scale, is the gimbal joint cover; it should be removed only by an ordnance repairman.

(h) To the right of the eyepiece is a small glass window about the size of a dime. This is the correction wedge window. Inside the window is the correction wedge scale, graduated in 30 equal spaces. This scale is used only in making the range adjustment. The scale is turned by means of a key inserted over the square shaft, protruding from the housing below the correction wedge window.

(i) To the right of the correction wedge shaft is a small slide on which are etched the words, "halving adjuster." This slide covers the halving adjusting knob.

(j) The triangular-shaped piece of metal carrying two hooks and a stud, mounted on the tube opposite the eyepiece, is called the adapter. It is used to attach the instrument to the small tripod.

(k) Two tripods are provided with the range finder (see figs. 64 and 65). Both tripods are interchangeable among the M1914, M1914M1, and the azimuth type, M1917. The small tripod, type S, has a spindle that divides into three legs and can be used when a low mount is desired for the instrument. It has an elevating knob, used to elevate or depress the field of vision, and a tilting knob, used to tilt the ends of the instrument up or down on its vertical axis. On top of the small tripod is the support on which the adapter is locked when the instrument is attached to the tripod. The large tripod, type R, is provided for use when a higher mount is desired for the instrument. When in use, the spindle of the type S tripod is inserted into the head of the type R tripod

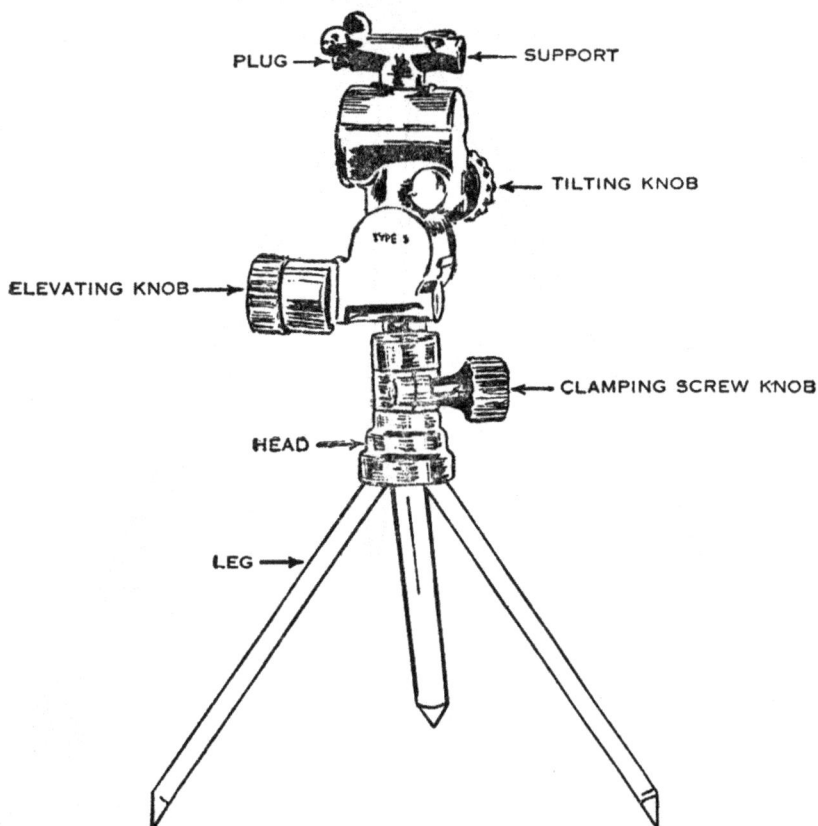

FIGURE 64.—Tripod, type S.

and clamped by means of the type R tripod clamping screw knob.

(2) *To set up the instrument.*—Select the tripod to be used and set it up on the ground. Remove the range finder from its case, rotate the sleeves to expose the two objective windows, and mount the instrument on the tripod by fastening the adapter to the support.

195

(3) *Operation.*—(a) Train the instrument on the target. Focus the eyepiece and bring the lower upright image of the target into the center of the field, just below the halving line, by means of the elevating knob. By use of the tilting knob, bring the most clearly defined line on the target so as to make it appear at right angles to the halving line. The pic-

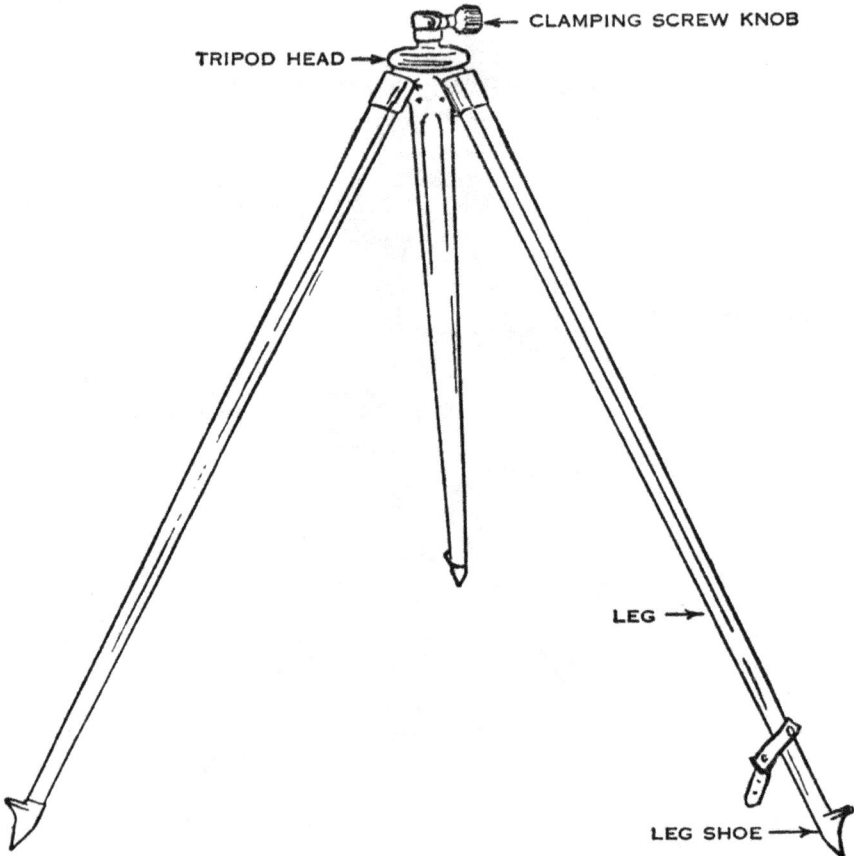

FIGURE 65.—Tripod, type R.

ture seen will then be similar to figure 66①. To line up the inverted image of the target with the upright image, rotate the range drum knob until the images appear as in figure 66②. When a picture similar to figure 66② has been obtained, the range to the target may be read from the yard scale.

(b) Ranges to horizontal objects such as roads, trenches, or skyline, may be measured by removing the range finder from the mount and placing it vertically on one end. This method is comparatively inaccurate and should be used only when there is no vertical object near the target.

(4) *Adjustments.*—Because of unavoidable jolts and bumps incident to transporting the range finder, the mechanism is frequently shaken out of true adjustment. When this occurs, the instrument will need readjustment. This may be done as explained below.

(a) *Halving adjustment.*—When the halving line (see (1) (c) above) is out of adjustment, the inverted image may

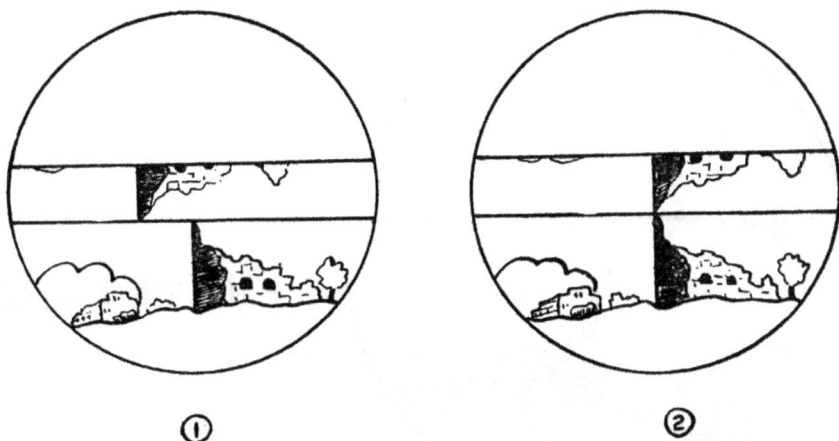

FIGURE 66.—Images, range finder, roller type.

appear misplaced vertically as in figure 67, or it may not be visible at all. To make the halving adjustment properly, first bring the upright image into contact with the halving line by means of the elevating knob. Then aline the inverted image, with that of the upright figure (see fig. 66①), by rotating the halving adjusting knob. While making this adjustment, the upright image must be kept in its correct position.

(b) *Range adjustment.*—When the instrument is out of adjustment for range, so that the true range is not indicated on the yard scale when the correct picture is obtained, the instrument may be readjusted as follows:

1. Known range method.—Select a target with an accurately known range, such as the target on a rifle range as seen from the 500 yard firing point. Set the yard scale so that it indicates the known range to the target. If the images appear as in figure 66②, no adjustment is necessary. If the images appear as in figure 66①, turn the correction wedge shift by means of the correction wedge key until the picture appears as in figure 66②. Note the reading on the correction wedge scale. Throw the instrument out of adjustment by two turns of the key; look through the eye-

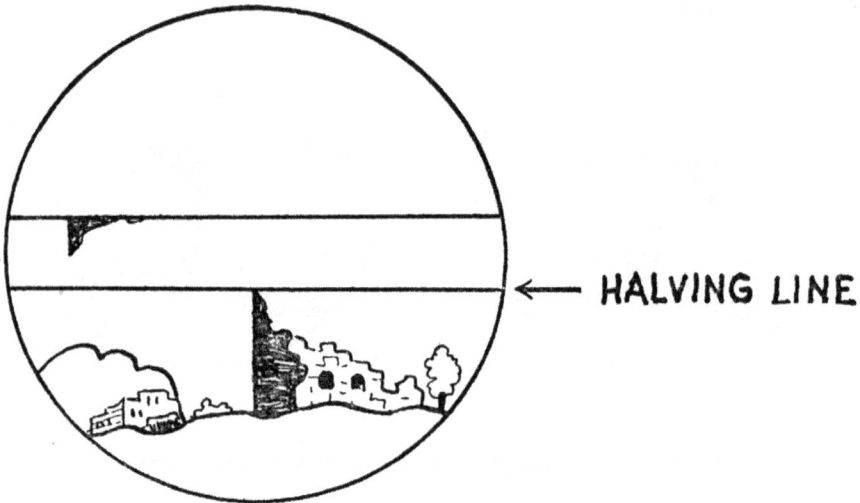

FIGURE 67.—Images, range finder, showing faulty halving adjustment.

piece, and by use of the key, bring the images into line again until they appear as in figure 66②. Note the reading on the correction wedge scale. This reading should be the same, or nearly the same, as that of the first one taken. Repeat this process at least five times. Disregard any readings that are obviously in error and take the average of the rest. Set this average reading on the correction wedge scale; the instrument should then be in adjustment. Caution: In case the average reading on the correction wedge scale is greater than **27** or less than **3**, the instrument, complete, should be turned over to Ordnance maintenance personnel for repair.

2. *Infinity method.*—When the yard scale is set at infinity (∞), the lines of vision from both telescopes are parallel when the instrument is in correct adjustment. To obtain adjustment by the infinity method, the moon or any other object which is at a practically infinite range from the instrument, may be used as a target. The yard scale is set at the infinity mark. The procedure, thereafter, is identical with that outlined for the known range method. A variation of the infinity method which is less accurate and also less practical is to use the adjusting lath issued with the instrument. The lath is set up at least 200 yards from the instrument. By sighting through the peep sight on the lath, it can be alined parallel to the range finder. The yard scale is set at the infinity mark, and the range finder is focused on the adjusting lath. If the image appears as in figure 68①, the instrument is out of adjustment. It will then be necessary to bring the instrument into adjustment in the manner explained under the known range method. When the instrument is in correct adjustment, the image will appear as in figure 68②.

NOTE.—The lath furnished with each range finder has the same serial number as the range finder. These laths are not interchangeable; therefore, to obtain accurate results, the proper lath must be used.

d. Range finder, 80-centimeter base, M1917 (Bausch and Lomb, azimuth type).—(1) *Description.*—This instrument (see fig. 69) consists of the range finder, type S and type R tripods (see figs. 64 and 65), and carrying cases. No adjusting lath is issued with the azimuth type range finder. This instrument is similar to the roller type range finder, with the following exceptions:

(*a*) There are no open sights attached to the instrument.

(*b*) The yard scale appears directly in the field of vision just below the halving line. This scale runs from 450 to 10,000 yards (see fig. 71). Originally, all azimuth type range finders had the range scale graduated in meters from 400 to 10,000. Practically all of these instruments have been changed to read in yards, the word "yards" being engraved on the eyepiece bracket.

(*c*) There is no range drum knob on the azimuth type range finder. The two images in the field of view are brought

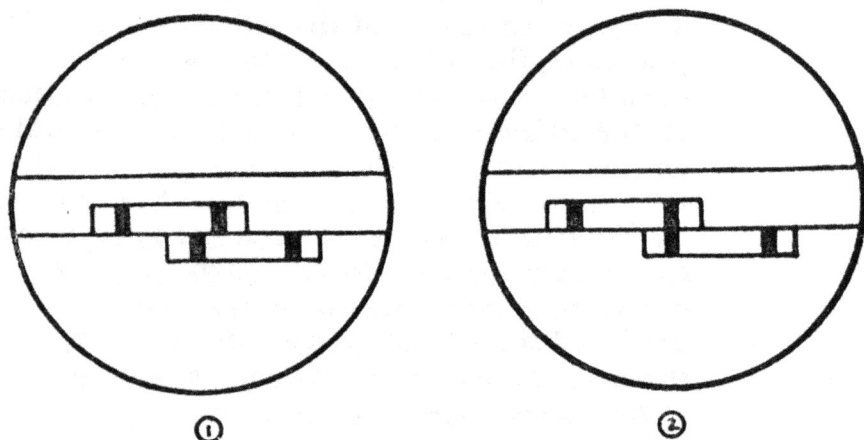

FIGURE 68.—Images, roller type range finder, showing adjusting lath.

into vertical alinement by moving one end of the entire instrument toward or away from the target.

(*d*) The halving adjusting knob is located to the left of the correction wedge shaft. It protrudes from the instrument and is covered by an outer housing which must be turned counterclockwise ¼ turn in order to expose the halving adjusting knob.

(2) *Operation.*—(*a*) Set up the instrument and loosen the type S clamping screw knob until the instrument can be turned easily on its axis.

(*b*) Train the instrument on the target. Focus the eyepiece and bring the lower upright image up to the halving line by means of the elevating knob. By means of the tilting knob, bring the most clearly defined line on the target perpendicular to the halving line. By turning the instrument from side to side about the spindle, bring the two images together until they appear as in figure 71②. Note the reading on the yard scale which appears immediately below the point on the target that has been used to aline the images. (Example: the range to the church steeple in figure 71② is 850 yards.)

(3) *Adjustments.*—Like the roller type range finder, the azimuth type may need frequent adjustment to correct maladjustments resulting from unavoidable shocks and jars incident to use.

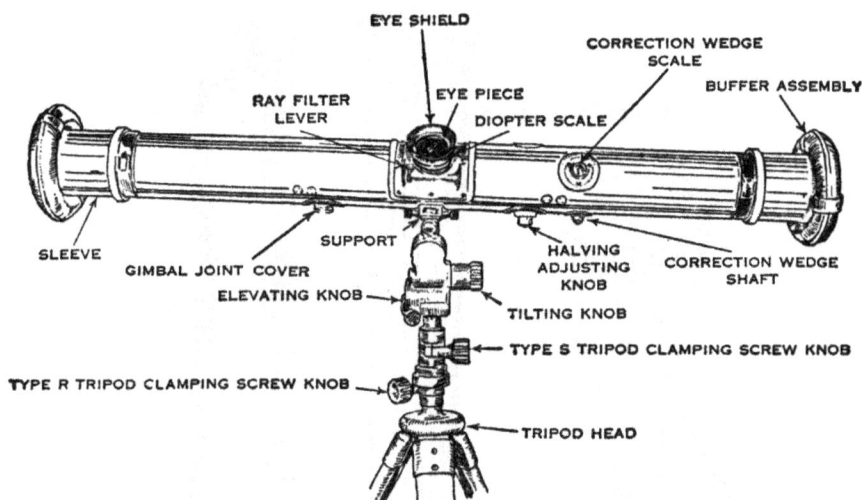

FIGURE 69.—Range finder M1917, 80-centimeter base, azimuth type E.

(a) *Halving adjustment.*—This adjustment is made on the azimuth type range finder exactly as for the roller type range finder.

(b) *Range adjustment.*—Adjustments for range may be made as follows:

1. *Known range method.*—The procedure used in making this adjustment on the azimuth type instrument is the same as that employed with the roller type range finder, except that the selected line on the upright image of the target is lined up opposite the graduation on the yard scale which corresponds to the known range distance to the target. While the correction wedge key is used

to move the inverted figure into correct alinement, every care must be taken to avoid disturbing the instrument. Repeat the process at least
five times, as explained for the roller type range
finder, and set the average reading on the correction wedge scale.

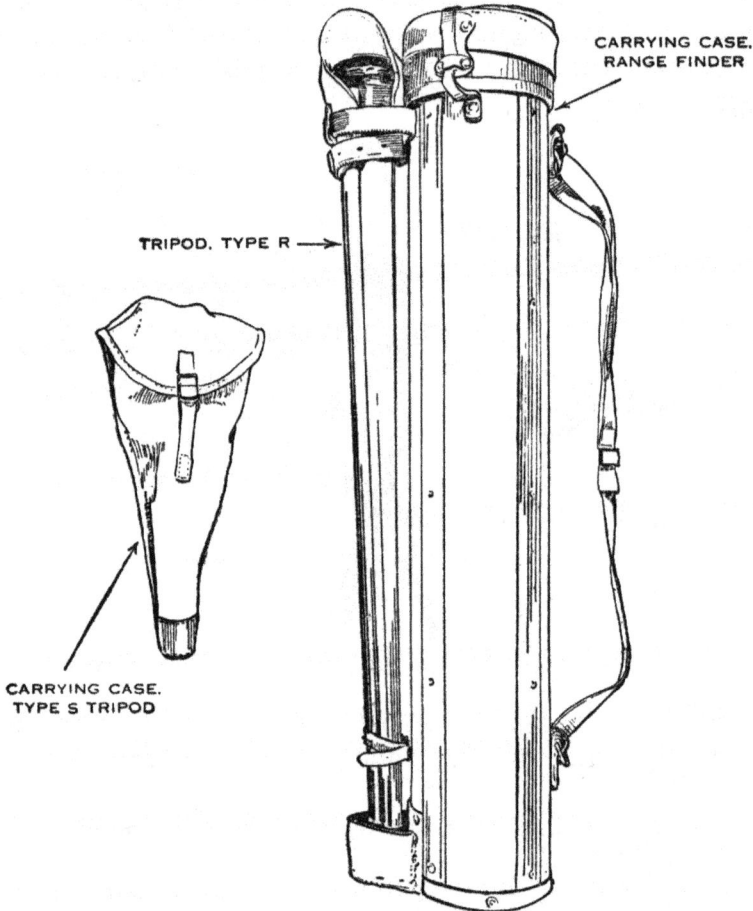

FIGURE 70.—Carrying cases, range finders, roller and azimuth types.

2. *Infinity method.*—The adjusting lath cannot be
used with the azimuth type instrument since the
width between the two lines of vision changes as
the instrument is rotated on its spindle. The
moon, or other targets at an infinite range, may
be used in the same manner as with the roller
type instrument.

(c) *Cautions.*—(1) All unnecessary turning of screws, shafts, and knobs is strictly forbidden. The range finder is a precision instrument; the use of force is prohibited.

(2) In making adjustments on the range finder and in taking ranges, extreme care must be taken to insure the highest degree of accuracy. A very slight error in alining the images in the field of view will be greatly magnified in the reading of the range in yards.

(3) If, when the instrument is properly adjusted, any targets are found in which the two images cannot be made to coincide by the use of the elevating knob, the instrument will have to be sent to the ordnance for repair.

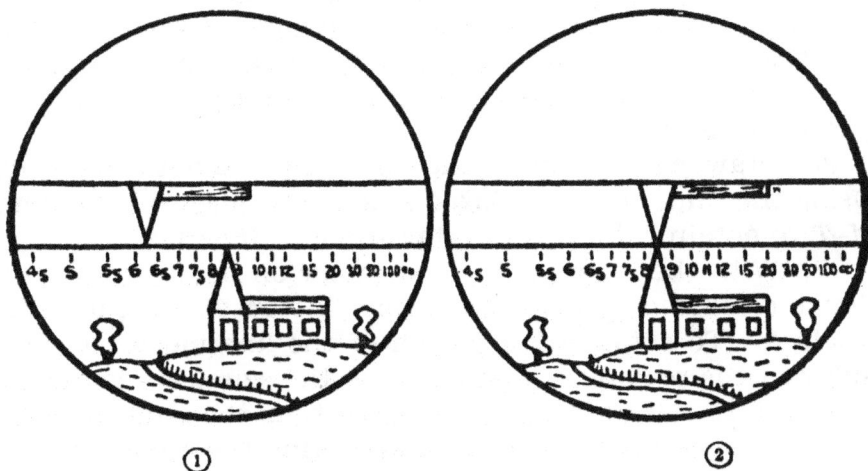

FIGURE 71.—Images, range finder, azimuth type.

SECTION IV

USE OF FIRE CONTROL INSTRUMENTS

■ 122. OBTAINING INITIAL FIRE DATA.—*a. Instrument method.*—It will sometimes be found necessary to select an observation post which will be at a considerable distance to the flank of the line mortar-target. (Par. 143c(1).) When this is the case, the instruments may be employed as follows:

(1) The instruments are set up with the platoon leader or platoon sergeant at the plotting board, the instrument corporal at the aiming circle, and the messenger or other trained private at the range finder.

(2) Draw an arbitrary north–south line on a piece of paper, so located as to facilitate plotting. This line represents the direction of magnetic north.

(3) On this line plot point O at any desired position. This point represents the position of the observer.

(4) Meanwhile the instrument corporal has read the azimuths, observer-mortar, and observer-target, with the aiming circle. These azimuth readings are plotted on the paper. In doing this, the index of the protractor is placed at point O and the diameter line coincident with the line O–M. Draw a ray representing the azimuth to the target and a ray representing the azimuth to the mortar.

(5) Concurrently, ranges to the target and mortar have been read with the range finder. Using any convenient scale, plot the distances to the target and the mortar on the appropriate rays. The positions of the target and the mortar are plotted accordingly.

(6) Draw a line connecting the target and the mortar. Using the same scale employed in step (5), measure the line M–T to obtain the range mortar-target. (See fig. 72.)

(7) With the index of the protractor on point M and the diameter line coincident with the line M–T, measure the angle A. To obtain the azimuth of the line mortar-target, subtract the reading of angle A from the azimuth reading to the mortar. (If the angle A is greater than the azimuth O–M, add 6,400 to the latter before substracting the angle A.)

(8) To obtain the distances from the observation post to the target and the mortar, any suitable method—such as pacing, use of maps or aerial photographs, or estimates—may be used instead of the range finder. The most accurate method available should be employed. The range finder will be the quickest and easiest to use in most situations, and the platoon leader should make early and frequent use of the instrument in order to furnish accurate ranges to key points to his section leaders. This information will assist them in the determination of the initial fire data, assist in obtaining surprise fire, and save time and ammunition.

b. *Aerial photograph method.*—(1) Frequently it is possible to request and receive vertical aerial photographs of a sector or zone of operation with very little delay. These photos contain the data necessary to compute their representative fractions (RF's). On them may be found the focal length of the camera in inches and the height, in feet, at which the photo was taken. For example, a photo may have the following information: V-49-740C-70BS (10-6-42-11:00) (6''-10,000). To obtain the RF, in this instance convert 6'' to ½ foot to get an RF of 1/20,000.

(2) Having determined the RF of a photo, it is necessary to convert the photographic distance to ground distance. When this has been done, it is desirable to construct a graphic

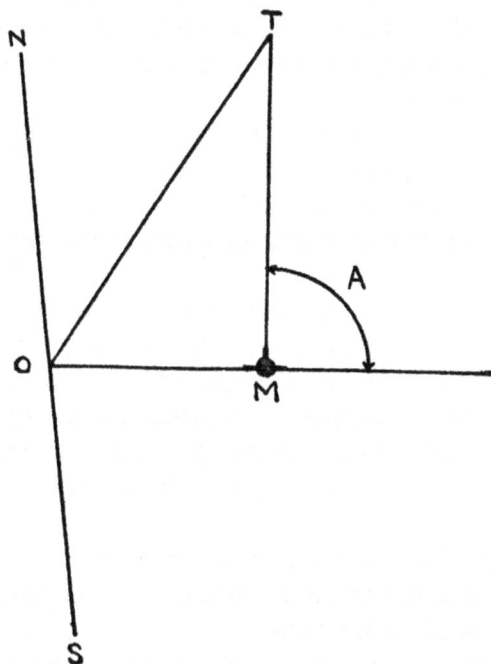

FIGURE 72.—Plotting initial fire data with instruments.

scale in order that ranges and distances may be measured directly without referring to the RF for each requirement.

(3) It is now necessary to consult the photo. If no north-south line has been placed on the photo, the following method will determine direction:

(a) Locate the observer's position accurately on the photo.

(b) Pick out some prominent terrain feature.

(c) By use of a compass or aiming circle, read the magnetic azimuth to this terrain feature.

(*d*) With the index of the protractor on the point which indicates the observer's location, move the protractor until the azimuth of the line, observer position-terrain feature is indicated by its proper reading on the protractor scale. The line established by the diameter line of the protractor will then indicate the magnetic north-south line.

(4) Having established the direction of magnetic north, the range and azimuth of any point on the photo may be read directly by use of the graphic scale and protractor.

c. Use of the photo with observer off line mortar-target.— When the observer is a considerable distance off the line mortar-target, the range and azimuth to the target may be obtained directly from the sector photo by use of the graphic scale and protractor.

d. Map method.—When a fire control map, either topographical or mosaic, is available, fire may be conducted from it in a manner similar to that used with the aerial photo. Maps, other than fire control, are not recommended for this purpose.

e. Adjustments.—(1) In the methods just outlined, it will be necessary, whenever possible, to use data which have been corrected as a result of fire for adjustment on the base point. In order to obtain the most accurate range to new targets, the fraction: $\frac{\text{(adjusted range to base point)}}{\text{(map range to base point)}}$ should be applied.

(2) The adjusted deflection used to register on the base point should be applied as a plus or minus constant on any subsequent azimuth readings.

(3) The corrections referred to are applicable only to targets that are within a range of 3/4 to 4/3 of the range distance to the base point and within a deflection bracket of 300 mils to either side of the base point.

■ 123. OBTAINING FIRE DATA FOR PREARRANGED FIRES.—*a.* Where prearranged fires are being prepared, the instrument corporal should measure the ranges to prominent terrain features to assist squad leaders in determining ranges to assigned target areas. This is particularly advisable when fire cannot be adjusted on base points because of the disposition of friendly troops, or where other aspects of the tactical situation, such as secrecy or surprise, will not permit adjustment of fire.

b. The aiming circle can be employed to determine accurately the azimuths on which mortars are to be laid, and to measure deflections.

CHAPTER 7

FIELD TRAINING

                                                              Paragraphs
SECTION I. General_____ 124–126
        II. Preparatory exercises_____ 127–130
       III. Elementary firing exercises_____ 131–137
        IV. Advanced training exercises_____ 138–143

SECTION I

GENERAL

■ 124. PURPOSE.—The purpose of this phase of training is to instruct leaders in the control of their units under simulated battle conditions and to instruct the individual soldier in the performance of his duties as a member of a fighting team so as to secure the maximum fire efficiency.

■ 125. PLACE IN TRAINING.—Before a unit receives training in firing at field targets, all men should be given instruction in mechanical training, training of the gunner, training for placing the mortar in action, marksmanship, and training of the observer.

■ 126. SCOPE.—Training in firing at field targets includes instruction in the selection and occupation of observation posts and mortar positions, range estimation, the use of cover and concealment, communication between observation posts and mortar positions, ammunition supply, technique of fire, and firing exercises.

SECTION II

PREPARATORY EXERCISES

■ 127. GENERAL.—*a*. Before a unit is given a field training exercise, it should receive preparatory instruction by means of conferences, demonstrations, and practical work, using non-firing exercises. These exercises are valuable because they eliminate to a great degree the problem of safety and allow the troops to give undivided attention to the instruction.

b. Officers who conduct preparatory exercises receive valuable experience. They learn quickly to present and conduct exercises, to judge solutions, and to conduct critiques. They can give their entire attention to these important points since they need not concern themselves with the safety precautions that must be enforced when live ammuniton is used.

c. Each of the following exercises should be conducted as if it were the last phase of training in the use of the weapon before going into combat. For this reason, it is important that each exercise be repeated until every member of the squad becomes highly proficient in all duties within the squad. During this process, every phase of training should come into play. Targets and observation posts should be varied so that initial direction of fire will be obtained by each method, so that all types of fire adjustment will be used, and so that both point targets and area targets will be engaged.

d. All of this is necessary in order to develop that state of proficiency which will insure skillful use of the mortar in combat.

e. Frequently in these exercises it may be desirable to disregard more usual means of communication such as radio, sound-powered telephone, or mesenger in order to provide training in arm-and-hand signaling. Radio and telephone equipment may be ruled out of use by designating them to be "out of order." To provide training in the use of "chain signaling," members of the squad may be stationed at intervals between the observer and the mortar position.

f. Ammunition for this firing will be taken from the combat allowance.

■ 128. Range Determination.—In the firing exercises, time and ammunition are greatly conserved by correct range determination. It is therefore advisable during this phase of instruction to review the methods of range estimation described in paragraph 60. Where tactical considerations indicate, appropriate use is made of the range finder.

■ 129. Selection of Positions.—*a. Mortar position.*—(1) Since a suitable observation post is the dominant factor in the selection of a mortar position, the observation post is located first. The mortar position selected must permit the accomplishment of the assigned mission. There must be a suitable observation post within the range of the available means of communication, as much cover and concealment from ground and aerial observation as possible, and a good route of approach from the rear for ammunition supply. The reverse slope of a hill or ridge usually offers a satisfactory mortar position. Alternate and supplementary positions should also be selected.

(2) These factors are pointed out in a demonstration showing several different positions. The favorable and unfavorable points of each position are discussed.

(3) This should be followed by exercises in which the men are required to select a number of possible mortar positions and to state the reasons for their selection. The advantages and disadvantages of each position are discussed to insure that all of the important factors governing the selection of a mortar position enumerated in *a* above have been considered.

b. Observation posts.—The observer must be able to see the target, or the area in which probable targets may appear, well enough to observe the accuracy and effect of his fire, and he must be able to control the fire of his mortar. If possible, the observation post should be located in the immediate vicinity of the mortar position or approximately on the line mortar–target.

c. Communication.—In order to control the fire of the mortar, the observer must be able to communicate with the personnel at the mortar position. This is done by sound-powered telephone, oral fire orders, arm-and-hand signals, or by radio.

■ 130. USE OF NATURAL COVER AND CONCEALMENT.—*a.* When a mortar can be definitely located by the enemy, either from the ground or air, an attempt will soon be made to put it out of action. It is necessary, therefore, that the crew take advantage of all natural cover and concealment available, both in approaching and in occupying the mortar position.

b. During training in the use of cover and concealment, the unit should be divided into a number of small groups. Two groups should work together as a team—one group selects the observation post and moves the mortar into position while the other group acts as observers. On completion of the exercises, the observers discuss the actions of the men of the group that occupied the positions and point out the errors that were made.

c. When an exercise is finished, the groups change places and another exercise is solved.

d. In training men in the use of cover and concealment, the following points are stressed:

(1) The observer should be concealed from enemy view and if possible should have cover from hostile fire.

(2) Positions should be concealed from enemy view and if possible should have cover from hostile fire.

(3) Shiny articles and sharply contrasting colors will not be worn.

(4) Steel helmets will be camouflaged so as to break the regular curved outline of the helmet.

(5) When crawling into a position in sight of the enemy, move straight toward him. Do not move sideways or zigzag.

(6) When crawling, keep the body well down. Do not let the arms and legs wave around.

(7) Avoid quick or jerky movements.

(8) All paths leading to the position must be carried past it for at least 100 yards in order to confuse air observation.

SECTION III

ELEMENTARY FIRING EXERCISES

■ 131. UNITS TO FIRE.—Each mortar squad and section engages in field firing exercises when local facilities permit.

■ 132. TERRAIN.—*a*. The availability of ground and the considerations for safety determine the selection of terrain for field firing. Where possible, varied ground suitable for the employment of mortar fire should be selected. It is a great advantage from the instructional viewpoint to use ground that is unfamiliar to the unit to be trained.

b. In the absence of other facilities, a known-distance range may be used by arranging the exercises so that they begin *off* the range and require the delivery of fire *on* the range and in a safe direction.

■ 133. TARGETS.—*a*. Targets for mortar firing exercises will be located with respect to the terrain in places corresponding

as nearly as possible to those in which mortar targets may be
expected to be found in combat. (For location of mortar
targets in combat situations, see par. 3d, FM 7–15.)

b. A simple tactical situation should be given with each
exercise in order that the exercise may approach combat
conditions as much as possible. For example, the location
of our own front lines on the ground should be given, and
some of the targets selected should be so close to our own
front lines that the creeping method of adjustment is clearly
indicated.

c. Artificial targets such as panels and silhouettes should
be used only when the terrain suitable for firing is not varied
enough to furnish reference points or natural terrain features. The silhouettes are most effective in establishing
fragmentation density when they are constructed and set up
as shown in figure 73①.

d. Targets may be outlined for scoring purposes in the
following manner:

(1) *Point target* (fig. 73②).—Three of the intersecting silhouette targets (fig. 73①) are placed within a circle of 1-yard
radius. An outer circle with a 25-yard radius is then outlined
by stakes driven at intervals along its circumference. The
stakes should be invisible to the observer. Any rounds fall-
ing within the large circle are scored as hits.

(2) *Target area for traversing fire* (fig. 74).—A rectangle
150 by 75 yards may be marked off by driving stakes at the
corners. This area may be divided into three segments, each
segment 50 yards wide. The center of either of the end
segments may be given as one end of a 100-yard traversing
target. Then the target may be scored for hits and for distribution of the hits. The target may be designated to an
observer as follows:

Front.

Reference: Lone tree on crest of ridge.

Left 150.

Target: Enemy group 50 yards beyond crest, extending
left 100 yards.

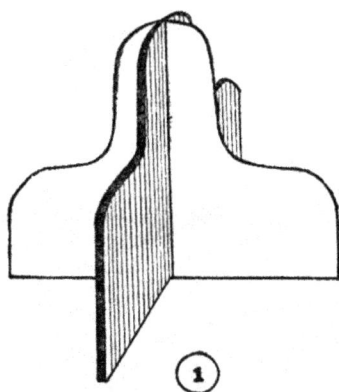

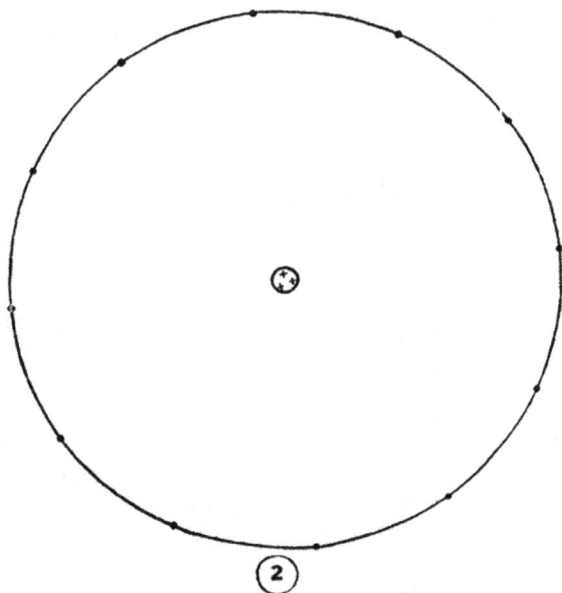

FIGURE 73.—Silhouette and scoring circle for point target.

Where the terrain permits, the target area should be defiladed from the observer in order to train him in engaging targets of that nature. The long axis of the target should extend

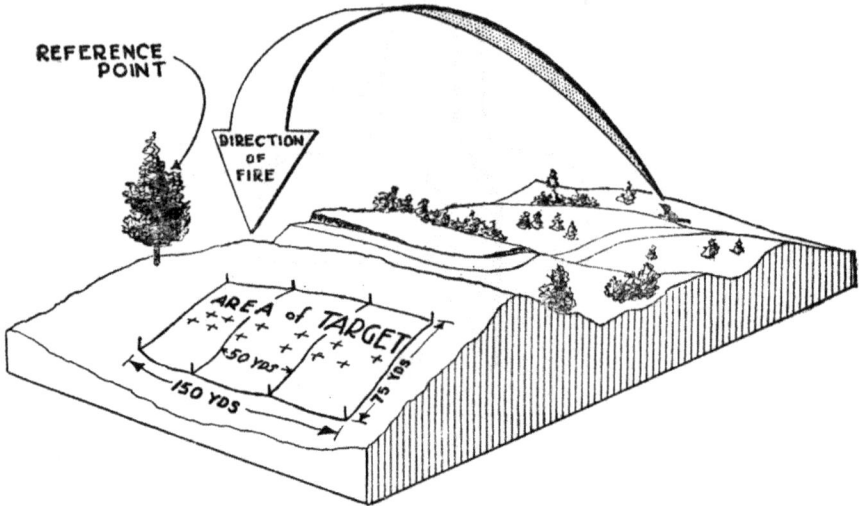

FIGURE 74.—Organization of traversing target area.

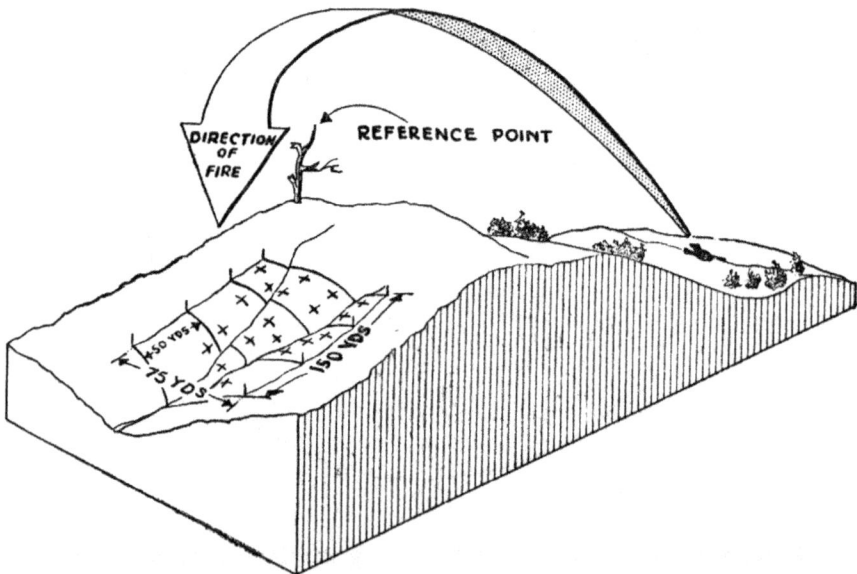

FIGURE 75.—Organization of searching target area.

generally perpendicular to the line of fire. Intersecting sil- houettes scattered throughout the target area will indicate the effect of the bursts.

(3) *Target area for searching fire* (fig. 75).—The target is laid out, designated, and scored in the same manner as for the traversing target, except that the long axis should extend generally along the direction of fire.

(4) *Target area for traversing and searching fire* (fig. 76).—The square 150 by 150 yards may be marked by driving stakes at the corners. The exact point of adjustment should be inside any designated corner and 25 yards from each of the adjacent sides (see point *P* in fig. 76). The rounds

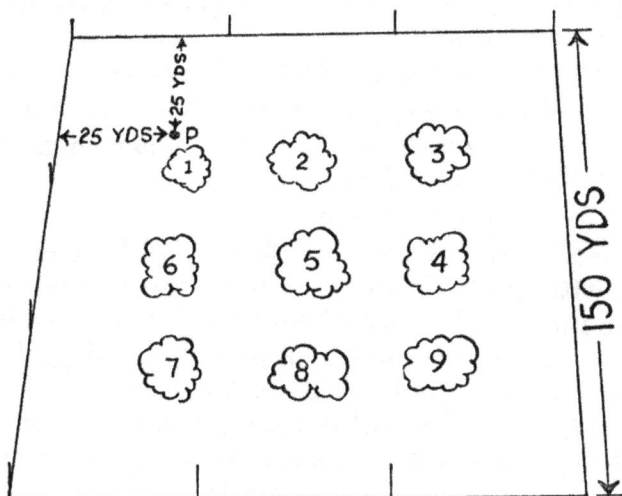

FIGURE 76.—Organization of traversing and searching target area.

should fall generally as indicated in the figure. Each burst in the area is scored as a hit.

■ 134. SAFETY.—The individual safety measures to be observed when firing combat ammunition will be those contained in paragraph 53. Prior to any firing exercise, the officer in charge will establish, by reference to definite objects on the terrain, lateral safety limits and will inform all leaders concerned as to the limits of the area. The officer will determine the maximum range and propelling charge needed to conduct the exercise. He will then direct that *as soon as a bundle of ammunition is opened,* all propellent increments in excess of those established as the maximum requirement for the exercise will be removed from the six rounds and laid aside. At the conclusion of the exercise, the officer will require all personnel to segregate for disposal any parts of the ammunition, particularly the propellent increments, before leaving the area. Discarded powder increments will be burned in the area. When duds occur, they will be located, marked, and reported to the range officer at the conclusion of the exercise.

■ 135. FIRING EXERCISE NO.. 1.—*a. Purpose.*—(1) *For the squad leaders.*—Practice in the control of the fire of their units by fire orders in order to engage properly the various types of mortar targets.

(2) *For the men.*—The application of factors which govern the selection of positions, the use of individual cover and concealment, operation of available communication, ammunition supply, and technique of fire.

b. Unit.—One mortar squad.

c. Situation.—The squad is deployed under cover. A sector of fire with safety limits and the general location for the mortar are indicated to the squad leader, who is now directed to place his mortar in a suitable location and to fire on any targets that are designated within the sector.

d. Method.—(1) The squad leader locates his observation post, definitely locates the mortar position, issues the necessary order for placing the mortar in position, and obtains initial direction to a base (reference) point in the sector of fire. When the squad leader has reached his observation post, a target is indicated. He issues his fire order, opens fire on the target, and adjusts his fire. Fire for effect is not a part of these exercises. As soon as fire for adjustment has been accomplished, the positions of the crew are changed, a new target is selected, and the exercise is repeated.

(2) With regard to the manner of adjusting fire, targets will be of two types:

(*a*) Those requiring adjustment by the creeping method to avoid endangering friendly troops.

(*b*) Those upon which adjustment may be made by the bracketing method without endangering friendly troops. Initially, each type of target is presented in a separate exercise. When the men have completed a simple exercise engaging each type of target, exercises are conducted of a similar type in which one or more surprise targets appear so that it is necessary to shift the fire of the squad to engage them.

■ 136. FIRING EXERCISE No. 2.—*a. Purpose.*—(1) *For the leaders.*—Practice in the selection of observation posts, firing positions, conducting the unit forward by covered routes, issuing orders for the occupation of the initial firing positions, fire orders, and fire control.

(2) *For the men.*—Movement into and occupation of initial firing positions with the minimum of exposure and application of the fundamentals of fire technique.

b. Unit.—One mortar section.

c. Situation.—The section is in approach march formation, halted under cover.

d. Method.—(1) The platoon leader indicates the initial targets to the section leader. The section leader then determines the general location of each squad observation post and the general location of each firing position in the designated area. (For selection of observation posts, see par. 199 and 207, FM 7–15.) He brings his section to a point near the mortar positions, where he issues his orders to the squad leaders. These orders will normally be concerning targets, the general location of observation posts, and the general location for the mortars. The squad leaders then reconnoiter for exact locations of observation posts and firing positions, lead their squads to the selected positions, and order the men into action. From this point on, the problem is conducted in a manner similar to that described in paragraph 135.

(2) The targets selected for this exercise should be of such a nature that distributed fire is clearly indicated. To permit the engagement of several types of targets through repetition of the exercise, fire for effect should not be delivered. However, for instructional purposes, the squad leaders should require their crews to "dry run" the necessary manipulations of the traversing handwheel or elevating crank.

■ 137. Critique.—At the completion of all exercises, the instructor should conduct a critique covering the following points:

a. Reconnaissance by section leader and squad leaders.

b. Actions and orders of section and squad leaders in getting their units on the ground without delay.

c. Suitability of observation posts.

d. Suitability of firing positions.

e. Suitability of alternate positions.

f. Use of cover and concealment.

g. Fire action of unit (all elements of technique used in delivering fire).

Section IV

ADVANCED TRAINING EXERCISES

■ 138. General.—The purpose of this section is to present type problems which will furnish varied field training. The exercises are presented in such a manner as to provide guidance to the instructor in their preparation and to give a solution as to the mortar technique which may be used. Herein, technique is of primary importance. The exercises may be fitted to any tactical situations desired. Combat ammunition should be fired whenever available. Exercises may be conducted in miniature by using the M68 training projectile.

■ 139. Firing in Woods.—*a. Purpose.*—The purpose of this exercise is to teach the technique required to provide close continuous support of a rifle unit by a section of mortars firing in dense woods.

b. First phase.—The forward elements of the supported infantry units are shown by broken line A–B (fig. 77). The direction of attack is indicated by the arrow. The disposition of the mortars is as shown by the mortar symbols. The observer is at an observation post in the front line (△ No. 1). A hostile machine gun (point target) has been located near *T*.

c. A solution.—(1) The section leader instructs the mortar crews to select positions and set up the mortars where they will have mask clearance (trees may have to be cut to accomplish this). The initial direction of fire is established by the most expeditious means (usually the azimuth method in woods). When the mortars are mounted, the ammunition bearers (Nos. 4, 5, and 6) return to the weapon carrier or company ammunition point for an additional load of shells. As an early advance of the troops with a corresponding advance of the OP is anticipated, observation from the vicin-

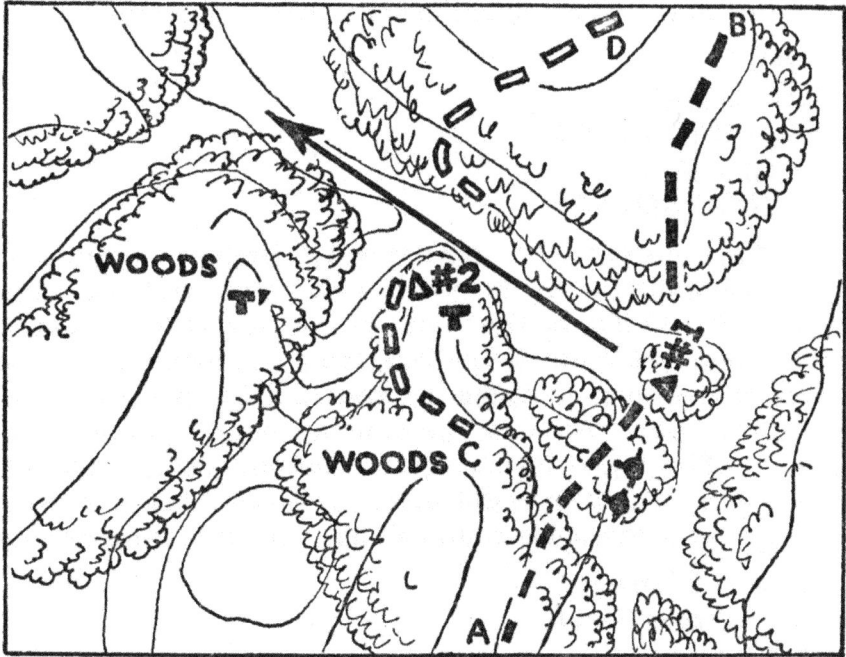

FIGURE 77.—Firing in woods.

ity of the newly selected mortar positions will soon become ineffective. Therefore, the section leader decides to control at least one of the mortars personally, and both of them if the situation permits. He estimates the range to the enemy machine gun to be 350 yards. As only one point target is to be engaged, but one mortar is employed initially (No. 1). Observation, because of the density of the woods, will be difficult; therefore, the section leader directs the squad leader of the second mortar squad to assist him in observing and sensing. They so place themselves, in separate locations, that each can observe the target. They are near enough to each other to communicate by voice or signals. They endeavor to place themselves so that one of them can observe to the right and the other to the left of the target in order to insure that the first rounds fired for adjustment will be visible to one of them. Both observers are practically in the front line. The section leader then commands:

NO. 1
HE, LIGHT
SEARCH 375–325
CHARGE 0
THREE ROUNDS

(2) No. 1 mortar fires, and the squad leader of the second squad, from his place of observation, notes that the three rounds have fallen to the right of the target (the section leader could not observe the hits from his location). The section leader now instructs his assistant to give the subsequent fire order (each is carrying a sound-powered telephone). The squad leader sensed the bursts to be 30 mils to the right; the first round over, the second round correct for range, and the third round short. He therefore orders:

LEFT TWO TURNS
DOWN THREE TURNS
THREE ROUNDS

(3) No. 1 mortar fires. The section leader is able to see these bursts and notes that they have neutralized the target. (If the target is not hit, it is now easy for the section leader to correct the laying and fire three more rounds.) His mission completed, he commands:

NO. 1
MARK BASE DEFLECTION

He directs that two additional aiming stakes be placed at 150-mil intervals to the left and right of the base stake. For future reference, he notes the azimuth in which No. 1 mortar has fired.

d. Second phase.—The forward elements of the rifle units

are moving forward.   The section leader and the squad leader, each with a sound-powered telephone (or radio), move forward parallel to each other until they reach the vicinity of the point marked *T* on the sketch (fig. 77) where the hostile machine gun previously was located.   The forward elements of the supported unit are now as shown by the broken line *C–D*.   Again an OP (△ No. 2) is established in the front line.   A new target appears at *T'*.

  e. A solution.—The section leader estimates the distance from his OP (△ #2) to *T'* to be 275 yards. He estimates that he is about 75 yards forward of *T*, placing him 425 yards ahead of the mortar. Adding his two estimates (275 and 425 yards), he obtains 700 yards. He has noted, however, that *T'* is off to one side of the line mortar–*T* and the range to *T'* would therefore be less than 700 yards. He estimates that this correction would indicate a range of 650 yards. He recalls that No. 1 mortar required an azimuth of 4,550 mils to hit the target at *T*. He now reads the azimuth from his OP (△ #2) to *T'* and finds it to be 3,800 mils. He subtracts 3,800 from 4,550 and obtains 750 mils. This is his change in deflection as calculated from the OP. To give the proper amount of shift to the mortar, he multiplies 750 mils by the factor *OT/MT*. The factor 275/650 is approximately $\frac{2}{5}$ and so, taking $\frac{2}{5}$ of 750 mils, a deflection of 300 mils is obtained. He now issues the following order (It will be recalled that additional aiming stakes were set out at his direction):

NO. 1
HE, LIGHT
ZERO
SECOND LEFT STAKE
SEARCH 675–625
CHARGE 1
THREE ROUNDS

The section leader and the leader of the second squad observe as before.   The section leader observes that the first round hits the target.   He now orders:

DOWN FOUR TURNS
THREE ROUNDS

without waiting for the remaining two rounds to fall. He then inquires by means of the telephone whether or not the ammunition bearers have returned. When they are back, he orders the No. 2 mortar and all its ammunition to be displaced forward to the vicinity of *T*. The squad leader of the second squad selects a position for the mortar with reference to his OP and mask clearance for the mortar, and guides it into position as he returns to recover the wire of the sound-powered telephone. After the No. 2 mortar is

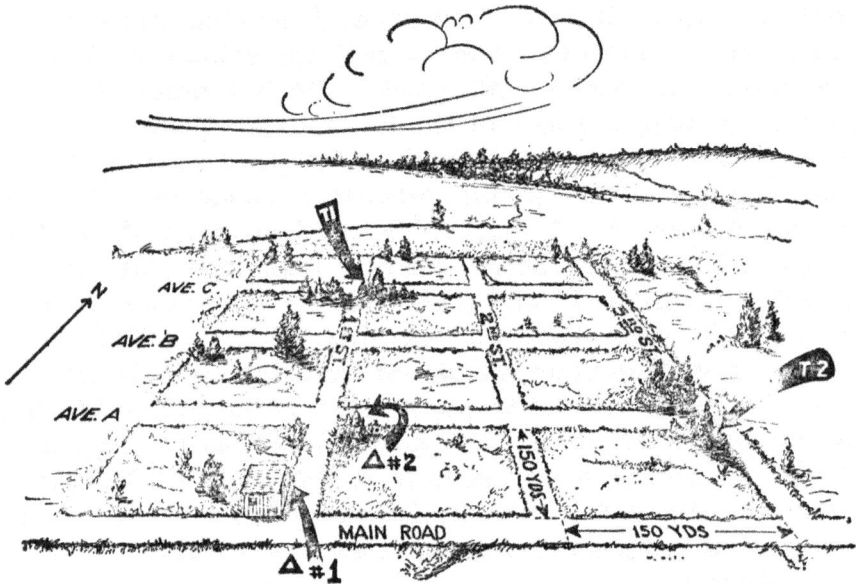

FIGURE 78.—Lay-out of training area for firing in villages.

displaced to its new position, the No. 1 mortar may be ordered out of action and brought forward.

f. Comments.—(1) If radio communication is available and the difficulties of ammunition supply are excessive, one or both mortars may be left in the rear while the observer moves forward at a greater distance. (In this instance, the distances were governed by the length of the sound-powered telephone line.) Whether the distances which the observer moves are great or small, as long as the observer remains with the troops in the front lines, communication with his mortar crews being available, the mortars will continue to give support within the limit of their effective range.

(2) If the observer moves a considereable distance ahead of his mortar position without firing, it may become necessary to fire a smoke shell, which will serve as a spotting round, because of difficulty of observing HE, light, in dense woods. If, however, the new OP is near a target on which fire has already been adjusted, it becomes an easy matter for the observer to adjust on any other target within several hundred yards of that OP.

■ 140. FIRING IN VILLAGES OR TOWNS.—*a. Purpose.*—The purpose of this exercise is to teach the technique of controlling mortar fire in areas containing buildings or similar masks.

b. An arrangement of target areas.—A portion of the firing range is laid out with cleared areas representing village streets, as shown in figure 78. Targets may be so placed with respect to existing trees or high brush that misses will be difficult to sense, as would be the case in a town with buildings on either side of the streets. A small mock-up of a building to mask the mortar and to furnish an OP will add realism.

c. First phase.—Assume that the forward elements of a rifle unit are near △ #1 prepared to attack up First Street. A mortar squad is under cover near the building, with the mortar dismounted. The leader of the rifle unit which is being supported requests fire on a hostile machine gun behind a street barricade at T1 (fig. 78). The squad leader, in his reconnaissance, has estimated that the length of a city block in this part of the town is about 150 yards.

d. A solution.—The mortar squad leader selects an OP near the buildings, reads the azimuth to T1, and orders the mortar mounted on that azimuth in a covered position, defiladed behind a building. He estimates the range to the target to be 450 and gives the following fire order:

HE, LIGHT

ZERO.

STAKE.

SEARCH 475–425.

CHARGE 0.

THREE ROUNDS.

He notes in his firing table that in charge zero (Charge 1 may have to be used in order to obtain mask clearance) the elevation for 475 is 59° (disregarding fractions) and the elevation for 425 is 63°, making a difference of 4°. Therefore, the gunner will have to elevate the mortar four turns between rounds. Assume that these rounds fall 15 mils to the right of the target and that the second round is observed to be correct for range. The squad leader now orders:

LEFT ONE TURN.

DOWN FOUR TURNS.

THREE ROUNDS.

These rounds should cover the target effectively. He then orders **MARK BASE DEFLECTION** and sends Nos. 4, 5, and 6 back to the company ammunition point for additional ammunition.

e. Second phase.—Assume that $T1$ (fig. 78) has been neutralized, friendly riflemen have reached the corner of First Street and Avenue A, and that the squad leader, having moved to △ No. 2 with his sound-powered telephone, has communication with the mortar position. The rifle unit commander asks for fire on another street barricade located at $T2$ (fig. 78).

f. A solution.—The squad leader realizes that to engage the new target, he will have to shift more than 900 mils, thus necessitating movement of the base plate. To save time that would be lost in computing the azimuth of the line mortar–$T2$ and in returning his compass to the mortar position for the squad to use in mounting the mortar on the computed azimuth, he orders No. 1 by means of the telephone to mount the mortar facing right on a line parallel to Main Road and to place out three additional aiming stakes to the left. To obtain the value of the angle $T2$–mortar–east on Main Road, he uses the mil formula. For simplicity, he substitutes distances in city blocks for distances in yards. That is, in the formula $M = \dfrac{1,000W}{R}$ he substitutes one block for W and two blocks for R and finds that M equals one-half of 1,000 or 500 mils. The squad leader is informed by means of the telephone that the mortar has been mounted as ordered and that the three additional stakes have been placed at 150-mil intervals to the left of the new aiming stake. Judging from the city blocks, he estimates the range to be 325 yards and orders:

    HE, LIGHT
    LEFT 50
    THIRD LEFT STAKE
    SEARCH 350–300
    CHARGE 0
    THREE ROUNDS

The squad leader senses these rounds, as he did in the first instance, orders the necessary adjustment to be made in turns, and requires the fire for effect to be delivered in the same manner as in the first phase. He marks the base deflection and determines whether or not the ammunition bearers have returned to the mortar.

g. *Comments.*—(1) As far as observation is concerned, the technique of firing the mortar in towns is similar to that of firing in woods. The observers must be in the front lines to be certain of the location of the leading elements. The mortar must be moved frequently to cover targets at short ranges, with correspondingly wide angles of shift, and to keep up with the observer. In this connection, suitable mortar positions may be hard to find where streets are paved. Mattresses taken from houses and jammed against a curbstone will help solve the problem. Marks on a wall or pavement will serve as a substitute for aiming stakes.

(2) This type of problem, as presented, is only workable in an area where streets are parallel and blocks are square. Where streets are curved and have irregular blocks, the compass will be needed for orientation, as in woods. It must be borne in mind that the compass tends to be unreliable in towns because of the frequent proximity of iron and electricity. Each problem may have several solutions. The most obvious and simple method should be employed.

(3) With ranges less than 500 yards (those most used in street fighting), use of the mil formula is frequently necessary, since the deflection-conversion table gives no data for those ranges. Because of the large fractions which result

when values in yards are substituted for the symbols W and R, many mortar men consider this formula impracticable unless paper and pencil and the necessary time to use them are available. It should be borne in mind that substitution of any linear unit of measure may be made and will give correct results, provided the same unit of measure is used for W and R. When the mortar is fired at targets located at close ranges, a relatively large error in deflection computed for the initial fire order will result in only a minor error in the result of the strike. Hence, approximations may be used more freely than at longer ranges. An example to illustrate the point in question may be helpful. An observer at a range of 300 yards estimates the amount of the required shift (W) to engage a new target to be about one-third of the range. He makes this deduction by comparing the two distances on the ground. Therefore, for his initial shift to the new target, he takes one-third of 1,000 or 335 (to the nearest 5) mils. Suppose, because of his hasty estimation, the observer incorporates what appears to be an enormous error, 80 mils. Even with this error, at this range, he will miss the target by less than 25 yards, keeping the target within effective bursting radius. As the ranges become greater, more accuracy will be required. However, the observer may use any convenient unit of measure in order to simplify the mental calculation of M in the mil formula, provided he applies this same unit to W and to R alike.

(4) The use of a 50-yard ladder for adjustment is suitable in the problem presented in (f) above. As the range is short, corrections may be readily made by observation and sensing. Besides making adjustment simple, this method should result in at least one—perhaps all—of the rounds producing effective fire as they fall at 25-yard intervals. Until the base plate is settled, the gunner must relevel his longitudinal as well as his cross-level bubbles between rounds. If the base plate does not become settled by the time the third round is fired, as sometimes happens in firing in charge zero, the gunner should inform the observer of this fact before fire for effect is ordered. The squad leader can then increase his range one or two turns when firing for effect and in this way overcome the effects of further settling of the base plate.

■ 141. THE MORTAR SECTION IN SUPPORT OF A RIFLE COMPANY IN THE ATTACK.—*a. Purpose.*—The purpose of this exercise is to train the mortar section in the technique of delivering fire in support of a rifle company in the attack.

b. First phase.—Prepare a situation along the following lines: The rifle company is reorganizing on one of its attack objectives preparatory to resuming the attack, and the mortar section has displaced to new firing positions in rear of the company (fig. 79). The section leader, staying as close to the rifle company commander as control of his section and its fire will permit, has given instructions to his section for its reorganization and is now en route to establish contact with the rifle company commander. Prior to his departure, he has directed the senior squad leader to be prepared to engage, on his own initiative, any surprise target which may require the fire of one or both of his mortars.

c. A solution.—The senior squad leader selects an observation post as near the mortars as practicable from which he can observe the area in which targets most probably will appear. (If there were two such areas, he would also select a supplementary observation post and station an observer there.) He then establishes initial direction for the mortars, by the most convenient method, on any clearly defined reference point near the center of the area in which mortar fire most probably will be required. (If there were an actual target already located in the area, he would establish initial direction on that target.) He next mounts the mortars so that they are laid in the direction he has established. (If he has a supplementary observation post, he may lay one mortar initially in the direction established from that observation post.) In this problem, he checks his ammunition and assures himself that he has enough to fire at each mortar position. He checks the camouflage and cover at the positions and leaves the other squad leader in charge of the mortars while he takes his position at the observation post.

d. Second phase.—The rifle company commander outlines to the section leader the company plan of attack. He points out the company's next objective (fig. 79①) and tells the section leader to be prepared to engage suitable targets on the ridge *A–B,* particularly any heavy weapons which might

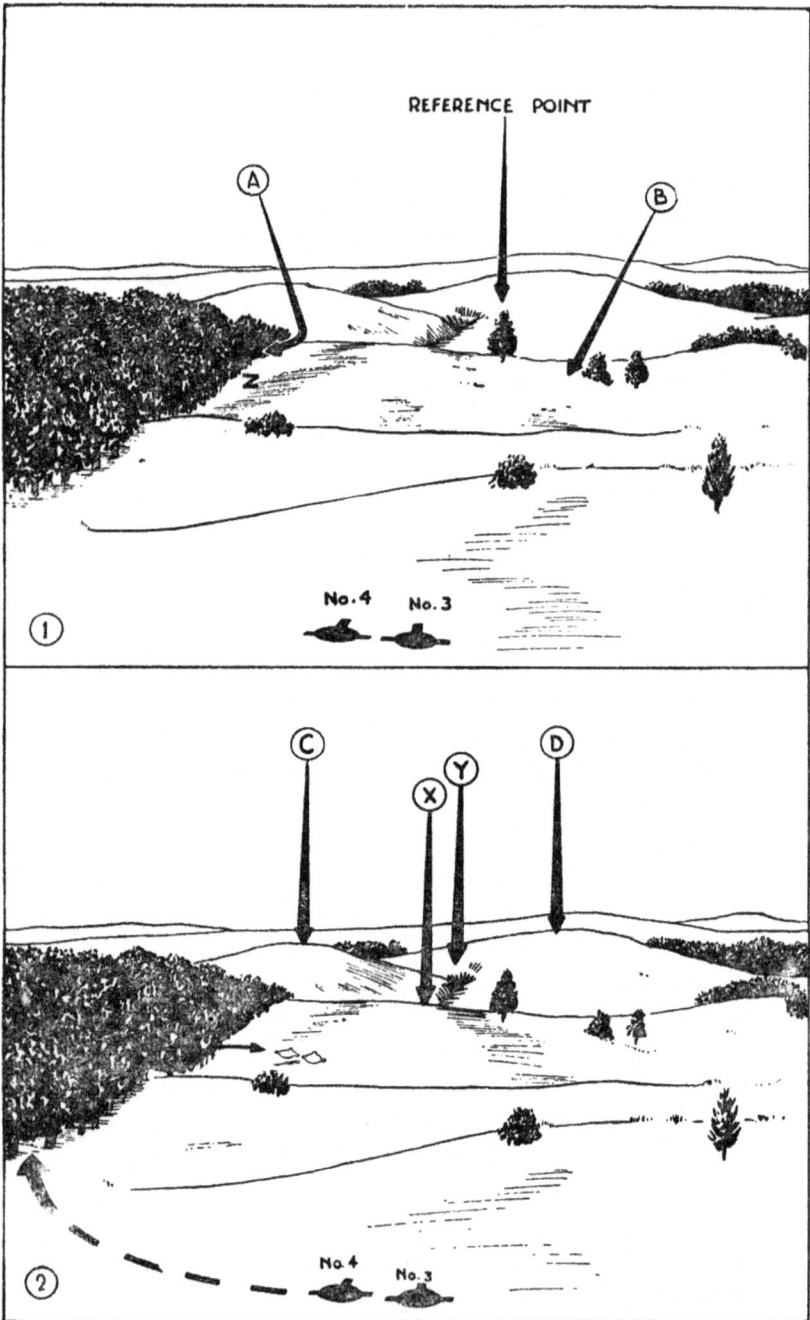

FIGURE 79.—Figures to accompany exercise: mortar section in support of a rifle company.

interfere with the continued attack of the company. He informs the section leader that his company will attack in 30 minutes and desires the section leader or his representative to remain near him during the attack.

e. A solution.—The section leader makes a brief reconnaissance, selects an initial observation post near the company command post from which he can observe the area over which the rifle company is to attack, and returns to the mortar positions. There, he learns that the squad leader in charge of the mortar positions has obtained direction on a reference point, a large tree near the center of the rifle company's next objective (fig. 79). Since this point is satisfactory for future needs, there is no need to change it. He explains any changes in the situation to the squad leaders. The section leader and both squad leaders estimate the range to the reference point and take the average of their estimates (in order to obtain the most accurate initial data possible). Assume that they estimate this range to be 800 yards. For future reference, the section leader paces the distance between mortars (assumed to be 40 yards). He then leaves one squad leader in charge of both mortars at the mortar position and takes the other squad leader forward with him to his observation post in the vicinity of the rifle company commander. Each carries a sound-powered telephone and sufficient wire to reach the next objective. In laying their wires, they endeavor to place the two lines so far apart that a single shell cannot break both wires. Before going forward, the section leader assures himself that one telephone is connected at each mortar and that there will be some one listening on each telephone at all times. This will insure that fire from both mortars will be instantly available at all times. After his arrival at the forward observation post which is near the rifle company commander, he informs the latter that either he or the squad leader with him will be available to bring mortar fire on designated targets. He instructs the squad leader to remain at such distance from him that both cannot become casualties from one shell. He directs the squad leader to observe the area near the company objective to the left of the reference point, to select in that area probable locations for targets, and to compute the initial fire data for each of these locations in order that fire may be delivered with minimum delay when needed. He computes similar data for target locations to the right of the reference point, and each makes a simple range card containing the data prepared by both. (This card may be a memorandum in a notebook referring to four or five probable targets. A sample notation would be: "Bushes near fence—No. 3–R95–base stake–800." This would give the observer data required to fire his initial round at that target.)

f. Third phase.—Assume that the attack progresses with slight resistance until the left leading elements reach the vicinity of point Z (see fig. 79①), where they are subjected to machine-gun fire from *B*. The company commander requests 81-mm mortar fire on *B* from the section leader, who is following him forward, reeling out wire as he goes. (The squad leader assisting the section leader is also advancing with his wire and is within signalling distance of the company commander and the section leader.)

g. A solution.—Assume that fire data for the target selected is not recorded on the section leader's range card. (For training in the use of the mil formula, deny the section leader his deflection-conversion table.) The section leader estimates the target to be 75 yards to the right of the tree (reference point) on which his mortars now are laid and estimates the range mortar-target to be 800 yards. Mentally he multiplies 1,000/800 (5/4) x 75, and finds that an angular shift of 95 mils is necessary to shift from the tree to the target. He telephones the order:

    NO. 3
    HE, LIGHT
    RIGHT 95
    BASE STAKE
    800
    ONE ROUND

He continues with subsequent fire orders, adjusts on the target, and fires for effect, using only the No. 3 mortar. After completion of fire for effect, he directs that this target be used as the base point (for, having adjusted fire thereon, it is more accurately located than the tree originally used as a reference). He directs that the mortars be paralleled.

with No. 3 as base mortar. To accomplish this, the squad leader left in charge of the mortars looks at the deflection setting on the sight of No. 3 mortar in order to obtain the final angle through which that mortar was shifted when registering on target *B*. Assume this angle to be 100 mils. He then gives the command to No. 3: MARK BASE DEFLECTION. He is now ready to compute the angle of shift which will be necessary in order to parallel No. 4 with No. 3. This angle is measured from the tree as reference point. He knows the distance between mortars to be 40 yards. He reasons that, since No. 4 mortar is still laid on the tree, to make it parallel to No. 3 it will have to shift so that it will be laid on a point 40 yards to the left of *B*. He notes the range used to fire on *B* for effect. Assume it is 800 yards. Glancing at his deflection-conversion table, he notes that an angular width of 40 yards at a range of 800 is 50 mils. Since the No. 3 mortar shifted 100 mils from the tree to target *B*, he need only shift the No. 4 mortar 100 minus 50 mils, or 50 mils, to parallel the mortars. Hence, he orders: NO. 4, RIGHT 50, and has the mortar mark base deflection. When this has been completed and additional aiming stakes are moved, the squad leader at the mortar positions informs both the section leader and the squad leader assisting him as to how the mortars are laid, so that they may change their range cards.

h. Fourth phase.—Assume that the rifle company captures the ridge *A–B* and is reorganizing preparatory to attacking the high ground *C–D* (fig. 79②). The section leader and one squad leader are forward with the rifle company commander. The section leader learns at this time that one weapon carrier is at the mortar position and that the other weapon carrier has been sent for ammunition but has not returned.

i. A solution.—The section leader takes advantage of this reorganization and orders No. 4 mortar displaced forward at once by hand along a covered route to the left of the zone of action (fig. 79②). He leaves the No. 3 mortar (its base plate is settled) in position to cover the reorganization of the rifle company. After the No. 4 mortar arrives with its ammunition, its squad leader selects an observation post and sets up the mortar, obtaining initial direction to a convenient reference point on the next ridge to the front.

The section leader then orders the No. 3 mortar brought forward on the carrier with the remaining ammunition. He directs that one private from the third squad remain at the old position to guide the other weapon carrier forward upon its return. He sends two privates back with the reels to pick up the wire. Upon the arrival of the No. 3 mortar at the new position, it is set up and paralleled with No. 4 by mounting it on the same azimuth. Sufficient ammunition is placed at each mortar position for current needs.

j. Fifth phase.—Assume that the attack on the crest *C–D* (fig. 79②) has been resumed and that the section leader and the squad leader who is assisting him are forward with the rifle company commander. The latter points out to the section leader the draw, **X–Y**, the visible portion of which extends about 200 yards into the enemy position. The rifle company commander indicates that the leading elements of the rifle company are held up by fire of automatic weapons which are generally located along the sides of the draw. Our forward elements are about 250 yards north of the ridge *A–B* (fig. 79①), and are unable to advance. The company commander calls for immediate fire down the length of the draw in order to neutralize the fire of the automatic weapons located there. (To conserve ammunition, simulate fire with one mortar, but actually fire with the other.)

k. A solution.—The section leader has No. 3 mortar adjust by the creeping method, enabling him to lay on the mouth of the draw located at *X*. (No. 4 mortar follows this procedure without firing. Thus, No. 3 adjusts, No. 4 is always parallel to No. 3.) Suppose No. 3 adjusts on this point with a range of 650 and that the mortars are 80 yards apart. The section leader wishes to search 650–750 with the right mortar and 750–850 with the left in order to cover the draw (simulating fire with the left mortar). (Deny the section leader the use of the deflection-conversion table.) To shift No. 4 mortar 80 yards to the right at a range of 750, he computes the angle by means of the mil formula. He reasons that since 1000 is $\frac{4}{3}$ of 750, he must shift the No. 4 mortar (right) $\frac{4}{3}$ x 80, or 105 mils. Therefore, he orders (a subsequent fire order, since he has been adjusting):

NO. 4

RIGHT 105

NO. 3, SEARCH 650—750

NO. 4, SEARCH 750—850

NO. 3

THREE ROUNDS.

l. Comments.—(1) It is necessary only to parallel the mortars when the use of fire by section can be foreseen. A method of paralleling them when the range to the target (or a reference point) is known was shown in phase three (*f* above).

(2) Although in the majority of cases the use of the deflection-conversion table is simpler than that of the mil formula, cases will occur where the fraction $1,000W/R$ can be readily simplified mentally, and the final result obtained in less time than would be normally consumed in referring to the table. Another reason familiarity with the mil formula and its use may be necessary is that a deflection-conversion table may not be available.

(3) The use of two observers is stressed for these reasons: With only one observer, the support of the entire mortar section becomes ineffective should the observer become a casualty; and in the event that individual mortars are required to engage separate targets simultaneously, one of the two observers can control each mortar. As two lines of communication are needed for this, the two wires have been laid. (Also, two wires double the chance of maintaining communication.)

(4) When mortars are laid on a reference point, a base stake and additional aiming stakes may be placed out, even though no firing is done for registration. These will serve to simplify the execution of fires on targets located more than 150 mils from the reference point.

(5) Most of the close-support fire in the attack will be adjusted of necessity by the creeping method. Delivery of fires on targets which are 200 or 300 yards in front of the leading elements of friendly troops requires that the mortars be as near the front line as possible. While firing at closer ranges, the dispersion is not only kept to a minimum but also the possibility of incurring errors in range estimation

is greatly reduced. While no fixed rule is laid down for the maximum range at which fires may be placed on targets which are located within ranges of from 200 to 300 yards ahead of the leading troop elements, field experience has indicated that such fires should be undertaken only at ranges of less than 1,200 yards. Even then, the rifle company commander will feel more confident if he knows the observer to be well qualified and that the observer is available to him near the front lines, where the fall of the shell can be clearly observed and the location of the leading elements of friendly troops accurately determined. The training of mortar observers in the technique of such fires should be conducted in conjunction with the training of rifle units they may have to support in combat. In this way mutual confidence and teamwork will be developed.

■ 142. Continuous Support From an Initial Position for Attacking Troops.—*a. Purpose.*—The purpose of this exercise is to provide training in furnishing close mortar support when for some reason the mortars cannot closely follow the advancing units. This exercise provides training for firing at medium and long ranges; also, for training of an advanced observer using radio communication. The exercise as presented may be broken down into a progressive series of smaller exercises.

b. Arrangement of target area.—A scoring circle for a point target (fig. 73) is placed in defilade at T–1 (fig. 80); a scoring area for a traversing target (fig. 74) is placed at T–2; a scoring area for a searching target (fig. 75) is placed at T–3; and a scoring area for a traversing and searching target (fig. 76) is placed at T–4.

c. First phase.—It is assumed that two sections, while affording close support to the attacking rifle units, have just crossed a stream. Their ammunition supply is limited to the section load. A third section, with an ample supply of ammunition, has been left on the near bank and is prepared to fire on targets designated by the platoon leader. The No. 1 mortar (fig. 80) actually fires; No. 2 mortar is in position 50 yards to the left (not shown) where it simulates fire for purposes of training. All of the smoke ammunition initially

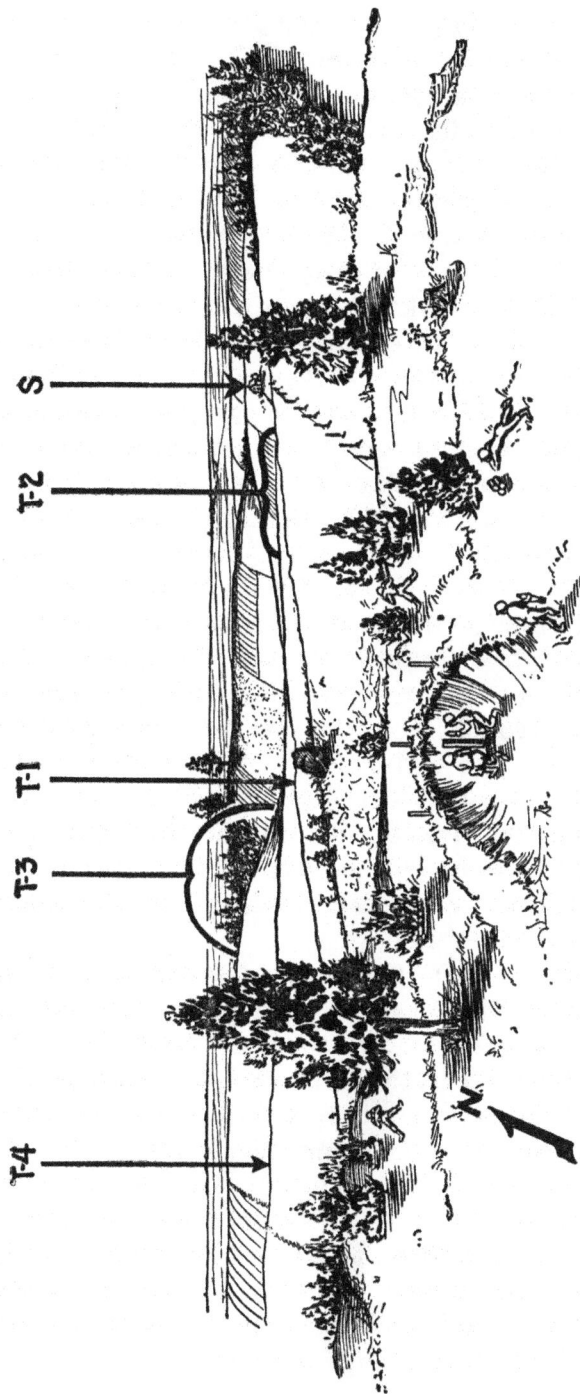

FIGURE 80.—Continuous support from an initial position for advancing infantry.

carried by the other two sections has been dumped near the positions, downwind, under cover. The battalion commander has assigned several radios SCR–536 to the heavy weapons company—one is with the mortar platoon leader and one is with this mortar section. All men are familiar with the situation except for information as to the location of the targets. The instrument corporal, before going forward with the platoon leader, set up the range finder, determined the range to prominent landmarks on each ridge in the zone of action, and passed on that information to the section leader. The platoon leader, in a fragmentary attack order issued before his departure, included primary and alternate observation posts and firing position areas. He indicated the initial target to the section leader with instructions to open fire as follows: "To your front, range 1,200, reference: large rock on ridge at head of draw, left three zero, target: machine gun concealed in draw (see T–1, fig. 80). Open fire at 0815. Use rapid adjustment, knock out the gun, then be prepared to switch to targets of opportunity as they appear. I am going to follow the leading rifle echelon, which is now about 150 yards to the front. My route will be generally along that row of trees on the right front. Keep a man on your radio so that I can get your fire when I need it. It is now 0701." Before leaving the section, the platoon leader noted the general line No. 1 mortar-base point (since No. 1 is the base mortar) and observes terrain features in extension of that line for future reference.

   d. A solution.—(1) The section leader assigns sectors of fire, squad observation posts, and firing positions areas, and directs both squad leaders to select their OPs, their exact mortar positions, to establish initial direction of fire on T–1 (fig. 80) individually, and to mount their mortars. When this is done, each squad leader selects alternate OPs and at least two alternate firing positions in the areas assigned, directs digging of slit trenches, and supervises camouflage of his position. In addition to computing fire data to his initial target, the section leader computes and records data to such other possible target or locations as time permits. Just before 0815, the section leader orders:

SECTION
HE, LIGHT
ZERO
STAKE
63 DEGREES
CHARGE 2
NO. 1
UPON COMMAND

Then, at 0815:

ONE ROUND

Immediately after firing this round, the gunner of mortar No. 1 replaces his sight, re-levels his longitudinal level bubble, cross-levels *without* re-laying on his stake, and again removes the sight. He does not replace the sight until after the next two rounds for adjustment have been fired. To save time, he cross-levels with the bubble in the yoke.

(2) Assume that the first round is on line for deflection and is a fairly near short. The observer decides to use the equivalent of a 100-yard bracket (he is adjusting with a modified ladder for, although his base plate was not settled, his orders were to adjust rapidly). He orders:

SECTION
DOWN THREE TURNS
NO. 1 WITHOUT COMMAND
ONE ROUND

Both gunners depress three turns and cross-level. Only No. 1 mortar fires. Immediately after that round leaves the muzzle, the observer orders:

SECTION
DOWN THREE TURNS
NO. 1
ONE ROUND

Both gunners depress three turns and cross-level. Only No. 1 mortar fires. Both of No. 1's rounds are in the air at once, a few seconds apart. Assume that they hit 15 mils to the right, the second on the near edge of the draw and the third on the far edge of the draw. The observer orders:

SECTION

LEFT ONE TURN

UP ONE AND ONE-HALF TURNS

NO. 1

THREE ROUNDS

Both gunners make the changes ordered. Only No. 1 mortar fires. The gunner cross-elevels between each round. All three should land squarely on the target.

NOTE: For scoring purposes, time may be taken between the first and last rounds to leave the muzzle. The maximum time for full credit should be 1½ minutes. The second squad, which is included in this exercise for the purpose of training in the technique of section firing, does not fire. If the No. 2 mortar were to register, it should be possible to adjust with a 50-yard bracket, since it has followed the changes for adjustment which No. 1 mortar required. However, if No. 2 fires, No. 1 cannot be scored for hits in the target areas.

After completion of the mission, the section leader, in order to parallel the mortars, commands:

NO. 2

LEFT 40

He then orders: SECTION, MARK BASE DEFLECTION.

NOTE: Since both mortars were directed at the base point, and since the mortars are 50 yards apart, it is necessary to shift the No. 2 mortar so that it will be directed at a point 50 yards to the left of the base point so that it will be parallel to the base mortar. Consulting the deflection-conversion table, the section leader finds that a shift of 50 yards at a range of approximately 1,200 yards amounts to 40 mils.

(3) After this is done, gunners place out additional aiming stakes, following required procedure. The section leader then directs the squad leader of the first squad to level his longitudinal level by use of the elevation micrometer knob only, without moving the mortar, and to announce the reading of the corresponding elevation at which fire for effect was delivered. Assume that the squad leader reports this reading to be 61°. The section leader consults his firing table and finds that for Charge 2 the range corresponding to that reading is 1,225. He makes a note of

that range for use in case he wishes to fire on that target again.

e. Second phase.—To designate the next target, the officer in charge of firing sets up an aiming circle with the index line of the reticle laid on the left extremity of the traversing target T–2 (fig. 80) as drawn in the figure. He calls the section leader to the instrument to look through the eyepiece and points out the exact flank of the target to him. He then tells the section leader, "Imagine you see the muzzle blast of a line of hostile automatic weapons firing from partial defilade behind the crest of that ridge, the left flank at the point just indicated to you, extending right 115 mils. You also see the leading elements of your own troops attacking up the ridge about 300 yards this side of the crest. Take necessary action." (This action should correspond with that taken in combat.)

f. A solution.—The section leader, assisted by the notes covering key ranges which were determined by the instrument corporal and by such fire data as he has already computed, estimates the range to the ridge to be 900. He reads the angle between the base point and the left flank of T–2 (fig. 80) with his binocular (assume he finds this reading to be 100 mils) and decides to adjust by the creeping method and to cover the target by using traversing fire. He directs the squad leader of the first squad to position his traversing screw nut near the right of the traversing screw so as to leave space on the screw to traverse to the right (the nut must be several turns away from the extreme right so that the gunner can adjust for deflection). He then issues the following order:

NO. 1
HE, LIGHT
RIGHT 100
BASE STAKE
66°
CHARGE 2
ONE ROUND

(The 66° were read from the firing table, being the elevation necessary to engage a target at a range of 1,100 yards when firing in Charge 2 zone.) From his firing table, he finds that

the elevation for a range of 900 yards firing in Charge 2 is 71°
(disregarding fractions).   The difference between 66 and 71
is 5, so, as soon as the first round is fired, he immediately
orders UP FIVE TURNS and awaits the fall of the first round.
Assume that it falls on the forward slope of the next ridge
beyond the target so that the observer is sure that it is over
between 100 and 200 yards (since tentatively he has just
decreased his range 100 yards by coming up five turns, he
does not consider it safe to fire at the present elevation of
the mortar until he is sure that the preceding round is at
least 100 yards over).   He senses the round as being 20 mils
to the right and orders:

LEFT ONE AND ONE-HALF TURNS
1 ROUND

Immediately after that round is fired, he prepares to creep
50 yards nearer the target on his next round (provided the
round just fired falls at least 50 yards beyond the crest);
to accomplish this, he orders a tentative change in elevation
UP TWO AND ONE-HALF TURNS.   Assume that the round now in
the air falls out of sight in the draw beyond the crest and
that after a few seconds he sees the dust and smoke of the
strike as it rises at a point estimated to be a good 50 yards
beyond the crest.   He orders ONE ROUND, and immediately
after the round is fired, orders UP ONE TURN.   With this last
tentative change on the mortar, which is the equivalent of
approximately 25 yards, he intends to fire his next round in
the event the round now in the air registers at least 25
yards beyond the target.   However, let us assume that the
round strikes just beyond the crest, where the machine guns
are located.   The observer senses the round to be correct for
range and deflection.   He therefore revokes this tentative
change in elevation and fires for effect by ordering:

DOWN 1 TURN
TRAVERSE RIGHT 4 TURNS
THREE ROUNDS

After the gunner has covered the target, he waits for a reasonable length of time to give the observer an opportunity
to decide whether or not the target is to be covered again

from the opposite direction. Receiving no word, he centers his traversing screw and lays on his base stake ready to fire a new mission.

g. Comments.—(1) Since a change of UP FIVE TURNS will cause a 100-yard decrease from the range at which the initial round was fired, if the initial round falls less than 100 yards over the target, a second round fired (after the change has been placed on the mortar) will fall short of the target. The latter must not happen. Therefore, when the initial round falls less than 100 yards over the target, one of two adjustments must be made, depending on the location of the strike with reference to the target. These adjustments are:

(*a*) If the round is definitely more than 50 yards over, reduce the tentative change (UP FIVE TURNS, in this case) by one-half; then fire the second round. By this procedure, the net change in range between the initial round and the second round is 50 yards; hence the second round should also be over. To accomplish this, the observer orders:

DOWN TWO AND ONE-HALF TURNS.

ONE ROUND

(*b*) If the initial round is less than 50 yards over, the observer removes the entire tentative change made after firing the initial round. He fires a confirming round at the original elevation by ordering:

DOWN FIVE TURNS

ONE ROUND

If this round falls in the same place as the first, he creeps back one or two turns and fires for effect.

(2) Experience has shown that the instance discussed in *g*(1)(*a*) above occurs infrequently; and that the instance discussed in *g*(1)(*b*) above occurs almost never.

h. Third phase.—Assume that target T–2 (fig. 80) has been neutralized and that forward elements of our rifle troops have reached the crest just short of T–2. The section leader receives a message from the platoon leader at 0900 directing him to place a smoke screen extending from the house at *S* (fig. 80) to the east 250 yards, in order to assist in an attack on the ridge northeast of the house. Starting at 0915, the screen is to be maintained for 10 minutes. There is an 8-mile wind from the west; the weather is partly cloudy and cool.

i. A solution.—The section leader, aided by his notes on key ranges secured from the instrument corporal, estimates the range to *S* to be 1,400 yards. He decides to use only the first squad in placing the smoke. He orders the squad leader to register on the house with HE, light, ammunition, using an initial range of 1,400, and to have his squad secure and prepare 35 rounds of smoke ammunition for Charge 3. He then consults his deflection-conversion table and discovers that at 1,400 yards the 250-yard front measures 180 mils across. He recalls that the traversing screw allows approximately 180 mils traverse and realizes that, at this range, he can cover the entire target without moving the bipod or placing out special stakes. He calculates from the deflection-conversion table that he can drop rounds at 50-yard intervals at a range of 1,400 yards by using two and one-half turns on the traversing handwheel for each interval, or that he can drop them 35 yards apart with one and one-half turns. He directs the squad leader to lay his mortar on the house at *S* with the traversing screw nut positioned to the extreme right of the traversing screw. He then orders:

NO. 1
SMOKE
1,400 (ASSUMED TO BE CORRECT RANGE)
UPON COMMAND

Then at 0915, he orders:

ONE ROUND

(This is a subsequent fire order, since the squad leader has adjusted initially with HE, light.) He observes this round to strike near *S* and notes that the smoke drifts slowly to the right in the desired direction. He decides, after studying the drift of the smoke from this round, to build up the screen by dropping rounds at 35-yard intervals and to drop two in the same spot, initially, on the left half of the target. He, therefore, orders (without command):

(1) TWO ROUNDS (they are fired)
RIGHT ONE AND ONE-HALF TURNS

(2) TWO ROUNDS (they are fired)
RIGHT ONE AND ONE-HALF TURNS
(3) TWO ROUNDS (they are fired)
RIGHT ONE AND ONE-HALF TURNS
(4) TWO ROUNDS (they are fired)
RIGHT ONE AND ONE-HALF TURNS
(5) TWO ROUNDS (they are fired)
RIGHT ONE AND ONE-HALF TURNS
(6) ONE ROUND (it is fired)
RIGHT ONE AND ONE-HALF TURNS
(7) ONE ROUND (it is fired)
RIGHT ONE AND ONE-HALF TURNS
(8) ONE ROUND (it is fired)
RIGHT ONE AND ONE-HALF TURNS.
(9) ONE ROUND (it is fired)
LEFT TWELVE TURNS.

He then observes the screen for gaps which he must fill at once. (Assume that he sees none. If he did, he would measure the mils from the left flank of the target to the gap, convert mils to turns, traverse to the gap, fire one or more rounds, then return to the starting point.) Assume that after a lapse of 3 or 4 minutes, the smoke on the left of the target begins to thin. He decides to maintain the screen by dropping smoke at 50-yard intervals and orders:

(1) TWO ROUNDS (they are fired)
RIGHT TWO AND ONE-HALF TURNS.
(2) TWO ROUNDS (they are fired)
RIGHT TWO AND ONE-HALF TURNS
(3) TWO ROUNDS (they are fired)
RIGHT TWO AND ONE-HALF TURNS
(4) ONE ROUND (it is fired)
RIGHT TWO AND ONE-HALF TURNS
(5) ONE ROUND (it is fired)
LEFT TEN TURNS.

(He need not drop any smoke on the extreme right after building up the screen as, in this case, the wind from the left will blow smoke over the right of the target.) After a lapse of 3 or 4 minutes, if the section leader notes that the smoke is beginning to thin out on the left, he repeats coverage of the target at 50-yard intervals. These should last the full 10 minutes.

j. Comments.—(1) Had the range been appreciably less than 1,400 yards, it would have been necessary for the squad leader to put out special stakes—one on the left flank of the target (the aiming stake used to adjust on the target will serve for that purpose, with the necessary deflection remaining on the sight) and one placed in line with the collimator of the sight after traversing right the entire length of the screw (par. 118). With good observation, it is more convenient to fire smoke missions on wide targets at ranges greater than 1,400 yards, since it eliminates need for special stakes and because the entire target can be covered without moving the legs of the bipod.

(2) Actually, while only 35 rounds of smoke were brought to the mortar and not all of those were used, more might well have been brought, if available. It is believed that 30 rounds will usually be more than ample for a mission of this type—this belief being based upon experience of actual firing—but, since wind and weather are unpredictable, it is well to pool as much ammunition as can be collected in case unforeseen weather conditions develop.

k. Fourth phase.—Assume that on the right of the sector of fire, leading elements of friendly troops are seen (through the binocular) advancing through the smoke; but that on the left they have been stopped on a line about 500 yards in front of the mortar. At this time, the platoon leader has just arrived at a point near the house at *S*. He knows the location of the base point of the base squad (first squad) and knows the range to it. The umpire now shows him the target T–4 (fig. 80), which is invisible to the section leader with the mortars, and tells him that this target represents enemy troops preparing to counterattack. He is directed to take whatever action he would take in combat. (*Exception:* Fire with the No. 1 mortar only will be executed; the other mortar will simulate fire.)

l. A solution.—Measuring the distance with his eye, the platoon leader estimates the target to be 400 yards to the left of the line mortar-base point. He estimates the range mortar-target to be 300 yards greater than that to the base

point, or about 1,500 yards. At this range, he finds from his
deflection-conversion table that to shift 400 yards to the left
of the base point he will have to shift 265 mils. He knows
that there are additional aiming stakes set out at 150-mil
intervals at the mortar, so he directs the section leader, by
means of his radio (*m* (2) below): "Chicago, this is Boston.
Read back. Base mortar. HE, light, Left 115, Left stake,
1,500, one round. Adjusting on right near corner, will observe. Over." The message is repeated back. The section
leader then issues the necessary orders so that only No. 1
will fire, while No. 2 follows all other commands. When the
round is fired, he calls back, "Boston, this is Chicago. On
the way. Out." Assume that the platoon leader senses the
round to be 150 yards (therefore, 100 mils) to the right and
a fairly near short. He directs the section leader, "Chicago,
this is Boston. Read back. Left 100–1,600, one round.
Over." He continues to sense by this method (used when
observer is off the line mortar-target more than one-tenth
the distance observer-target) until the base mortar is regis-
tered. He then directs the section leader to deliver traversing
and searching fire on an area extending 100 yards to the
rear and 200 yards to the left and stipulates that fire on
the left half of the target will be simulated. The section
leader computes the necessary shift for the left mortar as
follows: It is now located 50 yards to the left and on line
with No. 1. It is parallel to No. 1; hence it is now directed
at a point 50 yards to the left of the right near corner of
the target. He wishes to direct it at a point 100 yards to the
left of the right near corner, or 50 yards farther to the left
than it is now. To do this at 1,500 yards (the approximate
range to the target), he consults his deflection-conversion
table and finds that he must shift the No. 2 mortar left 35.
He then orders (assuming that fire was adjusted at 1,550
for both mortars):

NO. 2, LEFT 35
SECTION
SEARCH 1,550–1650
TRAVERSE LEFT TWO AND ONE-HALF TURNS
NO. 1
NINE ROUNDS

m. Comments.—(1) Were this problem actually fired with both mortars, it would be correct to register also the No. 2 mortar for range, bringing it in after establishing the initial bracket with the No. 1 mortar. At the command SECTION RIGHT, they would be fired from right to left at 5-second intervals in order to permit the observer to sense both rounds.

(2) When speaking over the radio (radio-telephone), alphabetical and numerical designations (for example AB, AC, or AB1, AB2), the names of towns (cities), or inanimate objects may be used as code names of individuals or stations (FM 24–9). If it is desired to have the message repeated, the body of the message is prefaced with "Read back" and is followed by the word "Over." Otherwise, the message is concluded with the word "Out."

n. Fifth phase.—Assume that the platoon leader has followed closely behind the advance elements, keeping to the high ground wherever possible so as to observe. As he proceeds, he paces the distance so that he always knows with fair accuracy how far to his rear he has left the target which was neutralized by his mortar section earlier in the attack. Knowing the range from the mortar to the neutralized target, he can, by the simple process of adding this range to the distance paced, estimate closely the distance between himself and the mortar. Assume that the leading elements of the left rifle company have reached a line 800 yards short of the battalion objective—the ridge with two tall trees on it (fig. 80) in the left center of the zone of action—and that they are about 1,700 yards ahead of the mortar positions. The umpire directs the platoon leader to place heavy mortar fire on enemy machine guns located generally in the draw at T–3. The platoon leader, from his position near the house, can see the draw, but is unable to see the mortar positions. He has, however, projected the line base mortar–base point along the ground and has noted terrain features near the extension of this line.

o. A solution.—The platoon leader directs his instrument corporal to read the range with the range finder from his present location to the mouth of the draw. By adding this range to the distance from his present position to the mortar, he estimates the range mortar–target to be 2,400 yards. He now estimates the lateral distance from the mouth of the draw to the nearest point on the extension of the line No. 1 mortar–base point to be 500 yards. A shift of 500 yards to the left at 2,400 yards range he finds to be 210 mils (see deflection-conversion table). He orders, CHICAGO FROM BOSTON, READ BACK, BASE MORTAR, HE, LIGHT, LEFT 60, LEFT STAKE, 2,400, 1 ROUND, OVER. This round is fired at the section leader's order. Assume it to be well over. The next round is similarly ordered at 2,200, using a 200-yard bracket. Suppose the base mortar to be finally adjusted on the mouth of the draw at 2,275. The platoon leader orders, CHICAGO FROM BOSTON, READ BACK, NO. 2, RIGHT 20; NO. 1, 2,275; NO. 2, 2,325; NO. 1, 5 ROUNDS, OVER. (Note that the mortars are both laid on the draw with ranges differing by 50 yards. With normal dispersion at this range, the two mortars fired together would cover the draw to a depth of 100 yards.) The platoon leader observes the fall of these rounds. Then, in order to place a similar concentration farther up the draw, he orders each mortar to increase its range by 100 yards and repeats the five rounds. This process is continued until the draw has been completely covered.

p. Comments.—(1) Additional ammunition was available to the section discussed in this problem, while the supply of the other two sections not under consideration was restricted to normal loads. Therefore, missions requiring large expenditures of ammunition were given to this section.

(2) In the last solution, it appears on the surface that searching fire is indicated, since the platoon leader has to cover the draw leading away from him. However, it is believed that the solution given is more suitable in this case for two reasons. First, *heavy* fire was ordered to be placed in the draw. Unless searching fire were repeated, it would result in fewer rounds being fired and so would be less effective than the method used. Second, searching fire as normally delivered tends to be inaccurate for range when fired with Charge 4, 5, or 6 because with these heavy charges the base plate continues to settle. To prevent errors in range when firing searching fire with those charges, it is necessary to level the longitudinal level for each round by means of the ele-

vating crank and then to make the necessary change in turns of the elevating crank before firing the next round. This will result in accurate fire but will cause the fire for effect to be delivered more slowly. The method used in this problem takes advantage of the normal longitudinal dispersion of the weapon at long ranges to obtain the desired distribution of fire in depth.

(3) This problem might be continued to a logical conclusion by adding other phases. For example, after the capture of the battalion objective, the mortar section might be able to assist in protecting it against counterattack by firing at targets beyond the objective, provided the latter were less than 3,000 yards forward of the mortars. In covering area targets 100 by 100 yards at this range, better results will be obtained by using alternate traverse instead of traversing and searching fire, since with the latter method of fire, it is impossible for the gunner to level the longitudinal bubble before each round is fired.

(4) The problem might be developed further by introducing a situation requiring the mortars to change to alternate positions between missions. Finally, the action might be concluded by assuming that the remainder of the platoon had arrived in positions close behind the battalion objective, that its ammunition supply had been replenished, and that the platoon leader had ordered this section to move forward as a unit.

(5) A suggested method of scoring is to give a credit of one point for every hit in a target area up to the number of rounds authorized to be fired for effect at that target. In segmented area targets (T–2 and T–4, fig. 80), allow one additional point for distribution if all segments are hit. When time is a factor, the score should be cut 10 percent for every additional minute consumed over the maximum time allowed, and one additional point should be credited for every minute saved below the minimum time, *in the event the target is hit.*

■ 143. PREPARATION OF PLANNED FIRES ON THE DEFENSE AND THE EXECUTION OF NIGHT FIRING.—*a. Purpose.*—The purpose of this problem is to teach technique necessary in the preparation of planned fires and in night firing.

b. Arrangement of target area.—Targets are selected with regard to the terrain and to missions normally assigned mortars in the defense (sec. IV, ch. 4). A scoring area for a traversing target (fig. 74) is outlined about the primary target. For the purpose of training in the various methods of computing fire data, targets are chosen so that it becomes necessary for unit leaders to use every means at their disposal in order to compute data for the various targets. In this problem it will be assumed that each of the targets listed below entails the difficulties of observation as indicated (see fig. 81):

Primary Target (M3)—Its outline can be vaguely determined from either the squad or section observation post, but its exact outline cannot be discerned from either position.

Target No. 6—Clearly visible and easy to observe.

Target No. 7—Clearly visible but difficult to sense.

Target No. 13—Visible only from battalion observation post or on an aerial photomap.

Target No. 14—Visible only from battalion observation post and from high ground in forward area.

Targets No. 17 and 18—Too far in rear of main line of resistance to be engaged from any but supplementary positions.

c. First phase.—(1) Assume that our troops are organizing a prepared defensive position. The platoon leader, at the section observation post, issues fragmentary orders to the section leader (see par. 180, FM 7–15) which include the following:

(*a*) Information that the enemy is about 5 hours away and is being delayed by security elements of our own forces.

(*b*) The exact location of working parties in front of our main line of resistance.

(*c*) Primary and alternate firing position areas for the section.

(*d*) Location of observation posts for each squad.

(*e*) Sectors of fire for each squad and their primary and secondary targets (pointed out on the ground and on a photomap).

(*f*) Supplementary firing position areas and supplementary missions (targets 17 and 18, for the right squad).

(*g*) Instructions that the signal for firing on the primary target should be a white star parachute fired from the battalion observation post (pointing).

(*h*) Instructions to emplace the mortar, to dig fox holes, and to camouflage the primary position.

(*i*) Information that one and one-half units of fire (150 rounds for each mortar) would shortly arrive and be dumped on the position with instructions that ammunition already on hand (previously dumped) be "dug in" at the primary positions and that additional ammunition, upon arrival, be dug in near the alternate and supplementary positions. (Ammunition in excess of that actually to be fired may be represented by billets of wood.)

(2) The section leader notes the location of his targets on a sketch. The platoon leader directs the section leader to compute data for all his targets, warns the squad leaders of the presence of working parties to the front, and authorizes the section leader to have each of the squads adjust fire on a target, by the creeping method, located at a range of at least 1,000 to 1,500 yards. He then informs the section leader that he will return later with the instrument corporal to assist him by furnishing a photomap and instrument data for some of the targets. The platoon leader then departs.

(3) Assume that the section leader has his squad leaders with him at the section observation post. Pursuant to the orders of the platoon leader, he indicates the location of those targets shown on sketch which can also be pointed out on the ground. He points out on the ground the squad sectors of fire, the squad observation posts, and the general areas for the mortar positions. He directs each squad leader to select his exact mortar position. (He will supervise this selection and, in the event a poor choice is made, he will instruct the squad leader as to the position he is to occupy.) He directs the squad leaders to conduct their squads to their primary positions, to dig mortar emplacements and fox holes, to dig in their ammunition, to camouflage, and to prepare their range cards. He tells them that he will compute data to certain targets and directs them to compute data for

the remainder. Assume that the squad leader of the right squad is unable to register on the primary target because of the activities of a wire party in that area. The section leader directs this squad leader to register on target No. 6 (after warning forward elements in that vicinity), thus enabling him to determine the data necessary for his range card.

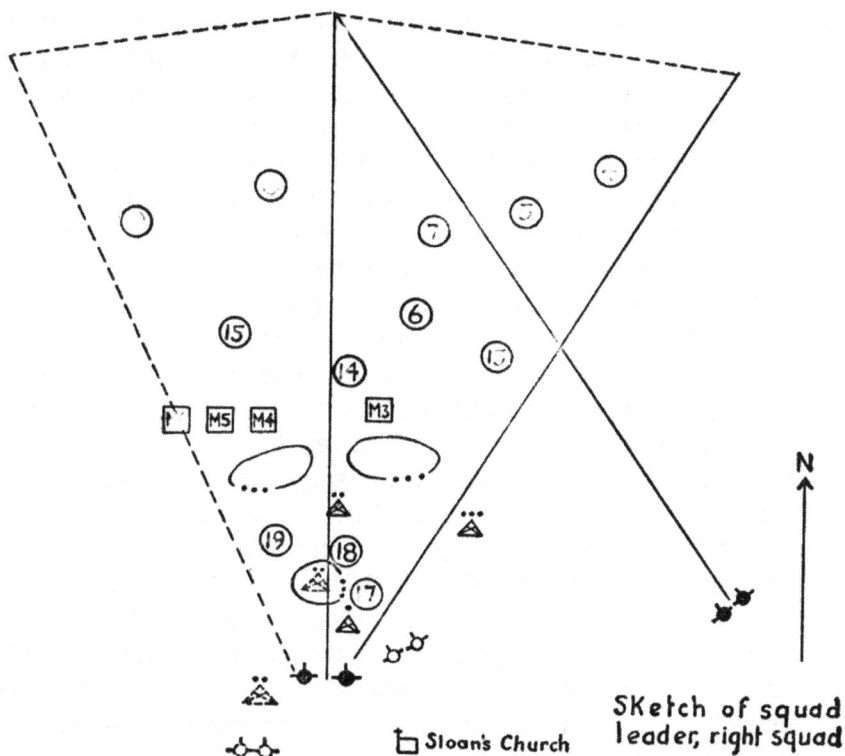

SKetch of squad leader, right squad

FIGURE 81.—Target assignment.

d. A solution.—(1) (For the right squad only, the solution will include computation of data for only enough targets to provide training in the different methods of computation. This procedure will avoid repetition. On the ground, the data for all targets should be computed.) The squad leader copies the section leader's sketch and moves to his observation post. He studies his sketch and outlines his squad sector with a heavy black line. He notes the additional area he is required to cover and outlines it with a heavy broken line (fig. 81). He brings up his squad, locates target No. 6 without delay, and sends a member of his squad forward to keep friendly troops away from its vicinity. He establishes initial direction of fire, selects the exact position for his mortar, has the mortar mounted and, upon signal from the member of his squad out front that all is clear, he fires for adjustment. Assume that he adjusts at a range of 1,200 yards. He reads and records the azimuth to target No. 6. He now reads an azimuth to one edge of a patch of woods in the vicinity of the ravine which is his primary target. Suppose this azimuth to be 115 mils. He cannot tell the exact location of the edge of the ravine from his observation post, so he directs No. 4 (or any other member of the squad) to march on an azimuth of 115 mils and to pace the range to a point opposite the ravine. He then tells No. 4 to pace the distance from his line of march to the edge of the ravine. No. 4 paces off 900 yards, taking care to march on the given azimuth, and arrives opposite the ravine. He then faces to his right and paces off a 50-yard offset from his line of march to the left edge of the target. He returns to the mortar, rechecking his pace on the way, and reports his findings to the squad leader. Upon receipt of these data, the squad leader consults his deflection-conversion table and finds that an angular shift of 50 yards at a range of 900 yards amounts to 57 mils. Since the shift is to the right, he adds 57 mils to 115 mils and obtains, to the nearest 5, 170 mils. He records this bearing on his range card as being the azimuth to his base point (fig. 82). Concurrently with the computation of these data, he issues necessary orders for the digging of the emplacements for the mortar and personnel.

(2) Upon the arrival of the instrument corporal at the section observation post, the section leader requests him to read the ranges to all targets visible to him from that location. He reads the range to target 7, among others, and by adding this range to the distance from this OP to the right mortar position (paced off), the section leader determines the range from the mortar to target No. 7 to be 1,750 yards. (The leader of the right squad determines the azimuth to target No. 7 from the squad observation post.)

(3) The section leader then has the instrument corporal move forward to a hill to the left front, from which target

RANGE CARD

LOCATION: _300 yds. N.W. of Gloria Church_   DATE _Jan. 11   1943_

RANGE	AZIMUTH	NO.	DESCRIPTION	DEF.	ELEV.	CH.	REMARKS
900	170	M3	Ravine (white star parachute)	0	71½	2	0 - Base stake - 3 rounds; Right 3½ turns, 3 rounds; Right 3½ turns, 3 rounds.
1200	370	6	Cross-road	R 200	63½	2	R50 - first Right Stake - Traverse right 3 turns, Search down 3 turns, 9 rounds.
1150	365	7	Dry stream bed	R195	60¾	3	R45 - first Right Stake - 3 rounds; right 2 turns, 3 rounds; right 2 turns, 3 rounds.
1000	5985	14	Ravine	L585	69¼	2	R15 - fourth Left Stake - 1 round; right 3½ turns, 1 round; right 3½ turns, 1 round.
1025	485	13	Road junction	R 315	68½	2	R15 - second Right Stake - 3 rounds; right 3½ turns, 3 rounds; right 3½ turns, 3 rounds.

FIGURE 82.—Squad leader's range card.

No. 14 is visible, in order to determine its range and azimuth. The corporal reads the range from the hill to the target, using the range finder, and finds it to be 550 yards. Using the aiming circle, he finds the azimuth to be 6,350 mils. He determines, by pacing, that this data was read from a point 200 yards to the left of the line mortar–target and 450 yards forward of the right mortar. By use of the deflection-conversion table, he finds that an angular width of 200 yards at a range of 550 yards amounts to an angle of 365 mils. Since the mortar is on the right of his observation post, he subtracts 365 mils from 6,350 and finds the azimuth mortar–target to be 5,985 mils. The range (550 plus 450) he finds to be 1,000 yards. He turns these data over to the section leader (informing him that it has been computed to the left near corner of the target), who turns it over to the leader of the right squad for entry on his range card.

(4) Upon the platoon leader's return to the section observation post, the section leader is furnished with data taken from the aerial photomap. These data are as follows:

Target	Range	Azimuth
6	1,250	345
13	1,075	460

The section leader already knows the adjusted range to target No. 6 to be 1,200 yards. Since the range to target No. 13 is between 3/4 and 4/3 the range to target No. 6, and since its azimuth is within 300 mils of the azimuth to target No. 6, it is sufficiently near to target No. 6 to allow the use of corrected map data. To correct the photomap data to target 13 for range, he divides the adjusted range by the photo range of target No. 6 and multiplies the quotient by the photo range to target No. 13. He computes these data to be as follows: $1,200/1,250 \times 1,075 = 1,025$, to the nearest 25 yards. To correct the photomap data to target 13 for deflection, he notes that the difference between the compass-azimuth and the photo-azimuth to target No. 6 is 370 less 345, or 25 mils. He knows that the same difference will exist between the compass-azimuth and the photo-azimuth to target No. 13; therefore, since the photo-azimuth is the smaller, he adds 25 mils to 460 mils and obtains a magnetic azimuth of 485 mils to target No. 13. He gives these data to the leader of the right squad to be recorded on his range card.

(5) As target data are computed for each mortar within its sector of fire, the section leader, where necessary, converts these data by use of the deflection-conversion table so that the data may be used by the other mortar if it should become necessary to fire on the same targets. In this instance, assume the mortars of the section to be on line approximately the same distance from all targets in both sectors. The section leader paces the distance between mortars and finds it to be 75 yards. He has already computed the azimuth from the left mortar to target No. 15 to be 6,150 and the range to that target 1,150. Using the deflection-conversion table, a shift of 75 yards at a range of 1,150 yards is found to be 65 mils, to the nearest 5. Hence, the azimuth to target No. 15 from the right mortar is 6,085.

NOTE.—If the mortars are staggered, instead of being on line, the necessary correction for the difference in range must be made.

(6) The squad leader, under the supervision and with the assistance of the section leader, continues the computation of data to all targets in his sector and for those targets in adjoining sectors upon which he may be required to fire. When the emplacement for his mortar is completed, he mounts his mortar therein, on the azimuth to his base point, the primary target. He then places out four additional aiming stakes at 150-mil intervals on each side of his base stake and is prepared to engage any target for which he has data on his range card or which may appear in his sector of fire as targets of opportunity.

(7) After work on the primary position is complete, the leader of the right squad places his men to work on the alternate and supplementary positions. He refigures all data for those positions and makes out separate range cards for each. In doing this, he employs the same method used by the section leader to convert data for the left squad into data for the right squad. (He finds it necessary, in addition, to pace off the difference in range, and to make allowance for that in his computations.) To obtain the data for the supplementary position, he adds the fire data for targets No. 17

and 18, which were too close in to be engaged from the other positions.

e. Second phase.—Assume that the section leader has directed the squad leader to be prepared to fire on his primary target upon signal after dark.

f. A solution.—The gunner cuts an ⅛-inch strip of adhesive tape, places it horizontally on the elevation scale index, sets the sight at the proper elevation for the primary target, and places a similar piece of tape on the scale opposite the first index marker. He then places another piece on the deflection scale index and another at the setting of 0 (the deflection setting for the primary target) on the deflection scale. He covers the glass of his flashlight with heavy black paper and pricks the paper at one point so that only a very small beam of light is visible. At night, when fire on his primary target is required, he feels the edges of the tape in order to assure himself that they are lined up (as they will be when his sights are properly set). Then, with his pin-point of light, he checks his bubbles. No. 2 turns on another similar light already placed in line with the left edge of the stake, pointing toward the mortar. Then he checks the alinement through the open sight as the fire order is issued.

NOTE.—If the night is very dark, No. 4 illuminates the collimator of the sight by shining the point of light through that part of the sight farthest from the gunner. To minimize the possibility of its being seen from a hostile position or by snipers, the light of the flashlight must be concealed. A raincoat or other covering will serve for this purpose.

g. Comments.—The process of preparing and checking data is continuous. The data which are first needed should be prepared first. If time permits, data are rechecked by all available methods until it is known to be accurate. Mere estimation by eye is relatively inadequate when there is time for pacing or for the use of the range finder.

(1) The instrument corporal might have computed the range to target No. 14 by another method. He could have read the azimuth back to the mortar position from his forward observation post. He would then have paced off the

distance from the observation post to the mortar or obtained the distance with his range finder. Since he has already determined the distance and azimuth from the observation post to the target, he needs only to lay off a north-south line on a piece of paper, selecting a convenient point "O" on that line and drawing two rays from the point at angles corresponding to the azimuths to the target and to the mortar. Using any convenient scale, he lays off a line on each ray proportional to the ground distance to the observation post and to the target. Then joining the ends of these lines, he completes a triangle. The length of the third side of this triangle so established, measured by the same scale as used above, will give the range mortar–target. Its direction, measured with a protractor with respect to the north-south line on the paper will give the azimuth mortar–target. Where distances are short, the method employed in the first solution is more simple; where distances are long, the latter method may prove desirable.

(2) Note that on the range card the point of adjustment for all targets is on the same side—in this instance, the left side. This procedure simplifies the delivery of fires for the gunner, since he positions his traversing screw nut on the same side for every target. Time is saved in this way.

(3) An alternate method which might be used to determine the range and azimuth to M3 is the following: The leader of the right squad sends No. 4 out to stand at the left edge of the target. The instrument corporal then reads the azimuth to No. 4 with the aiming circle, if available, or with the compass, which is, however, less accurate. Upon signal (having previously been instructed to this effect), No. 4 paces off a distance of 100 yards on a line perpendicular to the line observation post–target and stands still. Again, the instrument corporal reads the azimuth to where he is standing. The difference between the azimuths read is the angle in mils which is 100 yards wide at the unknown range. He then looks at his deflection-conversion table in the 100-yard column under "Deflection in yards." He follows this column down until he locates the mil value equal to the difference between the two azimuths read (suppose that difference to be 113 mils, in this case). Then he looks to the

left of the figure 113 under the column "Range in yards" and notes the range to the target to be 900 yards. At times, the corporal will have to interpolate when using this method, but if the angles are accurately read, the results will be quite accurate. In cases where the target is clearly visible, the base line of 100 yards may be paced off from the observation post and the azimuths read from each end of that line to the target.

(4) A combat outpost exercise may be drawn up, following principles outlined in FM 7–15. The technique involved in such an exercise is similar to that used in this exercise.

CHAPTER 8

ADVICE TO INSTRUCTORS

Paragraphs
SECTION I. General _____ 144-146
II. Mechanical training_____ 147-152
III. Training of gunner and observer_____ 153
IV. Training for placing mortar in action_____ 154
V. Marksmanship _____ 155-156
VI. Field training_____ 157-159
VII. Instruction on sand table_____ 160

SECTION I

GENERAL

■ 144. PURPOSE.—The provisions of this chapter are to be accepted as a guide and should not be considered as having the force of regulations.   They are particularly applicable to emergency conditions when large bodies of troops are being trained under officers and noncommissioned officers who are not thoroughly familiar with approved training methods.

■ 145. ASSISTANT INSTRUCTORS.—A sufficient number of noncommissioned officers and selected privates should be trained in advance for use as assistant instructors during the training of the remainder of the organization.

■ 146. DEMONSTRATION GROUPS.—Small groups of men, usally four to six, should be trained in advance to demonstrate exercises while the instructor is making the explanation.   They should be rehearsed carefully in the duties they are to perform so that when they present a demonstration it is correct in every detail and gives a clear picture of the work under discussion.

SECTION II

MECHANICAL TRAINING

■ 147. GENERAL.—a. The unit to be instructed should be divided into groups of eight men each.   Each group, under the direct supervision of an assistant instructor, with its own mortar and equipment should be assembled in a suitable area. With a crew-served weapon of this nature, there will not be sufficient equipment available to keep all men occupied at the same time. Accordingly, they must learn much from observing the actions of others.

b. The instruction is centralized under the unit instructor. Explanation and demonstration are concurrent, with each assistant demonstrating the element of the particular phase of instruction under discussion as the instructor explains it from the platform. For periods of practical work, the instruction is decentralized under the assistant instructors.

■ 148. NOMENCLATURE AND FUNCTIONING.—*a. Equipment for each group.*—Mortar, bipod, and base plate.

b. *Procedure.*—(1) The assistant instructor points out each part as the instructor names it and demonstrates the function of each part as the instructor explains the interrelation of parts.

(2) For practical work, the assistant instructor reviews the nomenclature and functioning of the mortar. He then places a pointer on individual parts and requires selected men to name the part and, where applicable, describe its function.

■ 149. MOUNTING AND DISMOUNTING.—*a. Equipment.*—Mortar, bipod, and base plate (fig. 83).

b. *Procedure.*—With the aid of demonstration personnel (Nos. 1, 2, and 3), the instructor explains the mounting and dismounting of the mortar without the sight. For practical work, each group performs these actions under the direction of the assistant instructor. Duties should be rotated so that every member of the group is able to perform the duties of Nos. 1, 2, and 3 in the prescribed manner. When the men have received instruction in sight setting and laying exercises (ch. 2), mounting and dismounting with the sight attached should be demonstrated and practical work conducted by the groups.

■ 150. SIGHTING EQUIPMENT.—The following training aid for use with the sight M4 should be constructed and explained by the instructor in conjunction with the exercise described in paragraph 41. It is generally known as the "Cook Demonstrator" (fig. 84).

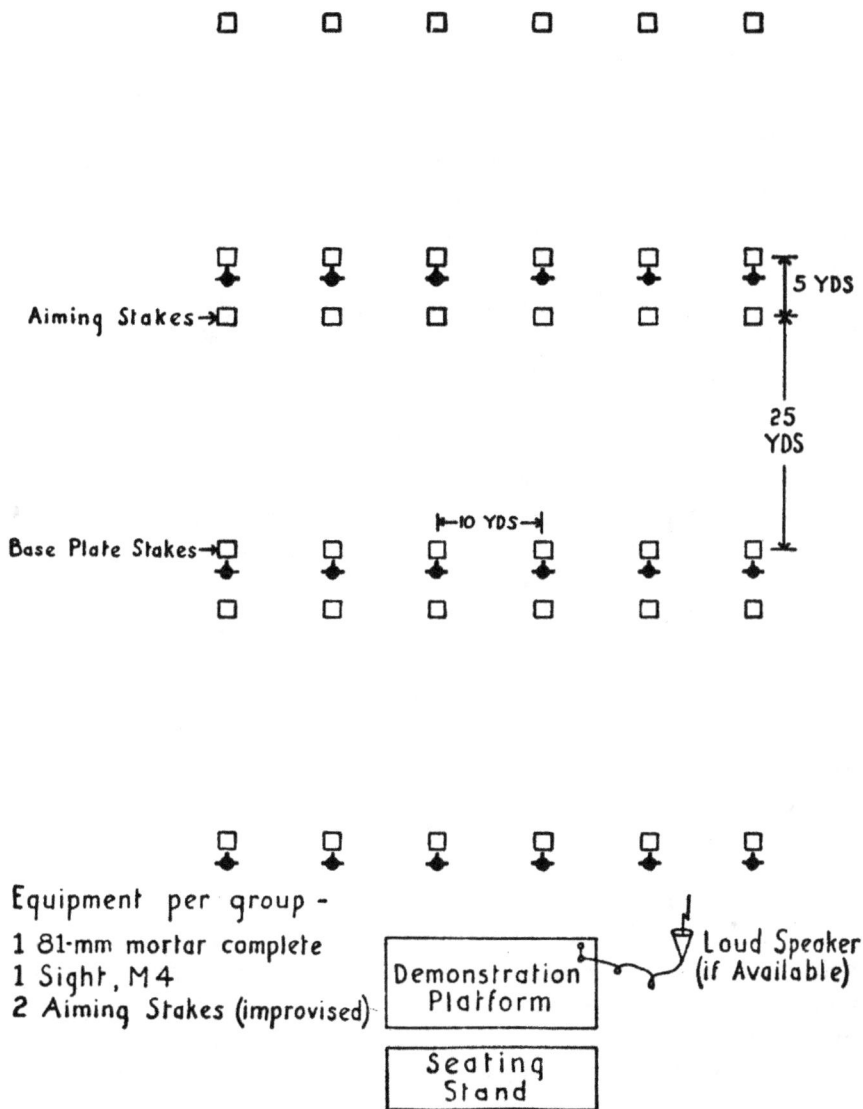

FIGURE 83.—Training area for regimental or training center instruction.

a. The light wood construction (*A*) inserted through the open sight is slotted at one end (*B*) to permit attachment. The horizontal arm (*A–B*) may be painted black to contrast with the vertical arm, which should be painted white, to represent the vertical line of the collimator. The muzzle attachment (*C*) indicates the vertical axis of the bore. The bar representing the axis of the bore can be adjusted by means of a wing nut and a bolt. Two stakes should be placed with their left edges alined with the vertical bars of the sight and muzzle attachments, with a slight clearance provided for manipulation.

b. The entire device illustrates two features of mortar technique which are likely to be confusing when the instructor attempts to correlate the movement of the vertical line of the collimator and the axis of the bore of the mortar. The device will illustrate that—

(1) A deflection set on the deflection scale of the sight (for example, right deflection) moves the vertical line of the collimator in the opposite direction (left) and requires manipulation of the traversing handwheel to the right to bring the vertical line back on the left edge of the aiming stake.

(2) The setting of a deflection on the deflection scale of the sight does not change the axis of the bore.

c. To illustrate the above principles, mount the mortar, attach the device, and follow the procedure indicated in figure 85. This training aid should clarify the fact that the sight is only an angle measuring instrument and that the mortar must be manipulated by means of the traversing handwheel to lay the mortar for direction.

d. The Cook Demonstrator may also be used to illustrate the necessity for cross-leveling the mortar, that is, taking the cant out of the barrel. Traverse the mortar to one end of the traversing screw and cross-level. Then traverse the entire width of the screw, cross-leveling at the same time. Reverse direction and traverse back again without turning the adjusting nut. Call attention to the cant of the bar representing the axis of the bore and then turn the adjusting nut to place the bar in a vertical plane.

■ **151.** CARE AND CLEANING.—A demonstration of the proper method of cleaning the mortar and points to be observed

before, during, and after firing should be given early in the
training schedule to insure that all equipment receives proper
care.

■ 152. AMMUNITION AND FIRING TABLES.—*a. Equipment.*—
Shell, HE, M43A1; shell, HE, M56; shell, smoke, M57; shell,

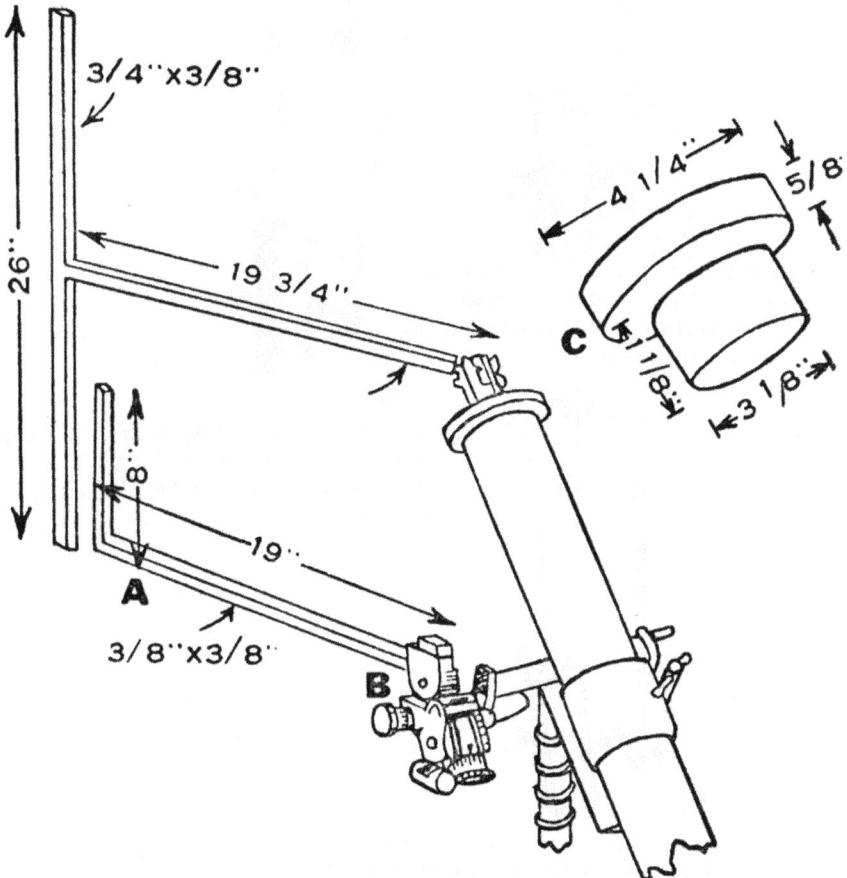

FIGURE 84.—Instructional device to illustrate laying procedure.

training, M68; and pertinent firing tables. (Ammunition
chart M26 for instruction is obtainable from the Ordnance
Department.)

b. Procedure.—(1) The instructor gives a general description of each type of combat ammunition and complete ballistic data for each shell. He then explains the functioning
of the M52 and M53 fuzes. A chart showing a cross-section

of each fuze will greatly assist in the explanation. Confidence in the ammunition is developed by emphasizing the safety features contained within each fuze.

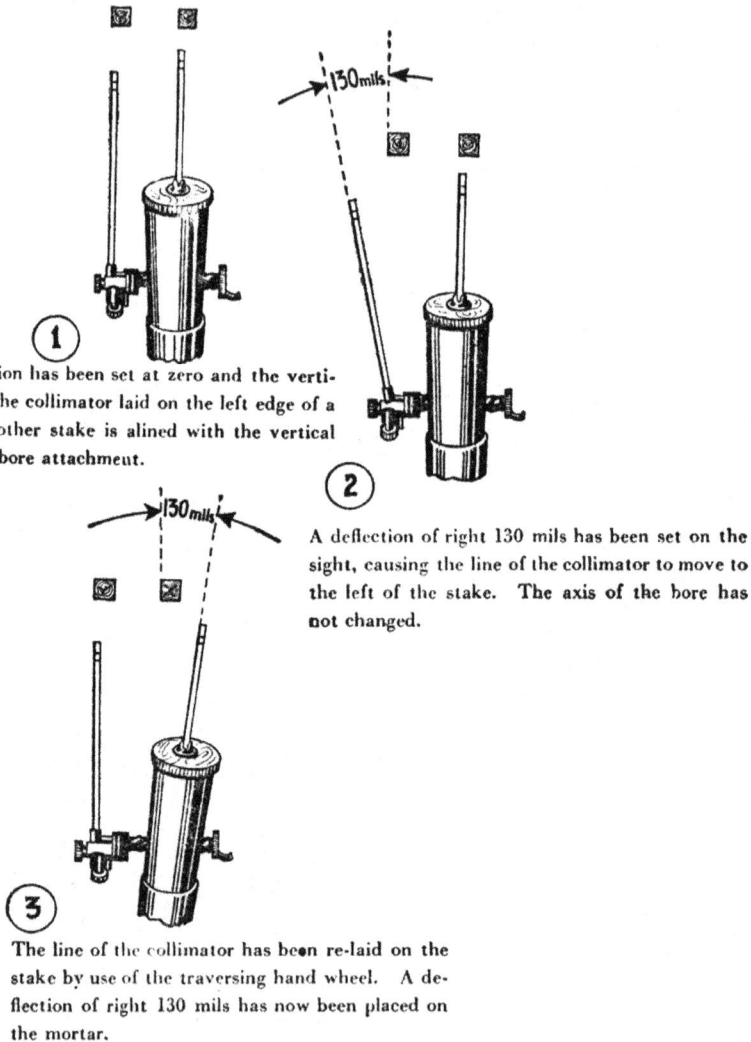

1

The deflection has been set at zero and the vertical line of the collimator laid on the left edge of a stake. Another stake is alined with the vertical axis of the bore attachment.

2

A deflection of right 130 mils has been set on the sight, causing the line of the collimator to move to the left of the stake. The axis of the bore has not changed.

3

The line of the collimator has been re-laid on the stake by use of the traversing hand wheel. A deflection of right 130 mils has now been placed on the mortar.

FIGURE 85.—Elements of instruction illustrating laying procedure.

(2) The instructor explains the use of the firing tables. Each man should be issued a copy of the table for the HE, light, shell to retain during training. The instructor then

announces various ranges and selects members of the class to give the proper elevation and charge to be employed.

Section III

TRAINING OF GUNNER AND OBSERVER

■ 153. GENERAL.—For the training of the gunner and the observer, the exercises described in chapters 2 and 4 for each phase of training should be followed as closely as possible. The necessary equipment should be apparent from a reading of the text for each exercise. The gunner or observer is required to execute the exercise as demonstrated. Emphasis is first placed on accuracy of execution; speed is gained as proficiency is attained. In the training of the observer, various types of terrain should be selected prior to each phase of training so that the observer will be presented with a problem requiring a solution by the method which has just been demonstrated.

Section IV

TRAINING FOR PLACING MORTAR IN ACTION

■ 154. MORTAR DRILL.—a. In the presentation of instruction in drill, demonstrations should be freely used. A demonstration unit of previously selected trained men is formed. Individuals or units to be instructed are arranged so that the demonstration can be plainly seen. The instructor explains that the demonstration unit will go through the movements very slowly, step by step, while he describes them. He cautions the men undergoing instruction to watch the demonstration unit and imitate the movements as demonstrated.

b. Units (usually squads) are then formed with their equipment by the assistant instructors, who require them to perform the movements demonstrated. Each movement is first executed, step by step, until the assistant instructor is satisfied with the performance of each man. Men are frequently rotated in the various squad positions.

c. The equipment necessary for each group is described in table I.

SECTION V

MARKSMANSHIP

■ **155. GENERAL.**—Preparatory instruction in marksmanship should follow mechanical training, training of gunner and observer, and mortar drill. In marksmanship, the element of speed has been added to the element of exactness in the performance of the duties of the various members of the mortar crew covered in the instructional exercises. The instructor must assure himself that each assistant thoroughly understands each exercise, is accurate in his explanations, and is insistent upon the exact performance of each sequence. The importance of exactness must be impressed upon the men at all times. For example, men in setting the sight for the sight-setting exercise are likely to say, "That is about right." There is no such thing as a sight that is about right; it is right or it is wrong. Once the habit of exactness is formed, speed follows as a matter of course. The various set-ups and the equipment necessary for each test are described in the beginning of each paragraph relating to the subject of the test. The instructor divides the unit to be tested into groups of from four to eight men, depending on the number of set-ups which can be made with the equipment available and the size of the unit undergoing instruction. When practicable, squad leaders act as assistant instructors in charge of each group. The groups contain the members of the squad leader's own squad to be tested plus a proportionate number of the unit overhead. If it becomes necessary to use noncommissioned officers or selected privates who are required to take the test, they should be tested with the first group in order that they may be free to assist in the instruction.

■ **156. PROCEDURE.**—*a.* Assistant instructors require each group to perform each of the subjects of test described in chapter 5.

b. They check each performance in the same manner as described for the board conducting the examination.

c. They mark the progress of each man on the progress chart shown in chapter 5.

d. They report to the senior instructor when the members of their groups are ready to qualify.

e. The senior instructor supervises the group instruction, notes the progress of the individuals on the progress charts, and calls for the board to meet when a sufficient number of men are ready to be tested.

SECTION VI

FIELD TRAINING

■ 157. GENERAL.—*a.* Field training exercises should be carefully and thoroughly prepared. The requirements should be simple and the instruction to be stressed should be clearly brought out by the exercises. Complicated exercises confuse the participants and do more harm than good.

b. Before preparing a field exercise, the instructor must make a personal reconnaissance of the terrain to be used for the exercise. In all demonstrations and exercises, emphasis should be placed on terrain.

■ 158. SEQUENCE OF TRAINING.—*a.* A minimum of 45 hours of instruction should be devoted to this phase of training. The schedule of instruction should be divided into training periods of from 3 to 4 hours in length.

b. The following is a suggested course:

(1) *First period.*—Preparatory exercise—Target designation and range estimation.

(2) *Second period.*—Preparatory exercise—Selection of observation posts and mortar positions.

(3) *Third period.*—Preparatory exercise—Occupation of positions, use of cover and concealment, preparation of fire data, means of communication.

(4) *Fourth and fifth periods.*—Firing exercises—Occupation of positions, preparation of fire data, means of communication, similar to those described in paragraph 135.

(5) *Sixth and seventh periods.*—Firing exercises similar to those described in paragraph 136.

(6) *Eighth period.*—Firing exercises similar to those described in paragraph 139.

(7) *Ninth period.*—Firing exercises similar to those described in paragraph 140.

(8) *Tenth period.*—Firing exercises similar to those described in paragraph 141.

(9) *Eleventh period.*—Firing exercises similar to those described in paragraph 142.

(10) *Twelfth period.*—Firing exercises similar to those described in paragraph 143.

■ 159. CRITIQUE.—*a.* The basis of good instruction in field training is intelligent, tactful, and constructive criticism. In his critique conducted after each exercise, the instructor discusses the solution offered and makes a comparison with other possible solutions. The critique should be given on the ground used for the exercise.

b. The instructor should commend that which was well done and call attention to that which was poorly or incorrectly done. Where errors have been committed, a correct solution should be indicated. In making corrections, the instructor should avoid ridicule, sarcasm, or any remarks which might be harmful to morale or initiative or which might lead the men to dread assuming responsibility.

c. The critique should not convey the impression that there is but one correct method of solving the exercise. Such a misconception is apt to lead to the adoption of fixed forms and attempts to guess what the instructor wants with the resulting destruction of initiative and independent thought.

SECTION VII

INSTRUCTION ON SAND TABLE

■ 160. PLACE IN TRAINING.—The sand table offers an effective means of teaching certain phases of technique and combat fundamentals. Exercises in conduct of fire, selection of mortar positions, and use of cover can be adapted readily to the terrain of the sand table. This type of instruction is valuable particularly during inclement weather or when facilities do not permit the use of adequate terrain. It engenders an appreciation for terrain by presenting terrain features and dispositions so that the pupil may view them perspectively.   The various kinds of sand tables used in teaching military subjects may be compared mainly according to simplicity of construction.   It is not necessary in teaching small units to use elaborate models, nor is it desirable.   Simple reproductions can be changed easily and frequently to present a variety of situations.

Appendix I

FIRING TABLES

Extracts of published firing tables (fire-control tables) applicable to the 81-mm mortar are contained in *a*, *b*, and *c* below. These tables give the range in yards and the elevation in degrees as indicated. The appropriate elevation for a given range and propelling charge is shown in the columns headed "Elevation" and "Charge." A firing table for use with the training projectile M68 is also included.

a. Shell, HE, M43, M43A1, and shell, practice, M43, M43A1 and M44 (fuze, PD, M52; weight of fuzed projectile 6.92 pounds).

FT 81–B–3 (abridged)

Range (yards)	Elevation (degrees)	Charge	Elevation (degrees)	Charge	Range (yards)	Elevation (degrees)	Charge	Elevation (degrees)	Charge
200	79¼	0			700			68½	1
225	77¾	0			725			67½	1
250	76¼	0			750	75	2	66½	1
275	74¾	0	82¼	1	775	74½	2	65¼	1
300	73	0	81¼	1	800	74	2	64¼	1
325	71¼	0	80¾	1	825	73¼	2	63	1
350	69½	0	80	1	850	72¾	2	61¾	1
375	67¾	0	79¼	1	875	72¼	2	60½	1
400	65¾	0	78½	1	900	71½	2	59	1
425	63¾	0	77¾	1	925	71	2	57¼	1
450	61½	0	77	1	950	70½	2	55¼	1
475	59	0	76¼	1	975	69¾	2	52¾	1
500	55¾	0	75½	1	1000	69¼	2	49¼	1
525			74½	1	1025	68½	2		
550			73¾	1	1050	67¾	2		
575			73	1	1075	67¼	2		
600			72	1	1100	66½	2		
625			71¼	1	1125	65¾	2		
650			70¼	1	1150	65	2		
675			69¼	1	1175	64¼	2		

Range (yards)	Elevation (degrees)	Charge	Elevation (degrees)	Charge	Range (yards)	Elevation (degrees)	Charge	Elevation (degrees)	Charge
1200	63½	2			2000	63½	4	51	3
1225	62¾	2			2025	63	4		
1250	61¾	2			2050	62½	4		
1275	61	2	71	3	2075	62	4		
1300	60	2	70½	3	2100	61½	4		
1325	59	2	70	3	2125	61	4		
1350	58	2	69½	3	2150	60½	4	66¾	5*
1375	56¾	2	69	3	2175	60	4	66¼	5*
1400	55½	2	68½	3	2200	59¼	4	66	5*
1425	54	2	68	3	2225	58¾	4	65¾	5*
1450	52½	2	67½	3	2250	58	4	65¼	5*
1475	50	2	67	3	2275	57½	4	65	5*
1500	46¼	2	66½	3	2300	56¾	4	64½	5*
1525			66	3	2325	56	4	64¼	5*
1550			65½	3	2350	55¼	4	63¾	5*
1575			65	3	2375	54¼	4	63¼	5*
1600			64½	3	2400	53½	4	63	5*
1625			63¾	3	2425	52½	4	62½	5*
1650			63¼	3	2450	51¼	4	62¼	5*
1675			62½	3	2475	50	4	61¾	5*
1700			62	3	2500	48	4	61¼	5*
1725			61¼	3	2600	64	6*	59½	5*
1750			60¾	3	2700	62¾	6*	57¼	5*
1775	67½	4	60	3	2800	61	6*	54¾	5*
1800	67¼	4	59¼	3	2900	59½	6*	51½	5*
1825	66¾	4	58½	3	3000	57½	6*		
1850	66¼	4	57¾	3	3100	55¼	6*		
1875	65¾	4	56¾	3	3200	52¼	6*		
1900	65½	4	56	3	3290	46	6*		
1925	65	4	55	3					
1950	64½	4	53¾	3					
1975	64	4	52½	3					

*Charges 5 and 6 are not to be used in the 3″ trench mortar Mk. 1A2.

NOTES

1. Deflection for one turn of traversing handwheel = 15 mils.
2. Elevation for one turn of elevating crank = ½°.
3. Where two elevations and two charges are available for selection, select the charge which will give the greatest latitude without changing the charge, for example, Range 1,000 use 69¼°, Charge 2 (par. 32).
4. In firing on targets involving searching fire, select elevation in degrees that will permit use of same charge throughout, for example, zone 950 to 1050 use charge 2 with corresponding elevations.
5. Note that for ranges greater than 2,500 yards, it is necessary to interpolate to obtain elevations corresponding to ranges containing 25-yard increments.

b. Shell, HE, M45 (fuze, PD, M53; weight of fuzed projectile, 15.05 pounds).

FT 81–D–1 (abridged)

Range	Elevation	Charge	Elevation	Charge
100	83½	1		
125	81¾	1		
150	80¼	1		
175	78½	1	82¾	2
200	76¾	1	81¾	2
225	75	1	80¾	2
250	73¼	1	79¾	2
275	71¼	1	78½	2
300	69	1	77½	2
325	66¾	1	76¼	2
350	64¼	1	75	2
375	61½	1	74	2
400	58½	1	72¾	2
425	54¼	1	71¼	2
450			70	2
475	75½	3	68¾	2
500	74¾	3	67¼	2
525	73¾	3	65¾	2
550	73	3	64¼	2
575	72	3	62½	2
600	71¼	3	60¾	2
625	70¼	3	58¾	2
650	69¼	3	56½	2
675	68¼	3	53¼	2
700	67¼	3	49¼	2
725	66	3		
750	65	3		
775	63¾	3	71	4

Range	Elevation	Charge	Elevation	Charge
800	62½	3	70½	4
825	61¼	3	69¾	4
850	59¾	3	69	4
875	58¼	3	68	4
900	56½	3	67¼	4
925	54¼	3	66½	4
950	51¾	3	65¾	4
975			64¾	4
1000			64	4
1025			63	4
1050			62	4
1075			61	4
1100			59¾	4
1125			58¾	4
1150			57½	4
1175			56	4
1200			54¼	4
1225			52¼	4
1250			49¾	4
1275			45	4

c. Shell, HE, M56 (fuze, PD, M53; weight of fuzed projectile, 10.62 pounds); shell, chemical, M57 (FS) (fuze, PD, M52; weight of fuzed projectile, 11.86 pounds); and shell, chemical, M57 (WP) (fuze, PD, M52; weight of fuzed projectile, 11.36 pounds).

FT 81-C-2 (abridged)

Range (yards)	Elevation (degrees)	Charge	Elevation (degrees)	Charge	Range (yards)	Elevation (degrees)	Charge	Elevation (degrees)	Charge
200	83	1			900			69¼	2
225	82	1			925			68½	2
250	81	1			950			67¾	2
275	80	1			975			67	2
300	79	1			1000			66	2
325	78	1			1025			65¼	2
350	77	1			1050	73¼	3	64½	2
375	76	1			1075	72¾	3	63½	2
400	75	1			1100	72¼	3	62½	2
425	74	1			1125	71¾	3	61¾	2
450	73	1	80½	2	1150	71¼	3	60¾	2
475	72	1	80	2	1175	70¾	3	59¾	2
500	70¾	1	79½	2	1200	70¼	3	58¾	2
525	69½	1	78¾	2	1225	69¾	3	57½	2
550	68¼	1	78¼	2	1250	69¼	3	56¼	2
575	67	1	77½	2	1275	68¾	3	54¾	2
600	65¾	1	77	2	1300	68	3	53¼	2
625	64¼	1	76½	2	1325	67½	3		
650	62¾	1	75¾	2	1350	67	3		
675	61¼	1	75¼	2	1375	66½	3		
700	59½	1	74½	2	1400	65¾	3		
725	57½	1	74	2	1425	65¼	3		
750	55¼	1	73¼	2	1450	64½	3		
775	52½	1	72¾	2	1475	64	3		
800	48	1	72	2	1500	63½	3		
825			71¼	2	1525	62¾	3		
850			70½	2	1550	62	3		
875			70	2	1575	61¼	3	69¼	4*

*Charge 4 is not to be used in the 3″ trench mortar Mk. 1A2.

Range (yards)	Elevation (degrees)	Charge	Elevation (degrees)	Charge	Range (yards)	Elevation (degrees)	Charge	Elevation (degrees)	Charge
1600	60½	3	68¾	4*	2100			58½	4*
1625	59¾	3	68½	4*	2125			58	4*
1650	59	3	68	4*	2150			57¼	4*
1675	58¼	3	67½	4*	2175			56½	4*
1700	57½	3	67	4*	2200			55¾	4*
1725	56½	3	66¾	4*	2225			55	4*
1750	55½	3	66¼	4*	2250			54¼	4*
1775	54½	3	65¾	4*	2275			53¼	4*
1800	53½	3	65¼	4*	2300			52½	4*
1825	52¼	3	64¾	4*	2325			51½	4*
1850	50¾	3	64¼	4*	2350			50¼	4*
1875	49¼	3	63¾	4*	2375			49	4*
1900	47	3	63¼	4*	2400			47½	4*
1925			62¾	4*	2425			45½	4*
1950			62	4*	2430			45	4*
1975			61½	4*					
2000			61	4*					
2025			60½	4*					
2050			59¾	4*					
2075			59¼	4*					

*Charge 4 is not to be used in the 3″ trench mortar Mk. 1A2.

d. Projectile, training M68.

FT 81–F–1 (abridged)

Range (yards)	Elevation	
	Degrees	Minimum
0	90	00
25	87	35
50	85	09
75	82	42
100	80	11
125	77	36
150	74	54
175	72	04
200	69	03
225	65	44
250	61	56
275	57	17
300	49	55
306	45	00

e. Deflection-conversion table.—This table is used by the observer to determine initial direction of fire by the compass and mil method (par. 59) and to convert yards to mils, when a sensing is necessary at some point off the line mortar–target (par. 68). This table is printed on the reverse side of the firing table for shell, HE, M43A1, which may be found in each bundle of ammunition.

Range in yards	Deflection in yards														
	1	10	20	30	40	50	75	100	125	150	175	200	300	400	500
500	2.0	20	41	61	81	102	152	201	250	297	343	388	550	687	800
600	1.7	17	34	51	68	85	127	168	209	250	289	328	472	599	708
700	1.5	15	29	44	58	73	109	145	180	215	250	284	412	529	632
800	1.3	13	25	38	51	64	95	127	158	189	219	250	365	472	569
900	1.1	11	22	34	45	57	85	113	141	168	195	223	328	426	517
1,000	1.0	10	20	31	41	51	76	102	127	152	176	201	297	388	473
1,100	.93	9	18	28	37	46	69	92	115	138	161	183	271	355	435
1,200	.85	8	17	25	34	42	64	85	106	127	148	168	249	328	402
1,300	.79	8	16	23	31	39	59	78	98	117	136	155	231	304	374
1,400	.73	7	15	22	29	36	55	73	91	109	127	145	215	283	349
1,500	.68	7	14	20	27	34	51	68	85	102	118	135	201	265	328
1,600	.63	6	13	19	25	32	48	64	80	95	111	127	189	250	309
1,700	.60	6	12	18	24	30	45	60	75	90	104	119	178	235	291
1,800	.57	6	11	17	23	28	42	57	71	85	99	113	168	223	276
1,900	.54	5	11	16	21	27	40	54	67	80	94	107	160	211	262
2,000	.51	5	10	15	20	25	38	51	64	76	89	102	152	201	250
2,100	.49	5	10	15	19	24	36	48	61	73	85	97	145	192	238
2,200	.46	5	9	14	19	23	35	46	58	69	81	92	138	183	228
2,300	.44	4	9	13	18	22	33	44	55	66	77	88	132	175	218
2,400	.43	4	8	13	17	21	32	42	53	63	74	85	127	168	209
2,500	.41	4	8	12	16	20	31	41	51	61	71	81	122	162	201
2,600	.39	4	8	12	16	20	29	39	49	59	68	78	117	155	194
2,700	.38	4	8	11	15	19	28	38	47	57	66	75	113	150	187
2,800	.37	4	7	11	15	18	27	36	45	55	64	73	109	145	180
2,900	.35	4	7	11	14	18	26	35	44	53	61	70	105	140	174
3,000	.34	3	7	10	14	17	25	34	42	51	59	68	102	135	168

APPENDIX II

INSTRUCTION CARD

The information contained in this card, which is printed on the reverse side of the ammunition data card, may be used for rapid calculations of turns between rounds, for distributed fire and rapid-method adjustment.

INSTRUCTION CARD

1. Turns of the traversing crank required between rounds to deliver traversing fire. (Target width—100 yards.)

2. Turns of the elevating crank required to deliver searching fire. (Target depth—100 yards.)

Range in yards	Number of turns
500	6½
600	5½
700	5
800	4
900	4
1,000	3½
1,100	3
1,200	3
1,300	2½
1,400	2½
1,500	2½
1,600 to 1,900	2
2,000 to 2,800	1½
2,900 to 3,200	1

Ranges

From	To	Charge	Turns
400	300	0	8
450	350	0	8
500	400	1	3
550	450	1	3
600	500	1	3
650	550	1	3
700	600	1	4
750	650	1	4
800	700	1	4
850	750	1	5
900	800	1	5
950	850	2	2
1,000	900	2	2
1,100	1,000	2	3
1,200	1,100	2	3
1,300	1,200	2	3
1,400	1,300	2	5
1,500	1,400	3	2

3. *Basis for table.*

a. To obtain the number of turns between rounds to cover a traversing target, measure the width of the target in mils (or refer to the deflection-conversion table) and divide by 30 (a constant).

b. To obtain the number of turns between rounds to cover a searching target, find the elevations, in degrees, for the limiting ranges (disregard fractions) and subtract the smaller from the greater. The difference will equal the number of turns required.

c. If, in the fire order for searching fire, the *longer range* is given *first*, the gunner will *elevate* the mortar the number of turns given on the table; if the *shorter range* is given *first*, then the gunner will *depress* the mortar the number of turns given above.

APPENDIX III

FIRE CONTROL INSTRUMENTS

NOMENCLATURE AND OPERATIVE PROCEDURE, MORTAR PLATOON

M1 AIMING CIRCLE

(In this order)
1. Shoes
2. Lower leg section
3. Leg clamping screws
4. Upper leg section
5. Tripod head
6. Sliding vertical support
7. Clamping screw
8. Ball and socket joint
9. Ball and socket joint clamping screw
10. Vertical wing nut
11. Orienting knobs
12. Azimuth scale (Back azimuth scale)
13. Plateau scale (for M1901 French sight)
14. Azimuth scale index (arrow on left of plateau scale)
15. Azimuth micrometer
16. Drum scale (Used with plateau scale)
17. Throwout lever
18. Celluloid plate (for marking magnetic declination constant)
19. Azimuth knob
20. Magnetic needle magnifier and reticle
21. Circular level
22. Compass needle
23. Needle release plunger (OD color)
24. Needle locking plunger (Red color)
25. Etched north line
26. Eyepiece (4 power, 10° field of view)
27. Eyepiece focusing sleeve
28. Illuminating window
29. Eyepiece reticle, with horizontal and vertical mil scales
30. Intersection of hairlines on reticle (Optical center of instrument)
31. Elevating knob
32. Angle of site spirit level

NOTE.—For further information on M1 aiming circle, see SNL F–160 and TM 9–1530.

AIMING CIRCLES

COMPLETE, the instrument consists of: Aiming circle proper, tripod, carrying case, lighting accessories.

USES: For measuring magnetic azimuths, horizontal angles, angles of site, and vertical angles.

TO ORIENT ON NORTH

M1916

1. Release magnetic needle. Set azimuth scale and micrometer at zero. Level instrument.
2. Loosen wing nut and lay approximately on magnetic north. Tighten wing nut.
3. Aline needle accurately on north arrow with orienting knob.
4. Look through magnetic needle magnifier and perfectly aline south seeking end of needle on middle hairline.

M1

1. Same as for M1916
2. Same as for M1916
3. Same as for M1916

TO MEASURE AZIMUTHS

M1916

1. Orient on north (see above).
2. Lay approximately on T, by using throwout lever.
3. Complete lay with azimuth knob.
4. Read azimuth from scale and micrometer.

M1

Same as for M1916

TO MEASURE HORIZONTAL ANGLES

M1916

1. Zero azimuth scale and micrometer.
2. Loosen wing nut, lay on left hand object, tighten wing nut. Complete lay with orienting knob.
3. Measure angle by means of throwout lever and azimuth knob.

M1

Same as for M1916

TO MEASURE ANGLES OF SITE

M1916

1. Lay optical center of instrument on T.
2. Level angle of site level by means of AS knob.
3. Take reading of AS scale and micrometer.
4. Difference between new reading and "zero" reading is AS.
5. If new reading is greater than zero, AS is positive; if less than zero, AS is negative.

M1

1. Lay on T.
2. Level angle of site level by means of elevating knob.
3. Look through telescope. Note on vertical mil scale the reading to T.
4. If T. appears below horizontal line, angle of site is negative. If it is above horizontal line, AS is positive.

METHODS OF OBTAINING ZERO READING OF ANGLE OF SITE MECHANISM ON 1916 AIMING CIRCLE

Distant horizon method

1. Lay on the distant horizon.
2. Level AS spirit level. Read AS scale and mircrometer.
3. Repeat steps 1 and 2 three times. Use average of readings as Zero.

Alternate method

1. Set up 2 instruments between 100 and 200 yards apart on sloping ground.
2. Lay optical center of each instrument on shutter of the other.
3. Level AS spirit level and record readings of scale and micrometer.
4. Without disturbing the tripods, switch instrument heads to opposite tripods and again take readings to shutters of opposite instruments.
5. The average of the two readings thus obtained on each instrument will be the "zero" of the AS mechanism for each respective instrument.

RANGE FINDERS

COMPLETE, the instrument consists of: Range finder, tripods (Types R & S), carrying case, adjusting lath.

USES: For determination of ranges—400 to 10,000 yards.

NOMENCLATURE: See FM 23–55.

DETERMINATION OF RANGES

M1914 and M1914M1 (range roller type)

1. Aline T in center of field.
2. Turn range drum knob until images coincide vertically.
3. Read range from range scale.

M1917 (azimuth type)

1. Select c l e a r l y defined point on T.
2. Turn i n s t r u m e n t i n azimuth until images coincide vertically.
3. Read range on scale at point of vertical coincidence.

M1914 AND M1914M1 HALVING ADJUSTMENT

Range roller type

1. Bring top of upright image to halving line using elevating knob.
2. Turn halving adjustment knob to bring lower edge of inverted image to halving line.

M1917 (azimuth type)

Same as for M1914.

RANGE ADJUSTMENT (KNOWN-RANGE METHOD)

M1914 and M1914M1 (range roller type)

1. Lay on T with range drum scale set at correct range.
2. Same as for M1917.

M1917 (azimuth type)

1. Turn i n s t r u m e n t i n azimuth until laid on T (at known range) with correct range.
2. Turn correction wedge shaft until images are in vertical coincidence. Note correction wedge scale reading. (Repeat 5 times. Use average of three readings for "zero".)

NOTE.—Both adjustments, once made correctly, need only to be checked occasionally, unless through accident or rough handling the internal parts of the instruments are affected.

INDEX

	Paragraphs	Pages
Accessories _____	36	42
Action, to place mortar in. (*See* Mortar.)		
Adjustment of fire. (*See* Fire.)		
Advice to instructors_____	144–160	259
Aiming circle_____	120	179
Aiming post_____	18	21
Aiming stake_____	46	54
Alidade_____	64	95
Ammunition_____ 20–32, 152		25, 263
Care, handling, and preservation_____	24	26
Classification _____	21	25
Fuze _____	29–30	29
Identification _____	23	25
Lot number_____	22	25
Preparation for firing_____	27	28
Propelling charge_____	28	29
Rounds _____	26	27
Storage _____	25	27
Training projectile_____	31	33
Arm-and-hand signals_____	61	86
Assembling mortar_____	4	6
Assistant instructor_____	145	259
Attack _____ 141, 142		227, 234
Azimuth _____ 43, 96		51, 148
Base deflection_____	45	53
Base plate_____	3	2
Binocular _____	63	90
Bipod _____	3	2
Board, examining_____ 88–90		141
Bracketing method (and bracketing method modified) _____	75	125
Care and cleaning of the mortar_____ 6–17, 151		10, 262
After firing_____	11	14
For storage_____	13	17
Gas attack, during_____	16	19
In extreme climates_____	15	18
In the field_____	12	16
On range_____	12	16
Preparatory to firing_____	10	14
When no firing is done_____	9	13
When received from storage_____	14	18
Charge, propelling_____	28	29
Cleaning:		
Agents _____	7	10
Instruments_____	8	12
Of the mortar. (*See* Care and cleaning of the mortar.)		
Climate effect on use of mortar_____	15	18
Combat expedients_____ 75–82		125
Commands. (*See* Fire orders.)		
Compass_____	34	39
Compass and mil method_____	59	71
Concealment _____	130	210
Conversion scale. (*See* Deflection-conversion table).		

	Paragraphs	Pages
Cover	130	210
Creeping method	69	105
Critique	137	218
Cross-leveling	40	48
Data, fire. (*See* Fire data.)		
Decontamination	16	19
Defense	77, 78, 123, 143	132, 206, 248
Deflection (*see also* Laying; Sight setting)	45	53
Deflection—conversion table	App. I; 59	270, 71
Demonstration group	146	259
Destruction of ordnance matériel in event of imminent capture in combat zone:		
General principles	32.1	34
Methods	32.2	35
Ammunition	32.3	37
Fire-control	32.4	38
Destruction of captured enemy matériel	32.5	38
Direct laying	49	57
Direction:		
Determination of initial firing	59	71
Laying for	41	49
Disassembling the mortar	4	6
Dismounting the mortar	5, 149	6, 260
Dispersion	66	96
Distributed fire	74	123
Drill, mortar	50–52, 154	58, 265
Elevation	39, 42	47, 50
Emplacement, mortar	81	137
Equipment	50	58
Examination	87–90	141
Examining board	88–90	141
Exercises	37–44, 127–143	45, 208
Conduct of fire	70	112
Distributed fire	74	123
Firing	136–137	217
Marksmanship	86	140
Preparation of range cards	82	138
Training, for gunner	37–44	45
Expedients, combat	75–82	125
Expert's test	99–104	151
Field:		
Firing	103, 131–137	155, 211
Targets. (*See* Targets.)		
Training	124–143, 157–159	208, 267
Fire (Firing):		
Adjustment	69, 75, 100	105, 125, 151
Bracketing method (and bracketing method modified)	75	125
Conduct of:		
By section	108–111	159
By squad	65–74	95

	Paragraphs	Pages
Fire (Firing)—Continued.		
Control instruments_____ App. III, 120–123		279, 179
Aiming circle_____	120	179
Improvised alidade and mil scale_____	64	95
Initial fire data, obtaining with_____	121	190
Range finder_____	121	190
Use of_____ 122, 123		203, 206
Creeping method_____	69	105
Data_____ 58, 78, 80, 102, 122, 123		71, 132, 135, 155, 203, 206
Direct laying_____	49	57
Direction, determination of initial_____	59	71
Distributed_____ 72, 74		116, 123
Exercises_____ 74, 131–137		123, 211
Field_____	103	155
For effect_____ 72, 111		116, 161
In towns_____	140	223
In villages_____	140	223
In woods_____	139	218
Ladder method_____	75	125
Mortar, to_____	54	66
Night_____ 47, 143		55, 248
Orders_____ 61, 62, 109		86, 89, 159
Positions_____	129	209
Prearranged_____ 76–82, 123, 143		131, 206, 248
Searching_____ 44, 72, 97		52, 116, 149
Tables_____ App. I, 32, 152		270, 33, 263
Technique of (see also Fire adjustment)__ 117, 118		166, 170
Traversing_____ 44, 72, 97		52, 116, 149
Without sights_____ 48, 71		56, 115
Firing. (See Fire.)		
Functioning_____	148	260
Fuze_____ 29, 30		29, 32
Gas, care of mortar during attack_____	16	19
Grades_____	87	141
Gunner_____ 33–49		39
Gunner's test_____ 91–98		142
Halving adjustment. (See Fire control instruments.)		
Improvised alidade and mil scale_____	64	95
Initial direction of fire_____	59	71
Initial fire data. (See Fire data.)		
Inspection of mortar_____	17	20
Instruction card_____ App. II		278
Instruction, marksmanship_____ 83–86, 155–156		139, 266
Instructors, advice to_____ 144–160		259
Instruments:		
Cleaning_____	8	12
Fire control. (See Fire control instruments.)		

	Paragraphs	Pages
Ladder, method (and Ladder method modified)	75	125
Laying of the mortar	93–95	144
Cross-leveling	40	48
Direct	49	57
For direction	41–43	49
For elevation	39, 42	47, 50
Lot number of ammunition	22	25
Lubricants	7	10
Manipulation of mortar	44, 97	52, 149
Marking base deflection	45	53
Marksmanship	83–107, 155, 156	139, 266
Examinations	89	141
Examining boards	88	141
Expert's test	99–104	151
Gunner's test	91–98	142
Instruction	84	139
Preparatory exercises	86	140
Qualification course	91–104	142
Mask clearance	39	47
Matériel	113	164
Mechanical training	1–3	1
Mil formula	59	71
Mil scale	64	95
Misfires	55	67
Mortar, 81-mm:		
Care and cleaning	6–16, 151	10, 262
Characteristics	1	1
Description	1–3	1
Drill	154	265
Emplacements	81	137
General data	2	2
Inspections	17	20
Preparation for firing	27	28
To fire	54	66
To place in action	50–56, 154	58, 265
Carry equipment	50	58
Ground equipment	50	58
Secure equipment	50	58
Mounting mortar	5, 92, 149	6, 143, 260
Night firing	47, 143	55, 248
Nomenclature	3, 148	2, 260
Observation	68	98
Observer	57–82, 153	71, 265
Orders. (*See* Fire orders.)		
Out of action	56	69
Parallel line method	59	71
Parts, spare	35	42
Planned fires. (*See* Prearranged fires.)		
Positions, firing	129	209
Prearranged fires	76–82, 123, 143	131, 206, 248
Preparatory exercises. (*See* Exercises.)		
Problems. (*See also* exercises)	73	122

	Paragraphs	Pages
Projectile, training. (*See* Ammunition.)		
Propellent increments. (*See* Propelling charge.)		
Propelling charge	28	29
Qualification course	87, 91–104	141, 142
Range	106	158
Card	79, 82, 101	133, 138, 151
Determination	60, 128	80, 209
Estimation. (*See* Range determination.)		
Finder	121	190
Precautions	106, 107	158
Round. (*See* Ammunition.)		
Rust preventives	7	10
Safety	53, 106, 107, 134	65, 158, 215
Sand table	160	268
Scoring. (*See* Qualification course.)		
Screen, smoke	116	165
Searching	44, 72, 97	52, 116, 149
Section, conduct of fire	108–111, 141	159, 227
Sensing	67–68	98
Sequence of training	158	267
Sight M4	19, 37–38	21, 45
Sighting equipment	18, 19, 150	21, 260
Sight setting	38	47
Signals, arm-and-hand	61	86
Smoke	112–119	163
Spare parts	35	42
Squad:		
Conduct of fire	65–74	95
Leader, combat expedients for	75	125
Storage of mortar	13, 14	17, 18
Support	141, 142	227, 234
Tables, firing. (*See* Fire.)		
Target areas	77	132
Targets	77, 105, 133	132, 158, 211
Technique of fire. (*See* Fire.)		
Terrain	100, 114, 132	151, 164, 211
Towns, firing in	140	223
Training. (*See also* Exercises.)	108–123 138–143, 153, 157–160	159, 218 265, 267
Field	124–143	208
Gunner	33–49, 153	39, 265
Mortar, to place in action	50–56	58
Observer	57–82	71
Training projectile	31	33
Traversing	72, 97	116, 149
Villages, firing in	140	223
Weather	114	164
Woods, firing in	139	218

www.ingramcontent.com/pod-product-compliance
Lightning Source LLC
Chambersburg PA
CBHW071408090426
42737CB00011B/1397